FALLOUT

Published by: 2605 Media LLC
21 Orinda Way C187
Orinda, CA 94563
www.falloutbook.com

Library of Congress Control Number: 2018901146

The publisher is not responsible for websites (or their content) that are not owned by the publisher.

Publisher's Cataloging-In-Publication Data
(Prepared by The Donohue Group, Inc.)

Names: Cole, Scott Edward.
Title: Fallout : the shocking true story of suffering, corporate greed, and a young lawyer's fight for justice / Scott Edward Cole.
Description: Orinda, CA : 2605 Media LLC, 2018.
Identifiers: ISBN 9780998535968 (paperback) | ISBN 9780998535975 (hardcover) | ISBN 9780998535982 (ebook)
Subjects: LCSH: Cole, Scott Edward--Career in law. | Class actions (Civil procedure)-- California--Crockett. | Environmental disasters--Law and legislation--California-- Crockett. | Environmental law--California--Crockett. | Unocal Corporation--Trials, litigation, etc. | Big business--California--Crockett. | LCGFT: True crime stories. | BISAC: TRUE CRIME / General. | SOCIAL SCIENCE / Disasters & Disaster Relief. | LAW / Environmental.
Classification: LCC KFC1017 .C65 2018 (print) | LCC KFC1017 (ebook) | DDC 347.794053--dc23

Printed in the United States of America

Published 2018.

Available on Kindle and online stores.

For Vincent

CONTENTS

FALLOUT

THE SHOCKING TRUE STORY
OF SUFFERING, CORPORATE GREED
AND A YOUNG LAWYER'S FIGHT FOR JUSTICE

SCOTT EDWARD COLE

AUTHOR'S NOTE

I'm a lawyer. Yes, I know what you're thinking, but don't hate me—at least not yet. Believe it or not, some of us went to law school to do what we considered "the right thing," which, to most people, means something that protects the little guy, the under-represented. I consider being a "people's lawyer" a noble calling, something worthy of long hours and personal sacrifices. Yes, I'm an idealist. I have always been an idealist and, luckily, the events this book brings to light didn't change that, but they sure shook my faith at times.

Other than changing the characters' names to "protect the innocent" and enjoying some slight literary license to keep the action moving—this is a true story. My opinions about why people did certain things will, undoubtedly, ruffle some feathers. If that happens, particularly to the lawyers, I'm sure they'll get over it. We all take hits in this profession from time to time. In other situations, such as where records still exist of the events recounted here, I tried to follow those records to the letter.

For the most part, however, no outside resources were needed since I was there. I was always there since, at least as to the legal battle that this book describes, I started that battle, and it was a fascinating one. Indeed, many lawyers, myself included, say that reality is often crazier than fiction. Many parts of this historical account illustrate why that's true.

This book is about a lot of things but, first and foremost, it's about me doing what I considered "the right thing." My late father always said about choosing a career that, first and foremost, "Do what you love" and, so, I hope this story makes it obvious I absolutely love the law and the good that its practice can do to help level the playing field between people who otherwise have little voices and the people with the power and volume to talk over them.

The story itself is classic. It's an account of horrible corruption and the legal battle waged to address it, but it also honors the stories and experiences of those whom I call the "little voices," the people traditionally without much power. And it's about big-business practices in furtherance of corporate greed and about powerful people choosing to stay quiet about the truth, or to outright lie, while the little voices— maybe I should just call them "heroes"—took brave steps and made a lasting difference. Finally, enmeshed with those themes, it's the story of me, at least a former version of me, when I was a bright-eyed 28-year-old kid, not even two years out of law school, who got a front-row seat to some amazing events and a remarkable level of human suffering, and who brought these happenings to light in a huge way.

There was a toxic airborne chemical release from what was then the Unocal Refinery in Rodeo, California, in the late summer of 1994. The big voices let it go on for 16 days and it hurt people, ruined families and even led to deaths of those given no warning they were even at risk. It was simply catastrophic and, like after most instances of corporate malfeasance, an apology never came. I discovered the corporate efforts to cover up the impact of the event and decided to risk everything to stop it—ultimately filing a class action lawsuit that was later joined by dozens of other firms.

With almost no resources, I represented nearly 1,100 people in the case born out of this tragic event and, in the process, witnessed a level of suffering that changed me. These people didn't deserve what happened to them. They were just small-town people living small-town lives. They were the elderly, the middle-aged, the very young—even a couple of animals somehow found their way onto my client list. What happened during those 16 days was shameful—there is no other way to say it. The chemical release could have easily been avoided and, even after its discovery, it could have easily been stopped, thereby preventing years of agony. But that wasn't in the cards because it would have limited profits.

I bet I know why action wasn't taken sooner, but it's inevitably speculative. You can probably guess too. Maybe it's because the victims lived in under-represented little blue-collar towns. Maybe Unocal really didn't realize how far the toxin stream was traveling, although I don't believe that for a second. Maybe Unocal didn't understand the science of it well enough to know the damage it might do to the locals and their property. Maybe big corporations are inherently greedy and just can't help themselves. While I may not know the reasons, I know the events and, for four years of my life, I helped lead the community in fighting back because what I saw disgusted me.

More than 20 years later, I'm still haunted by some of my clients' stories. Some of them I can't share because they were told to me in confidence and that's just how the privilege works. The ones I can share more than flesh out the aggregate experience of the victims of greed, laziness and indifference. While this book chronicles what I did during those years, I hope it's the client experiences that carry it because it is for them that I wrote it. Indeed, long after the Unocal case file was archived and the lawyers went their separate ways, I remember best the client meetings at my little, run-down office, and sitting in well-worn chairs in shabby living rooms, and handing out tissues to people to dab the tears so they'd feel just a little less humiliated.

Finally, as I journaled these events, I often asked myself: Does every good saga require that some lesson be extractable? Now that my journaling is done, I'm still not sure, but I think so—and it's the same thing I've mentored young lawyers about now for years. It taught me the importance of remaining passionate about something, taking chances and journeying into places, situations and emotions bigger than what you thought possible—just because you can. Everyone has bravery inside. That sounds preachy and trite, maybe, but it's so true.

As you'll see soon enough, I took a chance and it changed me, and that makes me think others can take big risks and make big changes too. It was my confidence in that which kept me going as I wrote this book. I like to witness people transform and recognize their capacity to influence others, policies and major events. But not everyone will have had that experience by the time they've finished this book and that's all right. If even one person is impassioned enough to say "hell no to the status quo," and stand up the next time his rights are threatened, even if on shaky legs, this effort to retell what happened back in 1994 will have been well worth it.

Unocal

San Francisco

San Francisco Bay Area

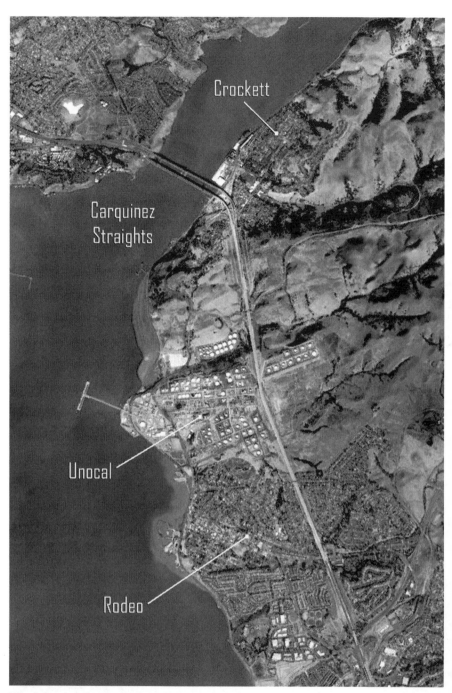

West Contra Costa County

CHAPTER 1

THE CALL

It all started with Ralph. It had to start somewhere because, frankly, I was too brash and eager for an adventure for it not to happen sooner or later. It was early afternoon on September 14, 1994 when Ralph caught me on the telephone in my ratty two-room law office in Alameda, a little island town across the bay from San Francisco. I had been practicing law for a little less than two years and, in that time, had done nothing particularly important.

"Scotty, I've got a case for you." It was Ralph, and I thought, *Oh, Christ.* Ralph's gravelly voice was distinctive—a voice much older than his 48 years. And it was with these words he started all our conversations so there could be no confusion it was him. Ralph called me a lot in those days and, with no office personnel to serve as gatekeepers for incoming calls, and desperate for new clients, I was compelled to answer the telephone whenever it rang. Yep, it was Ralph, and I was trapped.

I had represented Ralph the year before in a workplace discrimination case against a small company in Alameda, where I rented an equally ratty apartment. I got Ralph a decent cash settlement for not much work on his part, which made him very happy and gave him a taste of the power sometimes associated with bringing lawsuits. Since settling that case, he'd call me often, asking if I would represent him in disputes over, well, nearly anything; sometimes they involved conspiracy themes that were worthy of Hollywood movies or were calculated to champion issues he was certain supported the common good but were, more likely, exclusively of benefit to him.

Ralph was a funny guy and, boy, did he have some wild ideas. Perhaps the most interesting ever was his suggestion we sue the federal government to try to reverse major legislation concerning gun sales. *Yeah, no thanks, Ralph*, I thought, but he pushed me anyway. Apparently, since being fired from his last position, he'd opened a pawn shop which, among other things, sold guns. Bad timing for him though. In February of that year, the "Brady Bill" (requiring background checks be conducted on individuals before a firearm could be purchased) went into effect, and that made him mad.

According to Ralph, the new law's five-day waiting period was interfering with business and he wanted me to file a challenge to its constitutionality. What he didn't know, however, was that I really disliked guns, was very much in favor of gun control, and didn't want to hear about his cash-flow problems or how his customers wanted to get rifles in their mitts faster. No case. And none of his other calls yielded cases either. But, still, I had to hand it to him; he was creative and a hustler, kind of like how I saw myself, and so we developed a mutual respect. He was also just a really nice guy.

Ralph's tenacity made me grin when I heard his signature introduction this time. I'm not sure how he got to calling me "Scotty," but it was endearing. It may even have been part of the reason why I was always so open to listening. Nevertheless, I set the parameters for a short conversation this time, not expecting his case to have any legs. "Hey, Ralph. I'm getting ready right now for a court appearance, but what's up?"

Truthfully, I didn't have to be in court for a couple more hours and the appearance was routine, meaning no need for any preparatory work. Nevertheless, I thought it would be prudent to manufacture an exit strategy in case Ralph's sales pitch about our next proposed legal endeavor went long. Undeterred, he asked me if I knew about Unocal.

"You mean the gas stations?" I asked.

"No; I mean the refinery out here in Rodeo," he explained, referring to the next town over from his home, where the huge petroleum refining facility was situated. I knew Ralph was a homeowner in a little blue-collar unincorporated town called Crockett and I knew Crockett was next door to Rodeo, so at least these data points added up.

"That's the refinery you see to the left of the freeway as you head up I-80 toward the Carquinez Bridge, right?" I asked.

He confirmed that it was. As he continued talking, a visual entered my head of the various times I had driven that section of the Interstate, roughly 30 miles northeast of San Francisco, and curiously glanced over at all the heavy industry there. *So that refinery belongs to Unocal?* I thought. *That thing is enormous.*

As he talked, I put my feet up on my messy desk, stared out my second-floor window at the auto body shop and train tracks that ran in front of the old building where I rented space, and settled in for an adventure that might be more interesting than I first expected. That was sort of a habit of mine when clients called—to put my feet up on my desk. I suspect that this was my way of fooling myself into thinking I was in charge, that I didn't need clients, that everything was going fine and I had complete control over my career. But let's be honest—fooling myself that way just made it possible to not work in constant fear of malpractice claims, bankruptcy and being out-matched by lawyers with decades of experience. Whenever people like Ralph called me, I tried hard to tune out these realities.

Although Ralph didn't seem to mind, I was just a kid. In the field of law, 28 years of age still qualifies as a kid. Nor did he care that I was running my new law office on a shoestring budget, with only occasional volunteer help. And I had no safety net and no practical experience beyond a couple of short-term clerkships for firms while in law school and representing a couple dozen clients since passing the Bar examination and opening my solo practice. I barely had any business being a lawyer, much less talking with clients about cases against multi-national corporations. In other words, while I was hungry, I was very green and undoubtedly very foolish.

Divorcing my attention from these thoughts, I listened intently as Ralph's story picked up steam. He went on to explain how, just a day or two earlier, some managers, scientists and public relations people from the refinery had held a town-hall meeting at Crockett's Community Center on Pomona Street, not far from his home, and just a couple of miles northeast and downwind of the Unocal refinery. Several Crockett residents, including Ralph, had attended the meeting. According to Ralph, these residents were outraged and scared for themselves and their families, having been sickened by some airborne pollutants Unocal had recently released. Ralph was furious that Unocal wasn't, beyond this meeting, openly sharing what it had done.

The story was easy enough to track but I had serious doubts. I'd heard nothing about an airborne release until now. Plus, while I knew Crockett was a poor and a fairly small town, roughly 3,000 people in all, I wondered why there wouldn't be more than a few people attending this meeting if something so damaging had happened. Sure, I could hear fear and outrage in his voice, but I wasn't yet moved. My feet were still up on my desk—a telltale sign of disinterest—right where they usually stayed during most prospective client conversations.

In fact, my skepticism of any potential wrongdoing here ran deep. Refineries were hardly a major threat, I thought. Heck, I grew up in the 1970s in Richmond, California, about 15 miles south of where Ralph lived, with oil refineries, shipping companies and other heavy industry all around me. As a kid, I could see Chevron's 2,900-acre Richmond refinery from my house, with all the smoke and steam and Lord knows what else that would flare out of it, particularly on weekends when the health and safety watchdogs were off duty. In all those years, there were no major incidents, no catastrophes—at least none that I'd heard about.

And my dad was an expert on refineries because he, begrudgingly, worked much of his career at that Chevron refinery. That meant, in my mind, by my association to him, I was also an expert on refineries. And as an expert, I would have told you that living near refineries was not a big deal and not risky. After all, we lived there and even played there. No problems.

Indeed, on hot summer days back then, my parents would take us out through the Chevron refinery to the company's "Rod and Gun" club (originally known for its fishing and firing ranges) to swim and picnic. To get into the club, we had to drive through the nasty rotten egg smell that, to me, defined petroleum refining. But I didn't worry about it. Even my mom, the liberal environmentalist she was, seemed not to worry. She didn't like that my dad supported that kind of industry, but I wouldn't say she *worried*; at least she didn't show it. We all knew refineries stunk and yet, again, we turned out just fine.

But I continued to listen to Ralph's story, a little conspiratorial as it seemed. He explained that he and his wife had been suffering badly ever since gardening outside their Crockett home several weeks back. When they were outside in the yard, the air tasted funny, wet, and rough and, since that weekend, they'd been experiencing severe bronchial spasms, nausea, skin blisters, and high fevers. I listened intently, sympathetic to their injuries, but waiting for the punchline about extra-terrestrials or some other crazy theory that would allow me to quickly dismiss the story, just like I'd done with each of Ralph's prior stories. But the story wasn't crazy yet.

And there was more. He explained that his dog had also been acting peculiarly and had been scratching its fur so much that it was leaving raw, bare patches. Really sad, maybe even a little disgusting, but I thought, *How is any of this Unocal's fault?* I mean, let's be clear here; it's not that I didn't enjoy fighting the good fight against oppressive businesses, trying to level the playing field for the little guy and all. That's *why* I started my own law practice. But I wasn't about to sue some major corporation just because Ralph's dog was acting funky and the family had a weird flu.

On the appropriate pause, I explained my reluctance, pointing out that this just didn't add up. He immediately responded that I should talk to some of his neighbors—something a lot of potential clients say in desperation when you aren't immediately sold on their report. Purportedly, his neighbors were also very sick and some of them had even joined him at the recent town-hall meeting.

OK, now that's intriguing, I thought. Corroboration is key. Not exactly proof yet, I thought, but the story was getting a little more interesting. He suggested I go interview some of his neighbors, make some calls to the county, maybe even go out and get some samples before Unocal finished the job of washing down people's cars and houses.

And this is where the story really begins.

"I'm sorry, but Unocal is doing what?" I inquired, in a laughing, almost dismissive tone as my feet came down off my desk. Sitting up and reaching for a solid pencil and a clean tablet to scribble on, I asked the obvious question. "Why is Unocal washing down cars and houses?"

Feeling his power, Ralph slowed it way down, his voice deepening, recognizing I was a little slow on the uptake. "Scotty, they have a car wash set up in the refinery parking lot and they're washing everyone's car for free. And anyone who wants to get this sticky crap off their houses can call Unocal and they'll come around in their trucks and wash down your house for you. If you're getting sick from it, well, that's a different story. I guess you're on your own there."

I squinted with skepticism at what I just jotted down, but I was softening. *What the hell is he talking about*, but the possibility that he was on to something was gnawing at me, and the gnawing was giving way to anger. I hated recklessness and what some people did for control and money and I saw big business as being a common offender of my values in that regard. And my dad taught me that accountability—like not hurting other people with your misdeeds but owning up to it if you do—meant something. Dumping chemicals on your neighbors definitely qualified as a misdeed and merely washing down cars and houses didn't qualify as genuine accountability.

Too quickly I was getting swept up in his story and that wasn't good. I was taught in law school that you shouldn't get too emotional about your clients or their causes. Stay objective. Yet, while part of me remained doubtful about the accuracy of Ralph's details, another part of me was seething, already. I despise those who abuse their power, and I was getting a strong feeling that I was hearing an example of exactly this privilege and abuse of authority. I so badly wanted Ralph's story to prove me right. I should probably explain why.

First, understand that I didn't come from much and, whatever I had, I had to get for myself—and then fiercely protect it. I shared a modestly furnished, 1,200-square-foot house with my older brother and parents. A beat-up and unreliable orange camper was our family car. I started delivering newspapers when I was nine years old and then hustled my way into other jobs well before I turned 16. The Richmond high school I attended had no windows, only bars over the structural openings so students or members of the numerous local gangs couldn't come in after hours and vandalize or steal school property.

Ours was a racially charged, almost all-black high school and I was a short, skinny, freckled-faced redheaded kid who looked nothing like most of his classmates. Because I had to constantly watch over my shoulder and deal with a lot of bullies, I had to learn how to fight. It wasn't smart to turn my back on anyone. Moreover, my survival depended on exhibiting a tough-guy attitude, never backing down, taking risks to show I was brave. Being labeled a smart kid by the establishment and assigned to the school's gifted program didn't enhance my "street cred" and so, for that reason too, I over-compensated by openly rejecting what that establishment wanted to teach me, and I got bad grades as a result. Being labeled a "bookworm" would have just resulted in me getting beaten up more often. Out of all that rose a kid with a chip on his shoulder and something to prove.

With little interest in formal education, and barely passing grades in high school, it's a miracle I went to college at all. Now, listening to Ralph though, it was becoming clearer why I did go—and then went on to attend law school, but then rejected big-law-firm life or working for anyone else at all. I wanted the power and autonomy to help bring things back into balance whenever I saw the big voices—like those of the people of privilege—trying to take advantage of their positions. It looked like Ralph's town had been disrespected by such people and that wasn't fair. It threw everything off-kilter. This could be my chance to fix that.

I joined Ralph in slowing the conversation down. As you would expect, it's not unusual for prospective clients to overstate events, sometimes for no reason other than because their emotional response to their experience gets inadvertently blurred with the facts. Here, I might have concluded that Ralph was doing the same, maybe even intentionally trying to pique my interest by alleging his neighbors were equally sick. He'd cried wolf before. Moreover, I thought, *Hadn't Unocal been operating in that location, right on the edge of the bay, for almost a century?* I mean, given its track record of, at minimum, not killing the locals, wasn't it more likely that the company knew what it was doing and hadn't hurt anyone this time either?

But, then again, I never trusted big business.

In my mind, the big questions here were obvious: Why would a savvy, profit-minded corporation go to such effort and expense to wash potentially hundreds of cars and houses, and what exactly was it that was being washed off? The refineries I grew up around would release things like hydrogen sulfide into the air from time to time and, although that rotten-egg smell was pretty obnoxious, nothing was ever deposited on cars or houses that needed washing off. If that's all it was, there'd be nothing to remove. No, I thought—*big corporations never spend money unless it benefits them in some financial way. Couldn't that include hiding evidence of their mistakes?* I should have been getting ready for my court appearance, but I kept listening instead.

Ralph explained that, at least, one of the recent town-hall speakers admitted there had recently been an "over-spray" from the refinery. I thought the term "overspray" was intriguing since it suggested some lesser amount of spray was acceptable, but I decided to circle back to that issue later. Less concerned about generalities, I homed in on the juicier issue. "Ralph, what exactly was released?"

He didn't know the science behind it, but he had a name: Catacarb. And, while he didn't know what it was used for, he knew what it looked like—sticky, thick and brown, like molasses. I only later learned it contained a potential carcinogen known as diethanolamine (DEA) and some heavy metals. All Ralph knew was that it was making his town sick.

I pushed him for details he couldn't give but he assured me how obviously gross this compound would be if I came and took a look at the brown goop that now stuck to the house screens and their cars. *I'm not going out there,* I thought. *If this stuff is still in the air, I'm not risking my health.* But I was riveted.

"So, Ralph. What do you want me to do about all this?" I asked.

News flash—Ralph wanted to sue Unocal. No shocker there—and he wanted me to be his lawyer for it, and he knew a lot of people who might be interested in suing Unocal too. Something in the urgency of his tone and, at least, the specter of other people being interested in joining convinced me that this wasn't just another one of his wild legal schemes. I asked him to remind me of his address and then to hold on so I could grab a map of the area and check this out.

Studying the map, the Unocal oil refinery's dominance of the bay front was obvious. Sitting right there on the water's edge, the gusty winds coming off the San Pablo Bay would have taken anything the refinery spewed out and blown it right at Crockett to the east, or south into Rodeo, an even poorer neighboring community, barely twice the size of Ralph's hometown, and aptly named for the livestock roundups held by its original residents in the late 1800s.

Yeah, I knew this area, at least by reputation. Having grown up not far from these towns, I knew their close situation to so many refineries, electrical power plants and shipyards; heck, even the Southern Pacific Railroad had a main line that passed through these places to haul out major quantities of product. This was a heavily industrialized area, and heavy industry usually means filth.

Ralph's narrative was starting to get some traction with me and, I have to admit, the jury appeal was lovely. All the characters were accounted for: The big, bad oil company, sick residents of places where no traveler would have any reason to stop, a hard wind that whipped through the refinery, carrying away all the nastiness I'd seen and smelled in refineries growing up but, this time, perhaps something even more.

The story also had a great historical set-up; being from Contra Costa County, I'd forever heard of the area around Crockett and Rodeo referred to as "Cancer Alley," because of the high disease rates documented in people living there. I knew researchers had, for decades, been convinced of a link between industry there and many serious medical conditions. If Ralph's information panned out, this could be an important discovery. I thought that, if I got the chance to blow open a cover-up by Unocal, I'd let him call me "Scotty" forever. I ended our call with a promise that I'd do a little research, phone around to see if anyone could corroborate what he told me and then get back to him after my upcoming court appointment.

I sat for a minute in a bit of a fog after hanging up with Ralph. This was exciting, but I wasn't going to be made a fool. I needed to proceed carefully. I needed to hear this from someone beyond Ralph, *but where to begin?* Back in 1994, the Internet was an infant; there was no Google, no Yahoo!, and the World Wide Web (as it was then known) had been commercially available for a year at best and wasn't terribly useful. And so, I did what any other crack investigator would do to expose the insidious whitewashing of a multi-billion-dollar international corporation—I opened the phone book and started calling every government agency that I guessed knew anything at all about pollution issues. I didn't think it through. I just kept dialing.

I called the air quality management district offices (no answer there), fire and rescue services (no help), local hospitals (too busy). I even called the police department. I don't know why I called the police department. Apparently, they didn't know why I was calling them either and they seemed annoyed that I kept asking questions about an allegedly secret release of Catacarb that was hurting people and dogs. No one—and I mean no one—had any idea what I was talking about. There was no release, according to them. Maybe it was another refinery, according to them. Maybe my facts were just wrong. Maybe, I thought, I should just give up.

By the time I left for my court hearing, I was demoralized, convinced this was another one of Ralph's wild goose chases. It was quite a blow since it had all sounded so good. As I grabbed my court papers to go, I called and left Ralph a message that, despite 10 phone calls in that short time, no one had a clue what I was carrying on about, had heard anything about anyone getting sick or about any town-hall meeting. I told him that, for the people who didn't answer, I left messages, but that I absolutely had to leave then for court. I told him I would call him back later if something promising turned up. I then left the office, pissed off at myself for allowing my Robin Hood-ish leanings to cloud my judgment.

The drive to court was uneventful and the hearing went fine. I tried to push away all thoughts and dreams of the big case that wasn't, and I did my job well. Business as usual. I had made only a marginal investment in Ralph's fiction and, so, I ordered myself to give the conversation little weight. When so many cases that come your way end up being dogs—and as it was for me—you learn not to expect much.

Heading back to the office an hour later, however, my thoughts went back to Ralph. Was he confused or, more likely, just overplaying something insignificant? He'd certainly done the latter before. As I drove, I struggled to find closure since the alternative, of course, was that there was a colossal cover-up going on and, even for me, that was almost too much to stomach. I reminded myself that refineries sometimes release smoke or other particulates. While it was conceivable that had occurred here and that some of it may have indeed traveled downwind and landed on some cars and houses, this didn't necessarily mean there were lingering health hazards or, greater yet, grounds for a lawsuit. I walked back into my office, threw my suit jacket over a chair and hit the play button on my answering machine. One message.

One of the county officers I tried to reach earlier had called back. His message nonchalantly acknowledged that, indeed, Ralph was right; there had been a release, and it went toward Crockett. *Bingo! Well, that's corroboration*, I thought. And, sure enough, Unocal was responsible for it. According to him, it started on August 22nd and continued through the Labor Day weekend in early September. He said I could call him back if I had any questions.

Wait a minute...August 22? I thought. Labor Day was September 5th. Replaying the message, I wasn't sure if I was more alarmed by him telling me the event had gone on for more than two weeks or that his tone was so matter-of-fact. It sounded like he was just regurgitating a story he, mistakenly, assumed Unocal had already shared with the world. It also sounded like he had no idea anyone was sick.

I sat down for a minute, questioning the reason for the disconnect. If this chemical release was common knowledge, at least at the county level, why didn't Ralph and his neighbors know anything about it before the town-hall meeting? Had the county been complicit in this? Did it not take the event seriously? Had the county blindly trusted Unocal to share the proper information? I scribbled down a few critical questions and dialed him back.

When he answered, he blandly confirmed that Unocal had notified the county early on during the two-week period about an emergency of some kind being called at the plant, but was very vague about the report. He said that, indeed, chemicals had been released all the way through the Labor Day weekend, but he didn't know how much or exactly what they were. For a guy who allegedly held a high position at the county offices, I wondered why he was glossing over the details. I also wondered why he seemed so cavalier.

But I wasn't letting him off so easily. I asked if it was smoke. He confirmed that it was not. I asked if he knew about it settling on houses and cars in Crockett. He seemed surprised by the question and said he couldn't speak to that. I asked him if other towns in the area could have been affected by this and he adamantly and unequivocally said that they could not, because of the wind path and all. He very much wanted me to understand that the event was limited in scope, that the county was aware of it, and that there could be administrative fines against Unocal by his office or the air quality management district office if the event warranted it. I asked if this event warranted it. He couldn't answer that either.

I asked what the fine might be, and he gave another vague response about it depending on what happened and how much was released. This, of course, just begged the question: *How could he characterize this event as limited in scope if it also might be serious enough to warrant a fine?* None of this was adding up.

I ended the call thinking either he was right—albeit perhaps unprepared and rattled by my questions—that this situation wasn't worth my time or that the county was so worried about its own liability that he thought it better to tell me a half-truth than deny everything and virtually guarantee further investigation. I asked if there was anyone else there that I could talk to who might have more information.

"No," he said flatly. He was the person in charge of fielding such questions. *So much for our tax dollars at work*, I thought. Dismissively, he added that I could always call local emergency responders such as the police and fire department. He was done with this call, but I was now increasingly skeptical; by the inconsistency of his answers, I deduced his office had been too lazy or trusting to dig deeper and, now, he just wished it would all go away.

But I wasn't letting it just go away. You might chalk it up to an occupational necessity, but, even by this early point in my career, I had developed a keen aptitude for detecting liars. I think it had something to do with demanding respect, either for me or those I was supposed to be looking after, like the disenfranchised and oppressed people who ask for my help. Whatever the root, I absolutely couldn't stand bullshit. Here, I felt I was being lied to, and it was making my skin crawl. I knew I needed feet on the ground out in Crockett to uncover what was happening. I wanted an investigator to dig around there, turn over some stones, talk to the people and make sense of what I learned.

But that would cost money, and I had no money.

What I had was about 300 square feet of office space. What I had was a 1950s metal desk and a leather chair well-imprinted by my backside, and a few mismatched office pieces I acquired secondhand. My telephone and fax machine were new, but my file cabinet was covered with cartoonish stickers somebody else's kids must have placed there long before. What I did not have was money.

I called Ralph one more time and told him I wanted to keep fishing around, but would have to pull a favor from one of my very limited professional connections to make that happen. I told him I wanted to hire an investigator to spend a few hours in Crockett, hopefully at a reduced rate. He understood and accepted that, as my client, he might have to bear some of this cost in the end, whether or not the case was successful. For now, that was good enough for me.

"OK, Ralph," I said. "Let's do this."

CHAPTER 2

"DON'T TELL MEL"

I knew I needed to carefully investigate this new case, but I was really out of my league. I had handled relatively few cases since I started my law practice, all of them personal injury or workplace discrimination matters, and the only reason I even got those opportunities was through the referrals of an Oakland law firm that threw cases they considered beneath them in my direction from time to time. That was a win-win situation; I got a steady stream of clients and income, albeit a modest one, and they could divert unwanted people with one phone call (Ralph having been one of those). They never offered me any training, but I was ultra-aggressive and a perfectionist, and they were comforted by that.

I was fairly new to the practice of law but they could tell I was a person who'd research an issue I didn't fully understand for as long as it took—just to make sure I didn't miss anything. That was enough to convince them I could handle their referrals, at least those that panned out, but not enough to pay me anything for it. No money ever changed hands. I only got paid if I won for the client, and while I did collect on those sometimes, I still figured they owed me a favor, maybe in exchange for all the crazy people they sent my way, all the people to whom I had to say "no," after wasting a lot of telephone time. If I was right, if they did owe me a favor, now was the time to cash in.

Specifically, I needed a good investigator, someone who knew a lot more about sleuthing than flipping pages in a phone book. I talked to one of my contacts at their firm and was told they used a guy named John who was supposedly "the best." Great! I needed "the best." Well, candidly, what I really needed was "the cheapest," but "the best" would suffice. With John, I got both.

When I reached John that afternoon, I told him the story and asked if he was willing to work for me for a few hours as soon as he could. He was willing and explained that he would even do it at a special rate, given my relationship to the Oakland attorneys, but that he couldn't start until after work that day since this would be done on a moonlighting basis from his normal job. *He can do it today,* I thought. I certainly wasn't thinking it would be today, but I was fine with that.

In fact, I was fine with everything he said in that call, but was a little concerned about his loyalties. As he explained, his day job was for the late Melvin Belli, a preeminent personal injury attorney I knew only through his reputation as the "King of Torts." If John was good enough for Mel, he would be good enough for me, but I didn't want my scoop leaked to a far more experienced litigator before I even had the chance to investigate.

"OK, but don't tell Mel," I directed John, as we closed out our conversation. "And don't give my name out or try to sign up any clients for me. I already have a client. I just want you to interview people and see if this is as widespread as I suspect it might be. I'm not going to go learn all about environmental law if it's just for one person."

I had to be very specific about how I needed him to talk to people. What he said and didn't say in those interviews was important. I didn't want him trying to be a hero by drumming up business. That would just put me in ethical hot water with the State Bar for soliciting clients. "Go out and talk to as many people as you can and figure out what's happening," I told him. "I'll pay you for three hours, John, but please check in often. Good luck."

And then I told myself to let go, to let him do his job, to do some work on another case. No dice. I couldn't help myself. I found myself making lists of all the things I'd need to learn to litigate against Unocal. I tended to jump the gun like that.

Given my excitement, I decided to hang out at the office, make some more calls and stay available to get updates on John's progress. Around dinner time, I called him. He'd told me earlier that he could start in the late afternoon, and so I figured he'd already talked to several people by now and could tell me if the situation warranted further attention. In 1994, carrying a cellular phone was uncommon, so it impressed me that John did. But each time I tried his number, I'd get a message, or he'd answer in a hushed tone and promise to "call back," but almost never did. I was getting antsy.

Around 8:00 p.m., we connected for what I'd hoped would be a full report and he didn't disappoint. The anticipation was killing me, but his energy surpassed mine.

"Scott, there's something big going on out here," John explained excitedly, almost running over his own words. I grinned, reminiscing on Ralph's energetic preamble to our earlier conversation. John went on for a bit about reports from the residents he interviewed, including mention of a document someone handed him, a so-called "Fact Sheet" written by Unocal. *Ha. Gotcha!* I thought. This sheet talked about the release of this substance I already knew was Catacarb. John said Unocal had given out these sheets to some people a few days before, maybe even at that town-hall meeting. Some of the residents—and John had interviewed a lot of them—said they knew people who worked at local refineries and, therefore, had information even Unocal hadn't disclosed. John had been in the field for less than three hours and what he relayed was already quite eye-opening.

I asked him to tell me everything.

According to what he'd gathered, just before 7 a.m. on August 22, 1994, a few workers at the Unocal refinery noticed some kind of liquid solution leaking from a hole that developed around 140 feet up the side of one of its "unicracker" towers. They called the leaking unit "D-409," and it was one of these tall towers where hydrocarbons were cracked (i.e., broken down into their chemical pieces in a high-temperature, high-pressure system). This leaking solution was a highly alkaline substance which contained known carcinogens and was unquestionably known to Unocal to be highly toxic.

Workers at the tower quickly reported the leak to the refinery's management, a refinery-wide emergency was declared, and the County Health Services Department was notified. But, when it called the county, Unocal lied by claiming the leak didn't pose any danger. Blindly trusting this statement, the county did absolutely nothing. Beyond that call to the county, no agencies were informed of the leak, nor were residents of the neighboring towns, either by Unocal or by the county, until long after the end of this 16-day event.

Once aware of the leak, Unocal workers also started to shut down flows to D-409. This reaction was consistent with standard operating procedures, but what happened next was not; within a short time, the order to cease operations was countermanded by the refinery's second-in-command. After hastily-called meetings between some supervisors and engineers (but excluding health and safety consultants), Unocal's corporate office in Los Angeles ordered the unit be brought back up and to keep it running until its next scheduled maintenance on October 8. According to John, the workers at the tower were pretty pissed off at this decision but, despite their anger, continued to work the tower, trying to contain the release by hosing down the unit with water. All the while they kept running it, they were being lied to by upper management, being told that the toxic compound was safe.

John kept going.

Apparently, for more than two weeks that followed, the prevailing winds off San Pablo Bay blew the venting toxins over the neighboring communities of Crockett, Selby and Tormey and, to a lesser extent, over the cities of Port Costa, Hercules, Rodeo and the Bayo Vista public housing project that borders the refinery to the South, causing residents to develop sore throats, nausea, headaches, and dizziness. I knew what that meant. It meant the wind blew this garbage around for miles! As the hole increased in size around the Labor Day weekend, heightening exposure levels, even more serious health problems emerged, such as itchy skin, dry and itchy eyes, vomiting, nosebleeds, severe malaise, and a host of other symptoms. At least for the residents with whom John spoke, the symptoms persisted.

Perhaps most shocking, however, was that it wasn't these health problems that persuaded Unocal to stop operating the tower. When Unocal finally shut down the unit on September 6, it was because of a complaint from the Wickland oil terminal, a tiny industrial facility just north of Unocal. Someone at Wickland reported that Unocal's ever-worsening release was leaving greasy deposits on Wickland's equipment. Without this call, Unocal would surely have kept it going another month until the planned inspection on October 8. But it didn't matter. The damage was done by September 6. By that date, between 100 and 225 tons of the solution had already been dumped onto the surrounding communities and people were starting to become terrified.

I listened to John's report in absolute astonishment. I was amazed at how many details he had gotten and how people were apparently so willing to rat out their corporate neighbor. If this had been a scene from a movie, I'd have dropped the receiver.

Near-speechless, I stuttered out some questions about how these people had come by this information, and he told me. As it turned out, some of these people had been to the recent town-hall meeting, but, mostly, they had picked up details from insiders at the refinery or people with connections there. Clearly, something important was happening and the townspeople were starting to notice.

"These people are really sick," John continued, and I believed him. This guy was an investigator for one of the country's most successful personal injury lawyers. John knew sick.

"But you're not going to believe what just happened, Scott." I clenched my teeth and waited for the other shoe to drop. This was just too good to be true, and there had to be something wrong with the description. But that shoe never dropped. The tale just got better.

"Check this out. I go up to this lady's house and knock on her door and I tell her I'm from the law offices of Scott Edward Cole," John continued.

"You said what?" I interrupted, as I immediately recoiled.

I had specifically ordered him not to mention my name since it would look like I was canvassing for clients, and it might turn people off. Not wanting to slow him down though, I didn't get into it with him, but I braced myself.

John was clearly getting very excited. "So, I'm standing there, talking to this lady, when this truck pulls up in front of her house with the Unocal 76 sign on its door. And, as I'm talking to her, these two refinery workers come up the walkway toward her door."

"I'm listening," I cued him, hesitantly.

"So they walk up and say they're from Unocal and that they're there for an appointment to wash down her house. She says that's fine and that they can get started and then—I guess I looked suspicious or something—they asked me, kind of aggressively, who I was. And so I told them I was from your law offices."

Again. I recoiled. *Jesus, John,* I'm thinking. *This guy is really going to get me in trouble here. Now, Unocal is going to think I'm soliciting business, and that kind of thing is never good. OK, breathe,* I thought, calming myself.

"So, I told them, of course, that I was investigating the over-spray," John added. And then he paused. He already knew this was going to sound great.

"Scott, you should've seen the look of anger on their faces, and then this one guy gets really loud and he says, "Oh yeah? Well, you should get the fuck out of here!"

Whoa! Did my watch battery die or did time just stop?

You almost never hear things like that from representatives of big companies, especially if they might be facing a big lawsuit. I was a novice, but I already intuitively knew that. I didn't need to hear anything more, but I couldn't resist. I needed to be sure.

"Wait a minute—are you kidding me? Is that exactly what he said, verbatim?" I asked.

"Exactly what he said, Scott. I'm not kidding you."

And there it was. It was one of those moments when you feel like anything is possible. Sure, I thought, maybe this was just an overzealous investigator exaggerating the facts. Maybe he was even making up stories altogether so I might throw him more hours of work. I figured he'd must have seen his boss spin hundreds of stories in his clients' favor, but I really wanted to believe, and so I did. Trust is a decision and I decided to trust him. More accurately, I was *ready* to trust him. I would have to or else this story would have ended right there. The case might have gone nowhere and my career might have gone nowhere. But I already knew that I needed this experience. I was tired of waiting for something. I wanted to do something important. I decided this would be it.

Hearing all that I had, John got my enthusiastic thumbs-up to spend another hour or two in Crockett, at his discretion, but I already had what I needed. I had enough to know something big was brewing. Whatever had occurred, Unocal sure didn't seem to want people to know much about it, and, apparently, it had wound its workers pretty tightly. Those refinery guys must have been freaking out inside to have hassled my investigator as they did. Clearly, they'd been told to keep a lid on this event. I wanted to blow that lid clean off.

That night, I drove home in a mental fog. Despite still having more questions than answers, I tried to sum up these events to my fiancée, Liz, who undoubtedly had no idea what she was in for when she obligatorily asked about my day. Being an equally liberal-minded person, Liz immediately took offense to everything Unocal had done but warned me about getting involved in something that might be beyond my experience level or which could financially ruin us. I tuned her out, at least about her concerns.

Mostly, she was worried about money, and the unknown. We lived in a one-bedroom apartment with no real assets other than our cars and some cheap furniture left over from our college days. To her, a big case needed a big wallet. I disagreed.

"It's okay," I explained to Liz. "We'll just start small with the case, if it even becomes a case, and dial it back if it gets out of control. If we don't already have the revenue stream to support what might become expensive litigation, we can tighten our belts and ride it out. It'll be fine." But she wasn't persuaded.

"Our wedding is next month? Of course that's important," I conceded, yet rationalized that we had planned a short honeymoon anyway. I figured the case wouldn't interfere much with our nuptials or the trip. She had finished most of the legwork for the big event anyway. Plus, I thought, *How big could this thing really get?*

It was a one-sided conversation. I was interested only in hearing things that confirmed the decision I'd already made. They call that "confirmation bias"—when you search for and interpret information in a way that supports your preexisting theories and downplays everything else. It's not rational thinking, but I didn't care about rational thinking. I was mad, and everything else took second place to that. Unocal was a corporate bully and I don't tolerate bullies.

It wasn't our most agreeable evening, but I was adamant that this situation needed close attention, my attention, whether we could bankroll it or not. Liz and I fought, but I went to bed believing she'd come around to my way of thinking. And, if she didn't...well...she'd come around to my way of thinking.

As a rule, I pay close attention to my dreams, when I can remember them. When faced with complicated situations, I lie down and tell myself I need answers. By the time I wake up the next morning, I've usually worked it out with the right plan being obvious.

That night, I put my head down on the pillow and wondered how I'd embark on this journey, what needed my attention first, who I'd need to interview, what research I'd perform. It may not sound like the best way to calm down and fall asleep quickly, but it usually works for me. As someone who never needed more than five or six hours of sleep anyway, I wasn't worried that night about a few lost minutes.

As I lay there, I wondered, *What were those two Unocal workers so angry about anyway? Were they personally involved in allowing this to happen? Why would Unocal wind them up so tightly?* When businesses do bad things, I always assume a primary profit motive. Employers have a way of winding employees pretty tightly when loose lips could lead to financial ruin. Oddly, these thoughts gave me comfort since they fell right in line with my long-standing view of big business as overly privileged, untrustworthy, and dangerous.

Yes, this is all starting to fit together nicely, I thought as I flipped the pillow over to the cold side and cleared my head of everything else. I promised Liz we'd talk more about it later, but I was lying. I had no intention of debating this decision. I was hooked and my new sense of purpose calmed me. Wrapped warmly in self-righteousness, I closed my eyes and slept like a baby.

CHAPTER 3
CROCKETT

We woke up one morning; it was Labor Day weekend, 1994. We had a house that was on a hill, it's like the poor man's San Francisco. It's kind of like a town on the Mediterranean that comes up from the sea and all the houses are built terrace-like. And our house had a commanding view of the valleys and we faced the refinery which was west. And we woke up and I looked at the windows and they were covered with a sap-like substance like from a pine tree and I went, oh, God, what did those kids do?

— Crockett Resident

Having lived in San Francisco for many years as a college undergraduate, and then a graduate student, I can assure you of one thing: Crockett is nothing like The City. But that's not to derogate Crockett. Not one bit. Indeed, for a town that, from its many vista points, overlooks expansive bays, a panorama of mountains—Tamalpais, Mendocino, the Sierra Nevadas—and high-priced venues like Marin County and San Francisco, you might think Crockett's residents envy what they can only see from afar. But you'd be wrong.

The people of Crockett are not well-off financially, but they have a community pride reminiscent of any small Middle American town, despite their famous neighbors. Crockett is a provincial place where, despite being somewhat divided geographically by the Interstate and pockets of terrain so steep as to make further housing development impossible, people want to know their neighbors. To them, these community bonds are important for typical social reasons, but they're also a clever collective bargaining tool to better capture the attention of county officials, or when making demands upon any of the several petroleum refineries and other heavy industrial facilities that surround them.

In Crockett, nearly all the few dozen businesses nestled together along its tiny downtown strip are locally owned, mostly by the same townspeople who host the many yard sales, street clean-ups, barbecues, Easter egg hunts, bicycle races, fish fries, crab feeds, and bocce leagues you'll find there. And it is that down-home flavor that's kept families there for generations.

You could say that this is a forgotten place, but that might suggest that, at one point in time, it was anything more than an accident that someone from the outside world stopped here. That would simply be untrue. Suffice it to say that no one on Wall Street cares or probably ever heard about Crockett, but they have sure heard about the oil refining facilities there. Within a five-mile radius, you've got Shell Oil, Tosco, Chevron and dozens of other major corporations directly or indirectly tied to Big Oil, most of which have been there a very long time.

But, to Crockett at least, it wasn't the oil that brought the people and spawned this hilly little nugget. Without wheat and sugar, Crockett would probably never have made it on the map, despite its proximity to more popular cities, warm Mediterranean climate and convenient commercial situation along the south shore of the Carquinez Strait, the half-mile wide waterway that drains the Sacramento and San Joaquin rivers into the San Francisco Bay.

When first laid out as a town in 1881, it was a new flour mill that brought the people. Then, in 1906, it was sugar. In that year, the California and Hawaiian (C&H) Sugar Refining Company repurposed that flour

C&H Sugar Refinery in Crockett

mill and began processing pure cane sugar at the site. That's when Crockett took off. Indeed, during its early years, in the 1920s, roughly 95 percent of Crockett's several hundred residents worked in C&H's huge brick building along the waterfront, where cargo ships off-loaded raw cane sugar from the Hawaiian Islands. Sure, Crockett was always destined to remain a small town, but it was growing in significance.

Times were good for Crockett then and for decades to follow; the sugar plant served as the town's economic lifeblood, providing its plant workers and town residents access to a virtual fairyland of public amenities such as separate men's and women's clubs on the C&H grounds, a bowling alley, tennis courts, a shooting club and swimming pools. By 1956, when the 22-foot-high porcelain "C and H" sign was erected and illuminated by its 900 40-watt bulbs, Crockett had clearly entered its heyday.

By the time of the Catacarb chemical release in 1994, however, Crockett's prosperity was gone. Only a small percentage of the town's multi-generational families were employed at the C&H headquarters and, with most C&H workers living elsewhere, workers' wages were also going elsewhere. The sugar plant was still going strong but, by 1994, that strength wasn't helping Crockett. The town wasn't dead, but, with few local businesses to energize it, Crockett was on life support.

With that history, it's no wonder that Crockett's geo-footprint has stayed relatively constant. Indeed, Crockett's original town site of eighteen blocks, divided into lots of fifty by one hundred feet, still constitutes almost all of its unassuming downtown and flatland housing sections. And little has been done to change that. There are miles of cow-spotted grassy hills beyond its eastern and southern borders that have barely been tapped in the last half century, and when they have, for modest housing developments at best.

This is why the Census Bureau today still recognizes Crockett as having a total area of barely one square mile: almost no one is moving *into* Crockett. Indeed, even commercial developers with dreams of

Downtown Crockett

acquiring portions of the two rolling grassland expanses surrounding the town and operated by the East Bay Regional Park District would probably look elsewhere. There just isn't much to draw a crowd to Crockett and, even if there was, who would want to migrate to a region known for producing cancer clusters?

Similarly, before 1994 anyway, few people were moving out of Crockett. Although the intertwinement of the C&H plant and Crockett residents has unraveled over the decades, leading both residents and company to partner for work and workers elsewhere, the people in this town generally stayed put, simply commuting beyond its borders when necessary. With its relatively inexpensive housing, beautiful views and temperate climate, who could blame them? Sure, the refineries were poisoning the community, but just slowly and quietly enough that no alarm bells triggered an exodus.

In writing this book more than 20 years since the events described here, I went back to Crockett, naïvely expecting to see either a bustling metropolitan or a ghost town, but got neither. While there, I spent some time driving the neighborhoods, losing count of the number of American flags on front-porch flagpoles and the clucks of cooped-up chickens. I saw house address numbers burnt into wood and hanging on rusty chains by dirty screen doors and cars that hadn't been moved in years.

My first goal in going was little more than to reacquaint myself with the vibe and layout of the place, maybe snap a few photos and marvel at some of the best hilltop views anywhere—just stunning. I drove to one of the highest points in town, stood on one of its few legitimate sidewalks, while facing into a fierce wind at the edge of acres of tall golden grass. I gawked at a panoramic view of the shimmering bay.

With the majesty of the Carquinez Bridge and the Port of Crockett laid out below me, an elderly driver stopped his car behind me to brag. "Nice view, huh?" he asked, as I spun around. His tanned, pruned little face barely cleared the open car window, but I could see his pride.

"Sure is. Say, how long have you lived here?" I inquired, stepping toward his car, hoping to engage him in conversation, maybe even extract some anecdotal book fodder.

"All my life," he slowly boasted through his cracked smile and imperfect teeth. And, with that, he'd made his point. He turned his weathered face toward the road ahead, refocused, and drove on.

That's Crockett.

I told you how I pay attention to my dreams, how my sleep-turned-epiphany process never betrayed me, how my toughest riddles were often solved just by laying my head on a cool pillow. Well, apparently, it wasn't a perfect system. I'd like to say I woke the next morning after The Call with utter clarity, perhaps born out of some sense of righteousness in the cause. I'd like to say I had it all figured out. However, this is a true story, and so I can't.

In fact, I didn't recall any dreams and my thoughts were jumbled. By suggesting to Ralph I'd accept his case, I sensed I'd be committing to a lot. I'd be facing off with a corporation that aggressively pursued billions in revenue each year but was cavalier in its approach to protecting human health. *What does that say about how it will respond to me?* I wondered. What's more, I was promising to help even though I didn't have all the information about what had actually happened. I didn't know anything about Unocal's explanation. I wondered if I needed that and if I could reasonably expect to get it.

It wasn't realistic to think I could just call some source at the refinery who'd funnel inside information to me. All I knew for sure was that I needed to move fast and so I decided to take the morning to sit with it, to let marinate the information I already uncovered. I thought about that county representative who had confirmed the release had occurred. I remembered learning that the spray was constant for an entire weekend, maybe even an entire two-week period. I also had my very experienced investigator telling me something big was being covered up and who took notes of interviews with people who were very ill. And I remembered hearing that Unocal was spending a lot of time and money washing the evidence off houses and cars, and putting out an admission—its so-called Fact Sheet—that this company was the cause of this mess.

And, oh yeah, I had two Unocal workers telling my very pleasant investigator to stop snooping around—well—to "fuck off," actually. And I had Ralph.

Did I really need more? In the past, I would have thought so. Somewhere along the way, probably from watching too many legal television shows as a kid, I had been taught to sort of litigate backwards, to get all the evidence you needed for your case before you even filed it. It wasn't an unreasonable interpretation. After all, many of those television programs focused on the prep work, and not so much on the trial. They'd show the event or its immediate aftermath, the clever investigation, maybe even the big arrest. They'd focus on the dramatic exchanges between the investigators and the witnesses and the suspected wrongdoer. I thought lawyers simply watched that investigation from the sidelines, partnering loosely with the cops or private investigators who turned over those stones. But I didn't think the lawyers did much else at the outset and I thought they needed a fully-baked case assembled by somebody else before they did more.

The reality, however, is that lawyers do a lot of investigation but that doesn't mean that they need every fact before they file their cases. They just need the key ones. When I was younger, I didn't know about the "discovery process," and that's it's called a *process* because it's long and complicated and the way lawyers get all the additional facts they need for trial. That all happens after you file the lawsuit.

If I had to investigate for months, allowing the townspeople to forget about this event, allowing their outrage to grow cold, Unocal might have gotten away with it. I wasn't going to let that happen. I'd trust my gut on this one, not what I saw on some television show in my youth.

By the end of that morning, I'd calmed down, resigning myself to the fact that "where there's smoke, there's fire" and accepting that, while I already had some great intel, I was still pretty much going blindly into the unknown. I hadn't yet asked Ralph to sign a retention agreement, the contract that would allow me to act as his lawyer. I still had time to back out. But I couldn't. While I didn't know how harmful the chemicals were or where this case might go, Ralph was clearly on board. Whether based on intuition, the few data points I had or just my urge to stir the pot whenever possible, I finally admitted I was on board too.

When I reached Ralph that morning, I relayed everything John had told me the night before. That further fueled his excitement. I told Ralph we had a lot of work to do, but that we'd do it together. Ralph signed and faxed back my retention agreement within minutes and, with that, I was officially, categorically, hooked.

CHAPTER 4
THE WORM TURNS

It's always the same; the powerful can abuse the powerless, the disenfranchised—whether they are minorities, the poor, consumers or workers—for only so long. And then labor unions form, and civil rights movements begin. If it's true that most people inevitably get treated the way they permit themselves to be treated, and I think that is true, then change doesn't spring naturally from an acknowledgment by the ruling class of its immorality but, more often, out of the activism of the oppressed.

If you agree, then you'll understand why I work for the people, and not companies. It's not that I dislike companies. I own a company. But I work for the little guy because leveling the playing field requires organization and someone willing to lead others to action. I'm no Eugene Debs or some other famous modern-day social leader, but I yearn to mobilize people to demand better treatment. With the people of Crockett, in 1994, I got that chance.

Prior to the Unocal release, impoverished and discounted Crockett was like dry grass begging for a match. Unocal and its nearby industrial cousins had been spewing nastiness into the air for decades and the people were sick of it, literally. I had requested that Ralph give me contact information for his neighbors so I could conduct interviews and he obliged; I called them all, and every story I heard reinforced my conclusion that this town was fed up with the refinery and ready for a change.

It was immediately evident that everyone was suffering badly. This chemical release had done a number on them the likes of which they'd never experienced before. And each one of them had heard about others feeling ill too—all over town, some of them for nearly a month now. Some of them were second- or even third-generation Crockett residents and, while they spoke with fondness of the C&H Sugar plant and what that company had done for Crockett over the decades, they hated Unocal.

"That refinery always stinks," they'd tell me. "It's an eye sore," they'd complain. "Unocal doesn't contribute to or care about our community." They'd phoned the refinery before about odors, with no observable response. In nearly every conversation, I would try to keep the topic on the Catacarb release, but the floodgates opened the moment I mentioned the purpose of my call. They wanted to talk about what a horrible neighbor Unocal was, generally, and how they were tired of being ignored.

Concerning the Catacarb release, just like their eternal hatred of the polluter, their stories were the same—goop on their houses, cars, outdoor furniture, mailboxes, swing sets, garden fruits and vegetables, even the toys their kids forgot to bring inside. They were afraid to touch anything. Their stories about exposure to the chemical and lingering health effects also shared themes. Crockett has notoriously great weather and these people were often outside, particularly during the warm recent Labor Day weekend, when the release was most pronounced. They were gardening, barbecuing steaks, hiking in any one of the parks surrounding Crockett, swimming at the local community pool or just relaxing on their front porches socializing with neighbors. They were doing what many small-town people do—hanging out, walking their dogs, going to work, living easy.

During the release, they talked of a persistent metallic taste in the air and stickiness on their skin, much different than sweat. Their animals were also acting weird—jumpy and irritable—and their kids were lethargic, depressed and experiencing a host of other symptoms serious enough to make them miss school and seek medical treatment. Those were the saddest stories. No one likes hearing about sick kids.

Mimicking John's approach, I talked to a lot of people too. During the release, one woman was unable to walk outside without coming home with itchy skin and watery eyes. As the days passed, her symptoms progressed to frequent vomiting, nosebleeds and a severe malaise that now seemed permanent. She became one of my first clients.

As yet another resident later explained, "We thought we had landed in heaven when we bought our little house in Crockett. It's a friendly, nice community, and I kind of love it." That woman's health quickly deteriorated after the Catacarb leak too. She immediately experienced stinging eyes, a sore throat and upper respiratory irritation. Over time, her health worsened and her lungs were so damaged that they showed signs of lung disease and, for the first time in her life, she had asthma. Prior to the release, she had rarely called in sick to work. By the time we spoke, she'd used up all her accumulated sick time.

Not surprisingly, the children were even more susceptible, their relatively undeveloped immune systems less capable of rejecting the toxins. One homeowner spoke with a shaky voice about her kids having played with toys left in the backyard that were covered with a sticky, molasses-looking substance. Both of her children later developed chronic coughs and headaches and often cried, at times inconsolably, in pain. Her neighbor watched with horror the family's dog scratching off his own fur before it, too, got very sick and needed veterinary treatment. Other pets weren't so lucky and died in agony. These people worried about their children, their animals, about cancer, and about the apathy, perhaps even derision, of a company that could sit idly by, raking in billions in profits, while its product burned and poisoned so many. There was a case here all right—a big one.

Listening to all of this, I didn't care if Unocal, or the county for that matter, ever broke down and confessed their sins over this. I had everything I needed right there with those stories. These people were badly damaged, livid and terrified, and everyone was asking me what I intended to do about it. And then they asked for my contract so they could be a part of it. It didn't matter anymore that I knew we'd be out-matched. This town needed a change. This was a revolt and I was caught in its vortex.

The worm had turned all right.

I spent a good part of that day listening to stories, preparing and faxing around my retention contracts, establishing times to talk more. It was fast-paced, but I had still time to worry. I realized that if I was going to tackle something of this magnitude, not only did I need to clear my calendar, but I needed more help. I wasn't sure I could do this alone.

But even with help, I knew its management would undoubtedly fall on me. Luckily, I was poised well to accept that burden. I had the time, plenty of it. My fledgling law practice had no repeat business; everyone came to me through word-of-mouth. Also, fortunately, always being on the prosecution side of things meant I could speed up or slow down the momentum of my few other cases, pretty much as I saw fit, and without taking much grief from the defendant's lawyers. Those defense lawyers, wanting to protect their clients' resources, were usually quite content to sit back and wait if it didn't appear I was in any rush.

Moreover, I was a solo practitioner, meaning that, while I had no one, except the occasional volunteer intern, working for me, I also had no one to tell me how I should spend my time. I loved that. Therefore, as long as it didn't substantially impact my other clients, I could jump in to this case feet first. But I needed help. An intern couldn't serve well as a sounding board for complicated legal strategies and questions that were already beyond my experience. An intern also wouldn't stay around long enough to see the case to its conclusion. I needed another attorney, preferably someone with the same ambition and focus on efficiency I had. I needed someone with a street fighter's temperament, and that was Doug.

Talk to Doug today and he might disagree. He might say he was a bit more refined than all that, but that's not how I viewed him then. Doug was a guy who would replace his workweek suit-and-tie veneer with an obnoxious tie-dye shirt on Saturdays. Doug was a nonconformist. He cleaned up well but preferred to get dirt under his nails whenever possible. He was a problem solver and a fixer who loved to turn over stones in a lawsuit to see what he could find underneath. Well-educated and worldly, Doug's trademark was how he approached every case intuitively and aggressively, with an edge that suggested he had to prove something, just like I did. We both needed to stir things up. We just connected that way.

Like me, Doug possessed a "leap before looking" approach which I didn't see as reckless or inconsistent with great lawyering. In fact, so much of what I see exceptional attorneys do seems driven by instinct, passion, a want for justice, and an innate sense of how to move people to action. Let's face it: lawyers are glorified salespeople. We sell ideas. I think you're born with a knack for that or you aren't. I was. So was Doug. He was a salesperson, and a great attorney, and whatever he lacked in experience, he more than made up for in ambition and street-smarts.

Doug graduated law school a few years before me and started his practice soon thereafter. Interestingly, however, our introduction would not have occurred but for the legal matchmaking of his wife, Katy. I worked with Katy on what was, for me, a short-term project for the University of California at Berkeley while I awaited my bar results. Luckily, I had a big mouth and, so, as soon as I learned that I had passed the licensing exam and could start practicing law, I talked with whomever would listen around the workplace about my big plans to start an office and handle workplace discrimination cases. Katy overheard this and immediately suggested I meet with her husband, who also had a solo practice and who needed help with an employment law case referred to him by another law firm based in nearby Oakland.

My first meeting with Doug was at his downtown Berkeley office, just two blocks from where I worked for the University. We talked about our respective paths to law school, our dislike of big business and how fun it would be to sue the particular large corporation about which we were meeting. We became fast friends, filed that suit and, in doing so, were positioned against the biggest employment law firm in the country. Without regard for the risks of attacking such a Goliath or its representatives, we hit that company hard, and it felt great.

After settling that case, Doug and I continued as good friends and colleagues, taking on a few additional cases and having the time of our lives taking on companies and causes from which many lawyers would have run quickly. It was Doug who had given me that metal desk my heels were on when Ralph first called. It only seemed fitting that we would take on Unocal together.

Taking a break from my witness calls, I phoned Doug and invited him to work on the case with me. After a very cursory description of the events, his immediate acceptance wasn't any surprise. In his signature style, it was a simple, "Yeah, man. How can I help?" That's how he always was, never once complaining about being overworked or under-appreciated, and never afraid to take risks.

I worked a lot of evenings in those days and it's a good thing since those first few days brought in such a volume of calls that I had to return many of them after hours, and even direct some to Doug. Apparently, Ralph was a vocal guy, and his neighbors were getting bolder and increasingly motivated toward action as their symptoms persisted. Without Ralph's campaigning efforts in those early days it's hard to imagine where this case would have gone. He knew people in the most heavily-impacted area and that was invaluable.

As it happens, the hilltop in Crockett, where Ralph and his wife lived, was probably the most concentrated area of exposure, both according to the wind data and the disproportionate number of homeowners there who spent time outdoors during the release's heaviest period. And while inquiries came from all over town, the diversity of people—mothers, construction workers, local business owners, students—within a couple of blocks of Ralph's house convinced me that Catacarb was an equal opportunity pollutant that, in one way or another, touched everyone.

It's thrilling that every case I accept gives me the opportunity to learn something. It might be about the product or service of a particular company, or the various and weird jobs people do, or something more nerdy, as in an environmental case like Unocal, where disciplines of chemistry, medicine, meteorology, and toxicology intersected in a big way. That many lawyers can say they are perpetually learning is probably what keeps them practicing well beyond the age at which people in most other professions are retiring. The way I figure it, for the curious soul, being a perpetual student keeps you sharp and happy.

Because I had almost no background in the hard sciences (e.g., chemistry, meteorology), I knew I had much to learn if I didn't want to disappoint my clients. And yet, these were not disciplines that I could easily study. My undergraduate major was in Speech Communications. Yet, now, lacking the resources to hire experts, I needed to offer the residents telephoning me like crazy more than a bald recitation of the legal claims we'd make on their behalf. These people knew they lived in a cancer belt, and they suspected it was the fault of the several refineries that flanked their town. They were tired of living this way and welcomed a white knight who'd come in and shake things up, but the knight would need a sharp sword.

What's more, the townspeople were frightened that this Catacarb release would end up being the final straw, the catalyst to something life-threatening. For the clients who had kids, their terror meant they'd have little patience for any lawyer who wasn't able to hit the ground running. I needed to get up to speed quickly on exactly what had hit them and what it could do to their families.

Despite my recollection of the Cs and Ds I got in my high school science classes, I was ready to do this work because I couldn't be labeled "incompetent" or go down without a fight. Fear is a great motivator. As a young solo practitioner working without a safety net, embarking on something way beyond my expertise meant I had fear in spades.

To tackle this project without phenomenally embarrassing myself, I needed at least a rudimentary understanding of these areas of science, and I'd have to gain it within a few days. I had just heard from one of Ralph's neighbors about a *second* town-hall meeting, this one set for September 22. That was just one week away! Given my growing notoriety, I knew I needed to be there and, ideally, with a crisp new lawsuit in hand. I wasn't sure how I'd do it, but I had to work fast.

I also didn't know who would be presenting at the upcoming meeting, but I'd heard the ostensible agenda was about a land use permit being sought by Unocal and only secondarily about the Catacarb release. For the Catacarb portion, I suspected that Unocal's scientists and engineers would be there. I needed to at least pick up the basics, but I wasn't sure how to quickly learn enough about refining processes and exposure-symptom relationships to face off with Unocal's PhDs.

So, there I was, feeling lost again. I owned no reference books, the Internet wasn't even called that yet, and my college study of the works of Nietzsche and Plato, while perhaps mildly useful for picking up girls on campus, wouldn't make me particularly dangerous in court. Although my dad had been a chemist—and I certainly tapped him as a good starting place—I needed to learn specifically about Catacarb and its connection to my clients' mix of symptoms.

Completely out of other options, I figured it was time to swallow my pride and get a library card. I gathered all the loose change I could find and booked myself out for a little field trip.

Walking into the Oakland public library that Friday afternoon, I felt like a kid again. I hadn't stepped foot inside one of these things since I was a high school sophomore. What's more, as someone who had just squeaked through chemistry, I was a little reluctant to embark on any field of study that used terms that I could barely pronounce. In fact, I was the guy who always joked that avoiding studying any more science was one of the chief reasons I went to law school. And yet, there I was, standing at the Information desk, hands pushed deep into my front pockets, sheepishly trying to explain to the librarian my project.

"Excuse me, but do you have any books on petroleum refining processes?" I asked, "How would I find out what human organs are targeted by inhalation of particular chemicals? What magazines or other news sources do you carry that might discuss air pollution issues? Is there a section here on veterinary medicine?" Most of my law school colleagues had gone to work for big firms that had their own libraries. *What am I doing, at 28 years old, applying for a library card?*

It was a little embarrassing. Maybe I felt I deserved what my friends had. Maybe I thought the importance of this research exempted me from having to sit two tables down from a guy who smelled like wet dog and mumbled. But, luckily, the embarrassment didn't last long. When you're there, nobody knows you, and nobody cares enough to judge you when you're pulling a massive number of books off the shelf and stacking them around you like ramparts. And that was good since, not wanting to overlook anything, that's what I did. I grabbed every item that seemed remotely relevant and found a spot where I'd have anonymity, and be left alone.

And, with that, the work began, and I examined everything I could find, terrified I'd miss something critical. I've always been a first-class Funneler—a term I coined years ago to describe a researcher who spends a ridiculous amount of time identifying all possible information sources before really examining any one of them for substance. My official position is that funneling is about ensuring that the full breadth of sources are considered before dismissing any one of them, but, candidly, it's just code for being OCD. Whatever. Obsessive-compulsive? I'll own that. And it's not that being overly inclusive in collecting resources is, in itself, a groundbreaking concept; many careful researchers take such an approach, yet achieving first-class Funneler status virtually ignores the pragmatism associated with well-directed research. No, my method was more fear-based at a time when I really didn't have the luxury of letting fear slow me down.

Much to the bemusement of the children sitting at nearby tables, I brought my best funneling skills to the library that day, surrounding myself with tall-enough stacks of books and magazines to soothe my obsessive tendencies and quell my nerves. I reviewed microfiche and microfilm, and read newspapers and hauled out the oversized folios. If I was going to file this case for Ralph and his neighbors, it certainly wouldn't be out of reckless decision-making. This was going to be a monstrosity. I needed to go into it with eyes wide open.

My table must have been quite the sight, with no fewer than 35 books piled in a semicircle around me at any given time covering every scientific branch—Metallurgy, Toxicology, Chemistry, Human and Veterinary Medicine, Psychology, Horticulture, Meteorology and Wind Modeling, Chemical Engineering and Oil Refining—from which I suspected questions would be thrown at me from clients, friendly witnesses and litigation naysayers (every town has those, believe me).

Basically, I would need to grasp everything Unocal would be addressing at the upcoming meeting, yet without knowing much about its agenda.

One thing that I was sure of was that Unocal had been downplaying the toxicity of Catacarb. So, I'd need ammunition to show that it was lying. I also needed to know if the amount of chemical released was really enough, from a scientist's point of view, to cause the harms reported. That fact was *everything*.

You see, refineries emanate smells and smoke and other junk all the time, but whether the claims here could technically support a lawsuit required something more, but there wasn't more, not yet anyway. There were no studies on the impact of Catacarb, only that its components could injure or kill, even in small doses. Thus, I'd have to learn about those components too, and those answers would undoubtedly lead to more questions. I had to start from the bottom up, from scratch, and I'd need the resources at my fingertips. Thank God for libraries.

I knew that a Friday afternoon in the library wasn't going to make much of a dent in this volume of information, but I tried anyway, returning the next morning with a pocket full of change for the photocopying machine, and a full head of steam.

To see me sitting there, inside my fortress, speed-reading, tabbing and flipping pages in a furious effort to beat the clock and achieve maximum absorption before the library closed, must've looked like an exercise in futility, but it felt great. By the time I left, I wasn't thesis-ready but had gathered enough data to shine in front of my clients or anyone considering becoming one, and that was kind of the point. And it was also enough information to begin drafting the Complaint—the legal document that would initiate the lawsuit—and get it on file before the next community meeting. That was key.

I left the library late Saturday afternoon, found the nearest tavern that offered strong ale and deep corners to hide in, and started reviewing what I'd photocopied that day. I needed to focus, and to be among regular people. Two pints and several peer-reviewed articles later, I was ready to take on the world. It was probably the alcohol talking, but I didn't care. I had some power now and I liked it. For what was coming, I'd need to stock up on that. For what was coming, I'd need all the confidence I could get.

CHAPTER 5
CATACARB:
"A TOXIC SOUP"

The Occupational Safety and Health Administration of the United States Department of Labor requires that all employers, Unocal included, maintain and make available to employees what are known as "Material Safety Data Sheets" (MSDSs) for all potentially harmful substances handled in the workplace. You've probably seen these at your dry cleaners, and at gas stations, and any place of business that handles serious toxins. MSDSs must also be made available to local fire departments, local and state-emergency planning officials, and the public.

The regulations demanding this are extremely important ones. Mandating these disclosures supports emergency planning for response efforts to chemical accidents and provides the public with information about possible chemical hazards in their communities. Predictably, especially since it is used throughout the refining industry, there is an MSDS for the chemical solution Catacarb and, as you might have guessed, it reveals that it's pretty nasty stuff.

One of my newest clients reported she had been among the few to attend the first town-hall meeting—the one that Ralph had attended and that had made him so mad. At that meeting, Unocal representatives swore up and down that Catacarb was safe, particularly since, as they claimed, the release had been diluted by water and such. At the meeting, Unocal also promised that symptoms from exposure to it should be gone within a few days. Of course, they weren't.

And while the company's representatives did concede that Catacarb's abrasive nature could cause some irritation to eyes, ears, noses and throats, they were clear that there was no documented connection between Catacarb exposure and the kind of ongoing symptoms community members were reporting. It's true there was no documented connection, but only because no one had yet *studied* a connection. This was a total whitewashing. I knew it, and the community knew it. Even Unocal knew it.

Even more shockingly, at this meeting (and at subsequent meetings), Unocal also had the audacity to whitewash Catacarb's toxicity, likening it to soapy water. It was the same message it gave to its own workers for weeks. There was no denying that. Company managers had sent various memoranda to employees, including one sent a full seven days into the 16-day release, after they really thought about it, saying the solution was not harmful. Even one of Unocal's Incident Commanders was told by Unocal's management that Catacarb was no more dangerous than regular soap. I almost couldn't believe it was still perpetuating the myth.

This, of course, was nothing close to the truth and it wouldn't require days in a public library to figure that out. You could just ask the locals how they felt, which I did. They were in pain and, yet, no one could say exactly why—because the Catacarb release was of a mix of ingredients not entirely understood. For this reason, somebody—I think it was initially me—labeled the Catacarb compound a "toxic soup," and the label stuck.

So, what do we actually know about Catacarb? Well, within the unicracking tower D-409, which ultimately developed a hole near its roof, Catacarb's job was to purify hydrogen for gasoline production.

The system required that other compounds be steadily introduced into the tower and Catacarb then be pumped in to "scrub" (a term used for purifying or "washing" a gas or liquid) those compounds to break them into their elements—the way one might break water down into its hydrogen and oxygen building blocks under high heat and/or pressure. To do all this, however, Catacarb needed to be really abrasive, and it was, with an alkaline level roughly that of household lye. In fact, it was this abrasive quality that ultimately corroded the insides of this unicracking tower and opened a portal that blew hundreds of tons of the toxic soup into the air and miles downwind for 16 days and nights.

Clearly, Catacarb was nothing like soap. Among other things, the MSDS for Catacarb warned Unocal that the solution contained such things as vanadium (a heavy metal), borate (also nasty stuff) and diethanolamine (DEA), all commonly known by those in the refining industry to have a distinct profile making them extremely toxic to people. In fact, it's well-known that DEA commonly breaks down into something called nitroso-diethanolamine (N-DEA) in the open air, as well as in the human digestive system. N-DEA, for those few readers without advanced degrees in petrochemistry or toxicology, is a chemical known to cause cancer. Soap, by contrast, doesn't normally cause cancer.

Also, no one would have sued Unocal for soaping up Crockett, but they did over Catacarb because, under the Safe Drinking Water and Toxic Enforcement Act of 1986 (a.k.a. "Proposition 65"), it was illegal for Unocal to "knowingly and intentionally expose any individual to a chemical known to the [State of California] to cause cancer or reproductive toxicity without first giving clear and reasonable warning to such individual." N-DEA was a Proposition 65 chemical long before 1994 and, yet, Unocal gave no warning that it was sending an estimated 12 to 43 tons of its source compound (DEA) downwind. It wouldn't even matter if Unocal played dumb and said it didn't know how bad Catacarb was. Under Prop 65, Unocal was liable—strictly because it released it.

But, taking it a step further, even if it hadn't read the MSDS for Catacarb, or overlooked the bright hazard symbols on the Catacarb packaging put there by its Kansas City manufacturer, or read Proposition 65, there could be no real question that Unocal knew of Catacarb's toxic properties. I know this because, prior to the release, Unocal had also undertaken a study of Catacarb. It wasn't exactly the health study I would have wanted, but it examined what was inside the compound. The study identified its components as including a lot of tongue twisters—things like potassium metavanadate, potassium borate, polyhydroxyl alcohol, and the DEA material I mentioned already. Its report showed Catacarb was dangerous.

I also found out Unocal had received a report in February 1994, six months before the release, indicating that a substantial amount of the Catacarb solution consisted of material that was either already carcinogenic or could degrade upon its release into the air and become cancer causing. Some of this material could barely even be identified since it was so adulterated and distorted by the time it hit the atmosphere, but it was still clearly toxic. Unocal knew.

But wait, there's more. In May 1994, Unocal personnel prepared an application for issuance of a Material Safety Data Sheet for a hybrid of the Catacarb solution then also being used at the refinery, but no actual MSDS was ever issued, at least not before the August release. While it's still unclear why the MSDS never came, it doesn't matter. Under these strict environmental laws, you don't get an "E for Effort."

According to that May 1994 application, DEA constituted at least 10% of the overall Catacarb solution, which means as much as 45,000 pounds of this cancer-causing ingredient was dumped relentlessly onto Unocal's thousands of unsuspecting neighbors, their pets, their gardens and other property for those 16 days. And there is no denying it was dumped; after the release, one of Unocal's own contractors found carcinogenic N-DEA in a soil sample taken downwind of the refinery.

Through my own research, as well as through documents many witnesses were then bringing to my attention, I was learning a lot, and it was damning, and really frightening. Contrary to the assurances given by Unocal's representatives, this compound could cause blindness and death. Even in smaller doses, it could cause severe eye and skin irritation, kidney, liver and central nervous system damage, and the destruction of various body tissues, just to name a few. This is what pure Catacarb could do, all by itself. However, compounding the problem was that the stuff Unocal had unleashed wasn't pure Catacarb anymore. It was a blend of Catacarb and who knows what else. And, if it wasn't pure Catacarb anymore, the sky was the limit as to what damage it could do.

As I investigated further, the reason for this blending became clearer, and it had to do with what was happening inside that tower. Specifically, as Catacarb was introduced into the unit, it would get mixed with whatever else happened to already be in there. There was no fresh start each time the tower got a new shot of the compound.

Then, after each shot, the new soup recirculated inside for months, years sometimes, under high temperature and pressure before transforming into something else altogether—a dirty brown, viscous liquid full of unidentifiable materials that might be dramatically different from what anyone could predict. Hundreds of tons of that mysterious end-result were sprayed over the townspeople in those fateful weeks. No one knew exactly what it was—just that it was making people and animals extremely sick, and that was making them very scared.

So, exacerbating the townspeople's physical symptoms was this fear of the unknown, and they wanted explanations. Residents were starting to question Unocal, even forming a small group to negotiate with the company for increased air monitoring to track anything still in the air—but, predictably, getting no answers. I thought that lack of an honest response seemed cruel, but what I failed to consider at the time was that it didn't necessarily suggest evasion. Rather, it more likely suggested something even scarier—Unocal simply didn't know what this modified Catacarb could do.

The county didn't either and, while it tried to address some of the furious questioning, it was doing an equally poor job of it. Still, I thought the county *should* know, or at least go figure it out. It had been complicit in the event by not watchdogging the refinery better, especially after being notified of the leak. I thought it owed it to the citizens to obtain whatever information was needed to calm them, or at least to help them make informed health decisions. I even thought about suing the county, but decided against it, mostly in hopes of keeping it as an ally. I figured the specter of litigation would provide local government enough incentive to feed us documents which we might otherwise have to strong-arm away from Unocal. Plus, the damages permitted against government entities are always very limited.

No, to answer the questions residents really cared about, we couldn't rely on the county, and certainly not Unocal. So, I kept searching. With my newly acquired, albeit rudimentary, understanding of these fields, I called physicians, veterinarians, toxicologists, metallurgists, real estate experts, environmental engineers and experts in refining operations, asking for professional resumes from each of them, asking the questions locals had been asking me, asking whether they thought we had a case (they did). I knew I might have to retain some of these experts anyway, so I figured I'd better start making these connections early.

But even through expert interviews, my library time and resident interviews, the data I was collecting was just the tip of the iceberg. I was almost nowhere closer to determining what pockets of the community had been hit hardest, how long residents' symptoms might last, if it was safe to clean their own cars, or their houses, whether vegetables

The Rodeo Refinery

they'd grown in their gardens were safe to eat, and whether the many pregnant women now calling me had valid concerns about their unborn children. My clients, their refinery contacts and public agencies could only provide so much, and not one of them could explain *why* this horrible decision had been made.

Nonetheless, I needed to cut bait and file the lawsuit quickly, with or without knowing that motive, although I really wanted it. *How could Unocal not have considered the impact of its inaction?* I wondered. *Did it consider it but just not care?* Maybe I'd have to wait on those answers since, if I didn't take steps fast, it was questionable what would become of this event. Would it be pushed under the carpet and forgotten, or maybe just downplayed long enough that the community would let it go, like many unempowered communities do?

I had other good reasons to worry too. For example, I saw what was already happening around town: evidence was being taken and destroyed. Items like cars, houses, and backyard toys were being washed down by the company and no records were being kept. Few samples, if any, were being taken. Even when some residents asked Unocal for samples of the sticky goo being removed from their property, those requests fell on deaf ears.

What's more, Unocal was out there, culling the herd of potential plaintiffs, which demanded my swift response. Unocal was almost forcing residents to sign liability waivers which, once signed, could insulate the company. The stories of these efforts were sometimes alarming. One resident took his vehicle to the so-called free car wash at the refinery. Once his vehicle was cleaned, Unocal's crew wouldn't return his keys until he signed a statement promising not to sue the company. I knew that kind of coercive waiver probably wouldn't be enforceable, but other kinds might. I had to move fast. It had been only a few days since my first conversation with Ralph and just a few days before the next town-hall meeting, but things were happening at warp speed. I needed to keep up.

Hearing these stories of the refinery trying to avoid accountability, the decision to sue quickly was easy. I knew that, once a lawsuit was filed, Unocal had a heightened obligation to preserve relevant evidence, and that might include samples of what was being removed from my clients' homes and cars. By the speed of its cover-up work, the damning evidence might be gone within a few weeks. We needed it preserved, meaning we'd need to file now. To most lawyers, it would have mattered if they had almost no money to file the suit—and that the corporation they were attacking was worth billions. I simply didn't care.

Maybe I felt I had little to lose, or maybe I just felt righteous, but either belief can render a person very dangerous. Yep, I was suing Unocal. I was going to prepare a Complaint and try my best to make it hurt, but after just one more thing: I needed to face my opponent and, in particular, I wanted a closer look at tower D-409. So did Doug. We needed to drive out to the refinery. We had to see the magnitude of what we were about to take on.

The next day, I crammed some supplies into my convertible Miata and picked up Doug. As short as I knew our trip would be, I insisted we stop for gas to top off my soft-top's little tank. Ironically, despite our destination being a petroleum producing facility, I worried about running low on fuel.

Unocal's facility was only 30 minutes north of my Alameda office. Access roads to the refinery were limited, given its situation on the shoreline of San Pablo Bay and the tight security not unusual for an industrial facility capable of doing massive harm to the surrounding area. This meant that, unless we came in on one of the many cargo ships that routinely visited Unocal's docks—which didn't seem practical—it was going to be difficult for us to conduct a covert visit. Knowing this going in, we'd attempted to pre-map vantage points from which we could get good photographs of refinery equipment, yet work fast enough so that no one from the company would notice us. With my 35 mm camera and AAA maps on board, we advanced on Unocal.

Spanning more than 1,100 acres and with countless miles of piping, the refinery's size matched that of several small towns in the area. No matter what route you use to get there, its enormous holding tanks, some 50 feet high by 100 feet in diameter and adorning each neighboring hilltop, are visible for miles around. We came in from the north, a more dramatic entrance since it offered a glorious juxtaposition of the natural San Pablo bay on our right and several of Unocal's huge man-made vessels ahead and to our left. Most of that area is dry grassland, but the moment we rounded the bend of that old highway carved into the hillside, it was all Unocal, and there was no question we were in a whole different world.

It was an overwhelming place. I'd driven my fair share of American highways, but never before that day had I driven a road, looked up and seen pipes running overhead—in this case pipes connecting two massive sections of Unocal's operation. It was a warm afternoon, as Septembers in that area typically offer, and the ragtop was down in my car, providing me an excellent view of those massive pipes as we passed underneath. Craning my neck and slowing my car to get a better look, I thought, *Wow, how do you get the right to do that? Or is it just that Unocal has been here so long that the roads came later?* But which came first didn't matter. The facility had the money, determination and political clout to put its equipment wherever it wanted. That thought was just as awe-inspiring as the vision around us.

As we pulled to the side of the road near the Administration building's parking lot—the place we heard the car washes were being performed—we nervously checked our map. While still a public road, we were aware that normal public-access rules might not apply here, and I was jittery. This was Unocal Country and, from what I could see, it wasn't interested in sharing its land with anyone. Alternating between examining the map and pointing fingers at various processing units on all sides of us, I hurried to get our bearings before being pegged as outsiders.

Which is the tower that leaked? I wondered as I folded and flipped and turned the map in all directions, having heard only rumors about the infamous D-409's location. No luck. Frustrated, unsuccessful and impatient, I grabbed the bulky camera behind my seat, popped off its lens cap and rapidly took several photographs in a panoramic style. *It's lucky we're in a convertible,* I thought, as I hastily crammed the camera back behind my seat and drove down the road to what I hoped would be a less-conspicuous vantage point.

I understood the importance of having as many photos of the facility as possible. Since these shots might help determine distances to our clients' homes and workplaces, I figured we'd better determine where, within the refinery, the infamous tower stood. And, yet, this was a large facility and I had no idea what side anything was on. Our topographic maps were rudimentary and confusing, but I felt I needed to personally witness how exposed the tower was to the high winds common to the area. If sheltered behind a hill, for example, those winds would simply have whipped around the natural barrier, largely avoided the tower, and not carried the Catacarb very far. But, if that tower directly faced the Bay, the strong gusts could have blown the toxins for miles.

I also knew that getting a lay of the land would ease my conversation with refinery workers if and when we began interviewing them. It would also make it easier to describe to Unocal's attorneys what sections of the refinery we ultimately wanted to physically inspect. These were all legitimate justifications for a drive out there, but they weren't my principal reason for coming this day. Rather, I needed a mental imprint of the villain. I needed something I could carry with me as I embarked on what was to become the most challenging case of my career, as if sizing up the enemy early would motivate me to keep fighting when things looked bleak.

Determined to capture the perfect photograph, I stopped the car every few hundred feet, jumped out to take a few shots, hiding the camera behind my back each time a vehicle drove by. I had no real clue what I was recording. It just seemed important to document everything. It also didn't matter that, in those days long before digital cameras, processing film was expensive. I just kept snapping away, changing film canisters often, all the while recognizing how little of Unocal's overall operation I was really getting. *This place is just massive,* I thought, and it was. That's how oil refineries often are—massive, and efficient, and dangerous. Drive by one at nighttime and you'll see what I mean. Their thousands of eyes glow in the darkness because they never sleep and, if angered, the result can be catastrophic.

Unocal's facility was no exception. With its capacity to refine 80,000 barrels of crude oil and millions of gallons of fuel per day, this place was frightening in its potential to do harm. Plus, despite employing hundreds of local residents in all kinds of job positions that I still don't quite understand, the facility was in poor condition, either because it was just old, having operated in this community since the 1890s, or because Unocal just kept pushing its limits by greedily skipping necessary maintenance.

While I stood outside the car along Unocal's fence-line, peering into the labyrinth of piping which connected pumps, valves, compressors, heaters and coolers, I realized I had so much to learn. To those unfamiliar with the industry, petroleum refineries appear to be complex and confusing places and, as I quickly and humbly realized, I was still a neophyte, not having become as schooled on refinery operations as I'd hoped. That meant I was only a little closer to understanding the scene I was now witnessing than I was before Ralph's call. Honestly, I could not have identified D-409 if it stood right in front of me. Instead, I just trusted that, when I compared these photos to blueprints and operational flowcharts back at my office, it would somehow all come together. And so I just kept shooting.

The problem, of course, with driving up to an oil refinery in a bright red convertible, standing along the fence-line overlooking its various operations and taking photographs with a telephoto lens is that you tend to attract attention. This is particularly likely just after a major toxic chemical release. As such, it wasn't long before our leaps from one photo-op to the next were being mirrored by a white pickup truck with Unocal's insignia on its doors. It was following us. Whenever we stopped, it stopped, and when it did, I could see its driver speaking into his walkie-talkie. He was reporting back to somebody at headquarters—I just knew it. To what end, I didn't know.

While not entering into any space that the public couldn't legally access, these guys were intent on watching us, and letting us know we were being watched. They didn't try to hide it. *Are they getting my license number? Can Unocal figure out who I am? Are they trying to send me a message?* It was unnerving, but I tried hard to pretend it wasn't, at least when Doug was watching. I even considered taking a photograph of the guys in the truck, but thought it better not to make unnecessary waves with guys who were probably just foot soldiers.

Finishing our reconnaissance work, we left Unocal's territory, the mysterious truck following us down the exit road for another mile or so beyond the refinery limits. Apparently, it wanted to make sure we were really gone. Yeah, they were sending us a message all right: *Don't come back. We know you now,* or something along those lines. I even wondered if they might be the same guys who had cursed at John, my investigator. That would have been funny, but, if they were, I was even happier they'd stayed inside their truck. The hotheads who'd approached John were a little too unpredictable.

But, whoever they were, their tactic worked, and I was intimidated—still headstrong, but intimidated. I grew up in a rough town. I could take care of myself, but yet, I still felt very relieved this hadn't happened at night or somewhere more rural. I drove home angry and animated, thinking what nerve these people had for trying to scare us off, and how this motivated me even more. I didn't have to say it out loud. Doug was thinking it too.

CHAPTER 6
SENSIBLE SHOES

I endeavored to keep Ralph in the loop about our discoveries as they unfolded. I was excited about the information I was unearthing and approached our relationship like a real partnership, encouraging Ralph to talk to anyone he saw fit, so long as he didn't give out details I hadn't vetted first. Ralph liked being associated with something important; the fact that he got to tell people he had lawyers on his side and was going to take down the big, bad oil company seemed thrilling to him. And, oh, did he tell them.

So many calls came in those first few days that merely recruiting Doug didn't cut it, and I pressed my part-time assistant to work longer hours, so no calls would go to the answering machine. We needed to appear well-staffed, professional and available at all times and to send contracts to interested clients. Just as importantly though, we wanted everyone to know about the town-hall meeting just a few days away. There was simply no way we were letting Unocal off the hook and a packed community center at the upcoming meeting would ensure that its representatives knew that. But an enormous question still loomed over us. How would we get the word out about the meeting?

Crockett wasn't a big town to begin with, and what calls we were getting were from people living within a few-block radius of Ralph. Evidently, while Ralph was zealous, all his broadcasting was coming from off his front porch—figuratively speaking anyway. But we were convinced that all of Crockett, and maybe even a few of the towns beyond it, had been hit hard and that we could attract more than just Ralph's neighbors. That was essential. Without an impressive turnout for the next meeting, Unocal would never take the community's injuries seriously. This near-secret 16-day release would, largely, remain a secret. We needed that hall packed so Unocal would have a reason to act differently next time. Oil refineries are like time bombs. There's always a next time.

With just a few days before the meeting, we gamed out a few options, none of which looked particularly promising. Just having Ralph working overtime on the phones wouldn't help. The only telephone numbers any of us had were for his neighbors and they'd called me already. More calls wouldn't help us. E-mailing wouldn't either. It wasn't available yet.

Moreover, almost no government agencies knew about the release, nor did the media. Even if we had the resources to take out an advertisement in the county's newspaper, few Crockett residents would have likely read it, at least in time. How were we going to pack the hall with, say, a few hundred people, when the segments of town were so cut off from each other?

What became quickly apparent was that, if we were going to change either county, Unocal, or media perception about what had happened here, we'd need one-on-one face time with townspeople, at least to start, but it would need to be done in a nonthreatening way. We couldn't appear to be overbearing or ambulance chasers; that would virtually guarantee they wouldn't show up, much less participate in the anticipated lawsuit. We'd also have to keep our conversations focused on the upcoming meeting and not litigation, but the optics of our approach worried me since it might seem like we were soliciting business. I was probably overly concerned, but I was convinced that, if anyone reported me walking the streets of Crockett and knocking on doors, I could be throwing away my license to practice law.

As you may know, the term "solicitation," in legal parlance, is considered a dirty word. In fact, in some circumstances, it can result in you getting disbarred. For ethics purposes, the term is defined loosely, but generally means directly contacting potential clients with the goal of making money. When you consider that broad interpretation, you can see that, whether it'll get you in trouble depends on your intentions as well as how it's carried out.

Paying for a late-night television spot or sponsoring a local fun run, for example, won't get you exiled from law practice. Answering the legal questions posed by your uncle Ted, or the attractive man or woman you just met at a cocktail party, also won't get you into trouble. That's because, as everyone intuitively understands, giving legal advice, once you're asked for it, is the essence of what lawyers do. It's also acceptable because a lot of leeway is afforded to market your legal services when done in these more noble ways. When you start calling or visiting total strangers though, especially physically injured strangers, and with a lawsuit in mind, well, that's when the State Bar starts to frown upon what you're doing.

I've never improperly solicited a client, although I've known lawyers who routinely do. Honestly, I've never understood the need for it since just doing good work and remaining visible usually does the trick. But rallying strangers to attend a public meeting while staying above reproach required a different playbook. And, yet, it needed to be done. We knew that, if anyone in a position of power at Unocal was going to start taking this town (and our anticipated lawsuit) seriously, we either had to rent an ice cream truck with a bullhorn, or paper the area with information. We chose the latter.

To get this job done, we'd have to walk its streets, go door to door, visit places where people congregated, pass out flyers—really grassroots stuff. We knew climbing the hilly roads of Crockett would be labor-intensive and perhaps not particularly "lawyerly," but we had little choice. That this face time might also neutralize the popular cynicism about our occupation was just icing on the cake, especially insofar as it might demonstrate that Doug and I were "of the people" and willing to take proactive measures that, for us, held no particular economic benefit, but could assist the town enormously.

And so I cleared my calendar and persuaded Doug to join me for a day in Crockett the following Monday. As it turned out, our timing couldn't have been better since, by the end of the weekend, calls to our office were petering out and we were growing concerned. We had to jump-start the interest and make some noise. The more time that passed since the release, the less likely people were going to complain about it or demand long-term change.

With roughly a thousand households in town, we knew a day in Crockett wouldn't put us face-to-face with more than a small fraction of the people, but that would probably be enough to jump-start the interest. What we knew, what we conveyed to this audience, would get re-circulated around town. That would happen organically. We just had to re-fuel their excitement.

It was agreed that, for Monday's visit, I would draft a single-page flyer that provided information about the release—the dates, a short description of the harm Catacarb could do—and beckoned everyone to the Crockett Community Center on Thursday evening to make their voices heard. A few of these people had already received Unocal's confusing and ridiculous "Fact sheet," the one which likened deadly Catacarb to a bar of bath soap. Our flyer was also meant to neutralize that spin. And it was to warn residents not to waive their rights without first asking questions and getting both sides of the story.

The company, of course, didn't want that and we knew it. If Unocal's management found out what we were doing, we'd be thumbing our noses at some very powerful and influential people. But we liked that idea and welcomed the conflict. Our announcement would also show Unocal that lawyers were on the scene. The company, of course, didn't want that either. Unocal's Fact sheet and statements at the first community meeting explained that the company's public affairs and insurance adjusters were "quickly assembled" to address community concerns. I knew what that meant.

What that meant was residents were being asked to bring their questions to Unocal—not to each other, and certainly not to lawyers. It meant, once they did so, they'd probably get more misinformation from the company and its insurance carrier. And then, Unocal would have the green light to wash away all remaining evidence of its crimes from residents' cars and houses, while insurance adjusters handed out paltry settlement checks. Our handout warned residents about that and suggested they bring their questions to the meeting instead, where everybody could hear the answers and where Doug and I would be available to correct any misstatements.

That Monday morning, we were off in my little red car, briefcases full of flyers and heads full of practiced answers to the most anticipated questions. Exiting the freeway just before the Carquinez Bridge and driving downward into this little port town for my first time ever was exciting, given our purposes, and more than a little eye opening. I had already expected poverty, but a slightly different word came to my mind as we headed down Pomona, Crockett's main thoroughfare. The word was "Decay."

I wasn't prepared for the dated, neglected feel of the downtown area, barely three blocks long, nor did I expect the housing developments to be so disconnected. It made sense that the people in Crockett weren't talking outside of their immediate neighborhoods; many of their residential pockets were separated by steep hills and deep gulches, not to mention a transcontinental highway. As I noticed how vertical some of its residential streets were, I felt lucky we had dressed casually and wore sensible shoes.

And I'd forgotten about the historic C&H Sugar plant being there. It's the first thing you see when you approach the town from the south and it was an instant reminder we needed to be real with these blue-collar folks—don't use legal jargon or pretend we're going to change the world. Don't make promises we're not sure we can keep, I reminded myself. Just tell them why we're there, that we know they're hurt, that we know who did it, and that we could use their assistance to fix it. The "help us to help you" sort of thing. Remember, while we may be outsiders, that doesn't mean we can't work together and start making the refinery more accountable.

For Doug, this was a lot easier. He had a naturally breezy way about him that, for me, took more concentration. Doug was laid back, undemanding. I was always more impatient, less empathic, but I was working on that and this day was certain to provide some good practice. It was with that air of humility and concern I knew we needed to approach the project, and so we did, with every person who'd shake our hands. And we shook a lot of hands.

We parked and started to walk the town in no particular direction. In some areas, like the flatlands sections of town, the homes were separated by just a sliver of daylight. Those were the easiest to hit. There, we could finish with one house, walk 40 paces and be at the front door of another. We began there, with a plan to take an hour or two before moving toward the hills. We went to our first house and knocked. No answer. Next house. No answer. Third house, jackpot. Roughly half of the knocks yielded nothing. No worries. Just keep moving.

By and large, the people at home gave us time and they were cautious, but helpful and friendly. Occasionally, we'd confront some plaid-shirted codger on his rusty porch swing, or some middle-aged heavily bearded guys sitting on nylon garden chairs in their front yard smoking cigarettes. Those conversations required a little more finesse, more of an "ah shucks" approach in order to disarm them. They did start out as welcoming. Those guys might be just as sick as the little ole lady next door, but they often, at least at first, didn't want to talk about it. Before they warmed to us, they were apprehensive—about litigation, making waves, and their sickness needing attention. Complaining signaled weakness, and they weren't prepared to concede that.

If they did choose to talk, it was usually a flood of rage about the company's mistreatment of their town, maybe even their particular families. Then, when their venomous rants dried up, they'd watch for the recoil—to see if we were, as they first suspected, part of the same establishment that bred this inequity. They waited to see if we'd cringed at their disdain for the business that did this to them but, of course, we didn't waver. We explained that there was no collusion here, and that we hated Unocal too. Our job that day wasn't to change minds or practice our debating skills, or even to make friends, although we weren't against it. We just needed permission to stay on their property long enough to give them our flyer, explain why they should come to that week's meeting, and then let them get back to their light beers.

Despite the occasional assault, these people were forthright and authentic. I liked them for that, and I think they liked us. When you're new at something, it's hard to know if you're doing a good job. Our job that day was to be liked, just enough to build some trust, maybe even break down a misconception or two about lawyers. At some point, I assumed all these people would play a role in the case we were building. That would go more smoothly if they trusted us.

When we failed in our work, when they didn't like us, they told us, sometimes loudly. Sometimes, once merely announcing we were attorneys, doors were slammed in our faces. Sometimes we were directed to get off their front porches and leave Crockett alone. That was weird; it wasn't like we were asking all that much—just to consider attending a community meeting—but they had their preconceptions and I got it. That blurring of the message with the messenger kind of thing didn't faze me. I couldn't let it. If you don't have a thick skin, you've got no business being a plaintiffs' personal injury lawyer and I knew that. If we got booted off one porch, we'd just move on to the next house and likely be received more favorably.

For the homeowners willing to engage us throughout our walk, every account I'd heard over the telephone was being told again. For those generous with their time, it was because they were hurt and because Doug and I were pretty good listeners, whereas no one had listened before. The people talked of feeling unusually sick but didn't know why. Many didn't even know a chemical release had occurred, much less about any town meetings to discuss it. Others knew about the Unocal car wash or had seen Unocal trucks driving their neighborhoods, but figured none of that had anything to do with them.

We listened to stories about children getting sick after coming back from the local pool, and about pets that couldn't open their eyes. There were elderly people suddenly unable to leave their homes, a slowdown in commerce because local business owners were debilitated, and fitness-minded people now reluctant to run or bicycle in the area for fear of additional exposure. Mostly, at least for those who'd heard about the chemical release, they were scared, and not just for themselves and their families, but for their town.

These people never felt they had the collective influence to improve how local industry regarded their city and worried that might never change. But talking to us gave them a little hope—that, just maybe, things could change. At least that's how it seemed. I thought that was great, yet tragic that it took them getting so hurt for them to start feeling regarded.

Energizing as our little adventure was, pounding the pavement as we did was hard work and it gave me a huge appreciation for canvassers who make that their living. I sure couldn't do that every day. For the houses downtown, the walking was easy, but some of those Crockett hills really work your legs, no matter how young you may be. Not wanting to limit our attention to any particular area, we worked them all.

Fatigued from hours of this, we finally stopped at a delicatessen a few blocks from the freeway. It was a friendly enough place. A girl who couldn't have been older than 17 was working the register, arranging food on plates and hustling orders out to little bistro tables. I figured she had just gotten out of school for the day and, within a more few hours, she'd be gone again, out spending the few bucks she'd made during this late-afternoon rush.

She was quick and efficient and certainly had no time for our questions about how she, her friends or family, may have been affected by the release and so we asked her none. Nor did we ask any of the other people sitting and eating there. It seemed too intrusive, too intimate. This was still their town. We let them eat in peace.

Still, it was helpful to note the tables of high school kids with skateboards, the elderly couple undoubtedly wanting nothing to do with lawyers or courtrooms, the handful of industrial workers too dirty and exhausted from their long day of work to care about our agenda. It confirmed what I already suspected: these small-towners had little connection to the world of toxic tort litigation. Absent a bold statement from someone at least loosely connected to it, it was unlikely they would do anything to repair the damage their corporate neighbor had done.

Finished with our work, and dreading the commute back home, we paid for two waters, skipped the snack, and left. But for a few unequivocal commitments to attending the town-hall meeting, we had no idea what impact our efforts would have. It was enough that we knew we tried.

CHAPTER 7
CLASS ACTIONS

Filing a Complaint is the declaration of war in any civil suit. It announces to the world that you mean business and gives the court power to take action—hopefully, ultimately, in your favor. A Complaint identifies the parties bringing the case (the plaintiffs) and those who allegedly caused the harm and against whom damages, penalties or other remedies are being sought (the defendants). It also sets out, at least in general terms, the events alleged to have occurred, and how those events violated some duty recognized under the law. When you tell someone, "I'll see you in court," filing a Complaint tells them you weren't kidding around. Of course, whether you know how to properly draft a Complaint dictates whether the party receiving it is going to take you seriously or see you as a novice.

As you might expect, it's tough to intimidate a multi-national corporation and its robust team of seasoned and well-funded attorneys with virtually no support staff, almost no financial resources and little experience. If you decide to undertake litigation under these conditions anyway, then good luck to you. If you decide to up the ante and make your lawsuit a class action—especially one on behalf of thousands—then I hope you're an excellent poker player.

It was for these reasons I was more than a little tense when Doug suggested I draft a class action Complaint against Unocal.

"Are you kidding me?" I asked.

"No. It's your case. You should have the honor of writing up what it's all about," Doug explained.

But neither of us had ever done a class action before.

At the time, I thought he was being generous (albeit a tad sadistic) to offer me the gig, although I still wonder if he didn't want the undertaking because, like me, he never considered being involved in a case of this magnitude. In my mind, Doug was already a seasoned litigator, but in fact, he'd had only a few more years of legal experience than I did. But, he was right. This was my case and I was in too deep to back out now.

We'd just papered the town of Crockett two days before. That was Monday. Now, it was Wednesday afternoon, the day before what would be our first town-hall meeting and a potentially incendiary confrontation between Unocal's engineers and public relations representatives, on the one hand, and a likely swarm of residents on the other—people who had either already hired us or, at least, heard about or met us when we passed out our flyers. It was unlikely Unocal was going to satisfy anyone with its answers at that meeting and, so, I suspected people would be looking to me for information, to demonstrate my resolve and to take bold actions.

For these reasons, I knew it was mission-critical to get the lawsuit on file before the meeting, but, despite the stack of photocopies I had made at the library, I hadn't written a single word of the Complaint that would launch the case. Indeed, I felt I was quickly running out of time when I sat down at my office computer at around 1:30 that afternoon and settled in for what I suspected would be a long night.

The Internet was still in diapers back then, but I would have been dead in the water without it. To draft such an important document, I needed samples from similar cases pursued before. However, although a few environmental class action Complaints were visible online,

I couldn't find anything directly on point. Nor did I really understand what I was seeking. It was like finding a needle in a haystack without knowing quite what a needle looked like.

I started by printing out documents from every major class action lawsuit I could find, arranging them across the floor of my office and locking the door behind me so no one would accidentally walk in and step on my work. I also located a few environmental case descriptions and news stories about oil field pollution and dumping of toxic substances into bays or near ocean shorelines. But I found nothing about litigation over air pollution, which left me stuck and with no time to look elsewhere. Lawyers commonly spend days, sometimes weeks, drafting class action Complaints. I had 24 hours and, without more resources or experience, I'd have to wing it.

It's not that I was a complete stranger to writing Complaints; I had filed and prosecuted several cases in the year and a half since printing my first business card, but preparing a class action lawsuit is a lot different than just documenting how somebody bumped your car and hurt your neck. First and foremost, this Complaint was going to be filed for the people who had hired me, but it was also being brought for a larger *class* of people who had no idea who I was. That class was the ten to twenty thousand people who might never seek out their own lawyer, yet who'd been injured just by virtue of living or working in the affected towns—not just Crockett but also Rodeo, Hercules, and several other cities within a several-mile radius of the refinery. To successfully absorb that number of people (what class action lawyers refer to as "*absent* class members") into one case, I knew we'd have to start with an excellent Complaint.

If set up properly, a class action can be a beautiful thing. In a class action, you can start with just a few people as your clients, but then seek damages for everyone out there with similar claims, so long as you meet a few important criteria. Such cases can be extremely efficient vehicles for handling big-ticket litigation but are only viable when the class members (i.e., your clients *plus* the absent members) have been harmed by the same event, and seek similar remedies. If they don't have that connection, your class action will fail. The judge will reject it, compelling you to bring every person's claim separately or focus on an easier target elsewhere. If you don't move on, you may repeat, for every single victim, the same litigation efforts over and over again.

With this risk in mind, I first needed to carefully define who would compose the class. Too broad a definition and the case would get rejected. Too narrow a definition and I'd miss a lot of people who were hurt, and open the door even wider for other lawyers to file their own cases for the missed segments. I decided to identify the class of people as those "living, visiting and/or working" within a certain radius of the Unocal refinery at any time during the 16-day release. It was, ultimately, a more-formal-sounding description than this (a formality *expected* by the judicial system), but this was the gist of it.

Beyond the rough idea of how wide to cast the net, I also had a rudimentary understanding of what a class action was about. I recalled my law school Civil Procedure professor talking about it once or twice anyway. I knew, for example, that we needed to have something called "Numerosity," which meant pretty much what it sounds like—that enough injured claimants existed to make applying the special class action rules worthwhile.

Class actions are productive only in situations where there are too many people to manage all their claims separately, so the first question is about size, and here, size does matter. Because class actions are so favored for their efficiency, the system allows for a little less due process and some imperfections—a sort of rough justice that would never be tolerated in a case brought by one plaintiff against one defendant. Before a court will allow for those imperfections, though, there needs to be a benefit to enough people. That why Numerosity is required and why the Complaint I was drafting needed to address it.

I remembered 40 being a benchmark for the minimum number of people—not the number of plaintiffs who retained you but the total number of people affected. *Well, that shouldn't be a problem here*, I thought. *I've received that many calls already.* I also remembered that the plaintiffs who hired me, especially the one lead plaintiff, needed to have claims very much like those of the remaining victims—a requirement known as "Commonality." The facts surrounding the Catacarb release wouldn't change much if I polled different victims but their exposure stories and symptoms definitely would. This could pose a problem.

Some class action rules suggested I'd need a stronger thread running through this release's impact on community members. Weren't the exposure circumstances here very different from one person to the next? I mean, it's not like this was a case where everyone signed the same contract with the same bank and was then defrauded out of their money. This wasn't that clean. The release itself could certainly be described in the same way, whether we filed one or one thousand cases, but every client was *exposed* differently, and at different *concentrations*.

What's more, each person's medical history and physiology was different. They would, therefore, react differently to any particular exposure level, not to mention having a potentially unique mix of symptoms. Some people had migraine headaches for months thereafter, but some of them had no headaches at all, and some had suffered from migraines long before the release which were now worse. Others suffered tremendous levels of stress, partly because they had a low tolerance to stressful situations already. However, their neighbors might recognize their own anxiety as temporary or just no big deal.

Other differences were more categorical. For example, I heard stories of women suffering miscarriages, yet their male counterparts couldn't possibly claim that. Other symptoms and situations also seemed germane to certain groups, to the exclusion of others, whether based on location, occupation, gender, age or otherwise. If we couldn't prove Commonality, we'd have no class action; the judge would make us litigate every claimant's case separately and that would be prohibitively expensive. If they could stay joined in a class action, however, we'd be allowed to use the same evidence for everyone and, hopefully, enjoy one shared judgment. That would be great.

So far, I thought I had enough people to make the adventure worthwhile and similar-enough circumstances for the judge to allow our case to proceed. But one last element the Complaint needed was one that I was almost sure I couldn't back up. It's called "Adequacy," and it demands you prove two things: first, that your clients are able and willing to champion the interests of everybody else and, second, that the attorney bringing the case is qualified to pursue a case of that complexity. If you don't meet the test, you might be ordered to hand the case off to a more experienced practitioner.

In this way, becoming a class action lawyer is something of a paradox: generally, you're not allowed to pursue class actions until you are sufficiently experienced in pursuing class actions. There's the rub. Therefore, since I was not an experienced class action practitioner already, the best I could do was say in the Complaint that I'd become one. I'd make a promise and pray that it would be enough for the judge to take a chance on me.

And something told me I'd be persuasive enough when the time came to prove myself. I was eager and ready to read everything about these procedures I could get my hands on, and I ultimately did. I understood this kind of fight meant a steep learning curve, getting up to speed on special procedures, and that was fine. I'd have to earn my stripes at some point, so why not now?

Being my first foray into this kind of work, however, I had no clue about the magic words to put on these pages. This worried me; I knew this was one of the simpler documents I'd encounter in this field of practice and I was stuck already. *Was I really ready for this?* I was lost over how to draft one stupid document. *Why didn't they teach us these things in school?* I thought. I felt like I learned everything else there—all sorts of legal concepts—just not how to apply them. What good were all those esoteric theories today if I couldn't apply them?

Distracted by stress and the numerous piles of paper adorning my office floor, I briefly reminisced about law school. It's not like I wasn't paying attention those three years. I was. But the education I really needed there never came. Like me, many law students finish their education believing their careers will be built on little more than their encyclopedic knowledge of cases and statutes. Harboring this misconception, many budding lawyers graduate with almost no practical experience, and they really struggle.

This, in my opinion, is the biggest shortcoming of many law schools, particularly the more traditional ones. While these institutions offer introductory classes in contracts, civil and criminal procedure, evidence and constitutional law sufficient to pass their state's licensing examination, their curricula is often too light on specialty courses that teach new lawyers how to apply it all to real-life situations. Unless you're lucky enough to have found employment at a firm willing to teach you the nuts and bolts of litigation, you could be in big trouble as a solo practitioner.

Such it was for me when I graduated, notwithstanding having clerked for good firms while in school. Sure, I was taught the elements of various legal claims and how to research, but those were just the basics. Knowing how to work the pedals and back out of your driveway is a lot different from racing at the Indy 500.

If I drafted this Complaint incorrectly, I might look like a beginner to my clients. Unquestionably, I would look like one to the company we were suing and even more so to its lawyers. Those lawyers knew all about class actions. I needed to convince them at the outset that I was experienced—also sufficiently funded, staffed and tenacious—but, mostly, experienced. I needed them to presume I wouldn't botch the job in what could be a complicated case and trial. This was an optic that was doubly important if I had any aspiration for a meaningful settlement. If they thought I couldn't make it to trial anyway, why pay out much money to avoid it?

And, finally, mind you, these considerations would matter only if and when the case got off the ground. If I screwed up this Complaint, Unocal would file an immediate request in court to have the case dismissed on any number of grounds. If the judge agreed the Complaint was deficient in a big enough way and if I couldn't figure out how to repair it, dismissal is exactly what would happen. I'd lose the lawsuit. My clients might be barred from trying again. I'd be proven a fool, sued for malpractice, bankrupted, and probably sent looking for a new career.

Luckily, despite being a greenhorn, I was good at not reinventing the wheel. By the time my pepperoni and black olive pizza arrived that evening, I'd already spent several hours researching and printing countless documents from across the web, and now stood staring at a wall-to-wall carpet of paper. Then there came the hunt to determine what made them all similar, to grab those themes and paragraphs and phrases I liked and weave them together in some Frankensteinian fashion, with the endgame of massaging this diary until it honored the events it described. I always took offense to being labeled a "perfectionist," but I guess I was, at least this time. Every comma needed to be correctly placed, every conceivable claim included, and the amount of damages we sought had to reflect the severity of the company's recklessness. The damages had to be dramatic.

They say you don't get a second chance to make a first impression, and I knew I was writing for an audience of thousands, maybe tens of thousands. Even if it wasn't perfectionism, it was still with an eye toward not wanting to risk public humiliation. In either event, I was determined to get it right.

I've always functioned well on little sleep anyway and, so, obsessing about this project didn't worry me much. Actually, it was exhilarating. I'd grab a stack of papers, scour them to glean just a few choice words or a turn-of-phrase, type those into the master document, and chuck the source. And there were dozens of these stacks from all different places and my first draft was a mess. Draft. Polish. Re-draft. Cut and paste. Re-polish. I worked all night like this and, at 4:30 the next morning, I hit the "Print" key and powered down my computer. Stapling together the pages that would be the start to my most important legal adventure, I gently laid the Complaint on my desk blotter in anticipation of a fresh read when I returned later, and I went home.

In those days, while my volunteer was a great asset for answering phones, I had no dedicated administrative staff for tasks like driving to courthouses to file new cases. If I needed to visit the court clerk's window, where all new lawsuits were filed, I had to do it myself. Doug was in the same boat, yet, even if we had the help, we both knew the filing of this particular Complaint was just too important to delegate. When I returned to the office after breakfast, I called Doug about going to the courthouse. He begged to come along.

We timed it well. The town-hall meeting was set for 7 o'clock that evening at Crockett's community center, so we left early in the afternoon for Martinez, the county seat, with plenty of buffer. Our plan was to file the Complaint before the County Clerk's office got too busy and then, time permitting, either drive on to Crockett to pass out a few more flyers or just head home and beat rush-hour traffic. Later, we'd throw on suits and ties and head back up to Crockett in time for the community meeting. It was September 22, and just hours before the big event. Before I knew it, we were in my car with copies of the Complaint, the Summons and a check for the filing fee in hand, ready to wage war against one of the biggest corporations on the planet, and we were flying.

Doug didn't read the Complaint until we were already on the freeway. As he turned its pages, he chuckled, becoming particularly excited by my inclusion of a damage request that totaled $1 billion. That was the amount we were asking Unocal pay and, when he read it, his eyes bugged out of his head. Like me, Doug had a huge flair for the dramatic, but it's one thing to use a glove to slap your adversary's face, as you've probably seen actors do in Victorian-era period pieces, and it's another to use a brick. Doug and I always preferred the brick. In this case, the mere inclusion of such an astronomical number in a publicly filed document was our way of, finally, giving the middle finger to Big Business.

"Who's Ms. Santos?" Doug asked, referring to the first name on the Complaint's front page—what we call the "caption" page.

"Why?" I asked. "Are you wondering what happened to Ralph? He's in there. I just thought Ms. Santos would sell better. Young mother, struggling to make ends meet, doused by toxins, worried about her baby."

"That's great, man," was Doug's only response. This didn't need any more discussion.

Standing in line at the Clerk's office to file the documents, we were feeling giddy. We talked at high speed about how many plaintiffs might eventually sign on, how Unocal's conduct seemed downright criminal and how residents and company representatives alike might react that evening when we showed up with our shiny-new class action. We were giddy, for sure, and animated. Many Clerk's offices have signs posted prohibiting loud talking. If this one did, we were oblivious to it.

In those pre-Internet days, when newspapers were still king, inventive reporters working the "legal beat" would hang out near the Clerk's filing window from time to time, picking up information about interesting new lawsuits. They'd get their scoops, literally, by eavesdropping on other people's conversations—a brilliant approach to news reporting, both in its simplicity and conservation of effort.

This was one of those times and, since this lawsuit undoubtedly qualified as interesting, Doug and I were easy targets. We hadn't been in the Clerk's line more than two minutes, gabbing away, when a journalist standing against the wall overheard the loud talking and approached us. Lunging forward with his pale hand outstretched, he introduced himself as a reporter from the *Contra Costa County Times*, the top news rag for that region. He asked if we were filing a lawsuit against Unocal. I said we were as Doug stepped in, offered him an extra copy of the Complaint and made sure to spell his long last name very slowly. The timing of it all couldn't have been better.

The reporter seemed capable, but he really didn't need to be. We were craving publicity, wanting the world to know what Unocal had done and, frankly, to know us. The reporter had many questions about the symptoms suffered by our clients, whether we believed the county bore any responsibility for letting the leak to continue, how our first client came to us, and how many people we predicted had been hurt by Catacarb exposure.

Unlike the technical focus of my research, his focus was on human suffering and corporate fault. He wanted drama. He also wanted to know about that elusive motive—what evidence we had that Unocal knew Catacarb was dangerous and why the company let it continue for so long. I answered in a word—"Greed"—and then punted on the evidence we lacked to back up my accusation.

Admittedly, I wasn't interview-savvy or practiced in the art of manufacturing sound bites common in journalism. I offered all kinds of legal analyses, and he smiled graciously and listened, but he was largely tuning me out. He couldn't use all that jargon. From what I could see, he was taking notes only about the good stuff, the human drama. "If it bleeds, it leads," as they say in the media about prioritizing stories. I quickly recognized I needed to alter my overly cerebral approach to this interview or this was going to be a very dry piece.

And so I did. I changed my tone, made my words punchier, talked about the suffering, cut out the lawyer-speak. Sure, it may have cheapened the bigger, more important impact we hoped for the case by dumbing it down this way, but not making the story sexier would have just left the reporter to do it himself. He would write who knows what, demote the article to Page 8 status, and probably not quote me at all. This reporter had to convey the events in an interesting way, or the events I'd worked so hard to uncover would stay a relative secret. Plus, I have to admit, I wanted Unocal to know exactly who did this to them—and I wanted to finally see my name in the paper.

After thanking us for our time, the reporter left, we filed the documents and then drove home, thinking little about the interview. Instead, we buzzed about the meeting just a few hours out. Admittedly, we were feeling pretty smug about it all. Seeing how the audience, maybe even the company's spokespeople, reacted to a billion-dollar lawsuit was going to be fun. In what might be a long journey, we'd need to grab every opportunity for fun we could.

CHAPTER 8
FANNING THE FLAME

B ack home after filing the Complaint, and with only an hour before I had to leave for Unocal's presentation in Crockett, I had a difficult choice to make: *Red, yellow or blue?* Blue was supposed to represent calmness and confidence and integrity. I liked that. Red was too in-your-face and yellow seemed too cheery. I was picking out my tie and I was clearly overthinking things. In the end, I went with the blue tie, with a perfectly formed dimple below a perfectly tapered knot, just made for prime time. Fine-pinstriped, charcoal-gray wool suit. Crisp, white, unstarched, Windsor-collared shirt. *White connotes honesty.* I'd read a study about that. Black wing-tip brogues, shined. *Tie them up tight and I'm good to go.* I may have been a novice in the courtroom, but I knew how to dress.

I have no idea how many attorney retainer agreements I'd faxed to potential clients the few days before that Thursday, but it must have been dozens. Many of them had come back signed already, but I wanted a few extra copies in my bag that night for the folks who'd been dilatory about returning them. I also brought court-stamped copies of the Complaint and some research I assembled describing the evils of chemicals like Catacarb. I stuffed as much of it as I could fit into my briefcase, grabbed some paper, pens and business cards, and drove to meet Doug. As I pulled up to his house, he was waiting by his door and pacing. I smiled knowingly. He was never ready on time.

On our trek up to Crockett, we were so antsy that, to hear us talking, you'd think we were long-lost friends, eager to catch up. We discussed the reactions we might get from our clients when they heard the lawsuit had been filed, and how much interest we might get from their friends and neighbors. I'd tossed a handheld tape recorder into my briefcase to capture everything the Unocal officials might say. We found that plan hilarious—maybe it was the thought of how the panel might react to a couple of suited-up guys standing on the sidelines collecting evidence, keeping them on their toes, and then learning we'd be using their words to support a billion-dollar-damages request.

As we sailed along toward Crockett, Doug asked me how many plaintiffs I guessed would ultimately join. In the Complaint, we'd included only the best, a couple dozen, although many more had called. From that, I thought we might get a few dozen more. At that point, however, I figured it would slow down. The largest number of plaintiffs I'd represented in any case before this was four.

"Join how soon? Like, within a year? I don't know. A hundred or so?" I was guessing. I had no clue. I was just talking out of obligation to speak and sound knowledgeable.

But Doug wasn't buying it, and dismissed it as overly ambitious. "I don't think we'll get more than 100," he surmised. As it turns out, we were both wrong. By that year's end alone, we blew the doors off both estimates.

My little red convertible—the only car I owned in those days—wasn't fancy or expensive, but it was bright, and that meant I sometimes had to make parking decisions that resulted in a lot of walking. Crockett was a rusty old 4×4 kind of town, where not a lot of people drove small or shiny vehicles. Knowing this going in, I didn't think it would sell well to drive up, top down, all suited and tied, and park in front of the wooden-walled Community Center in my luminous carriage. Despite our crisp professional appearance, I wanted to blend in, not appear like outsiders looking to capitalize on the misery and grief of the townspeople. With this in mind, we parked a few blocks away, on a side street, and started walking.

By our estimate, the Community Center was probably the only place, other than the town's few dilapidated churches, where people gathered in big numbers. Still, everyone there seemed as shocked as I was to see the turnout. By the time we showed up, the Center was full, seemingly beyond its official capacity, hundreds of anxious victims wanting answers—standing room only. Being the only audience members in suits, we stood out like sore thumbs; seeing my car wouldn't have changed anything. We noticed a small space at the back wall and made our way there along the window line, trying our best to look tough—just in case the Unocal reps were watching.

There was a small raised stage at the front of the hall where several company spokespeople, a physician and a county representative had already taken their seats behind folding tables. Audience members had since scoped out their seats, occasionally placing personal items on the folding chairs so they could freely mingle with neighbors and friends before the presentation began. The energy was high, with the sort of nervous anticipation that commonly precedes high-conflict situations lacking agreed-upon rules of engagement. As we stood at the back of the auditorium, we felt very much out of our element, but worked hard to telegraph a faux-comfort as if we'd worked rooms like this a thousand times.

Had we not made such great time getting to Crockett and arrived 20 minutes before show time, we might have been stuck outside. The Unocal representatives were also way ahead of schedule. That was unfortunate for them since it gave the packed auditorium plenty of time to death-stare them and make derisive comments under their breath.

Apparently, the audience predicted this would be a public relations spin session, and the expectation itself seemed to incense them even more. The company spokespeople were reviewing their notes and trying to quietly chat amongst themselves, yet the citizens were already talking in loud, agitated voices, sometimes even at one another. All the while, the panel members struggled to stay calm while periodically and ineffectually encouraging spectators to take their seats.

But Doug and I weren't immune from the attention. With just minutes to go before the start, we were confronted by a small group of existing and would-be clients who quickly pegged us for guys who didn't fit in, wondering if we were who they suspected we were. Curiosity quickly turned to excitement once we divulged our identities, and the pack quickly grew to a mass of more than a dozen people. None of them had any remaining interest in listening to what Unocal's people might say; they sought a Q&A session with us about our investigation and litigation plans. We happily obliged.

Although I was glad we'd brought extra contracts for those victims who promised to meet us, I was oddly relieved we hadn't brought more. Everyone in this swarm wanted in on the lawsuit, yet, as the meeting was about to start, we hardly had time then to be vetting new claimants. Business cards came cheap, however, and we depleted our stack of them within minutes, furiously dropping them into open hands like Halloween candy into plastic pumpkins.

By the time the public relations staffers began talking, at least a quarter of the room had already approached us for information or, at least, had close eyes on us. Those who didn't come over watched us intently, judging our demeanor and our motives. But even these skeptical ones, while clinging to an optimism that their symptoms would soon resolve, undoubtedly wondered if they should make their introductions. Even they were starting to accept that they had a real problem, and that they might need us.

Those late in starting their visit with us were seemingly oblivious to the panel members who were now talking. They were relentless and continued to interview me despite my efforts to shush them with promises to speak later. I was eager to capture everything being said on the tape recorder I'd brought, thinking that this might provide good evidence for our newly filed case. I certainly didn't want stubborn residents offering voice-overs to whatever concessions Unocal might make and, yet, I didn't want to appear rude. I told these stragglers the company's comments might be invaluable to the town's chances of success and then successfully disengaged from the final interview as the panel's introductory comments were ending.

Pressing the record button on my handheld, I wasn't sure what I expected to hear that night. Admissions of guilt? Unlikely. Empathy? Well, maybe false empathy. Maybe Unocal would try to placate these people, handle them with soft talk and hollow statements of compassion. But none of it came. Not even a promise that "We understand." I didn't expect atonement or even a "We're sorry," but I, at least, expected charity, some token of kindness.

What was I thinking? Did I seriously expect this to be anything but another whitewashing of the event? I thought. With a room this full, I wondered how the company reps were going to escape alive without some acknowledgement of responsibility but, again, that never came. The statements made that evening were far too scripted or patently evasive to be of much use, but I captured them anyway. If we found them guilty at trial, maybe their continued cover-up this night, their ongoing denials in the face of overwhelming evidence, would inflame the jury. That could be useful.

Seemingly unaware of our outreach efforts or having predicted a turnout this large, the spokespeople were uncomfortable sticking to the script they'd rehearsed, but they forced themselves anyway. And it was what everyone should have expected: Catacarb is benign, they explained. The compound is mostly potassium. Potassium is an important element already found in the body. People even seek it out to complete a healthy diet, they told us.

I almost couldn't believe what I was hearing. *Are they seriously suggesting that people should welcome Catacarb exposure, that ingesting this toxic soup was as beneficial as popping a vitamin supplement?* Even if they were speaking out of turn, talking about things perhaps they weren't qualified to say, one thing was obvious: they were telling this room of terribly sick people that Catacarb couldn't be the cause. That was just making things worse.

The panel went on to explain how there was no documented connection between Catacarb exposure and illness, again suggesting no relation between the two. All distractions. Lack of a scientifically proven link didn't mean there wasn't a link. It just meant the association hadn't been made—because it hadn't been studied. *And whose fault is that?* I silently accused. The spokespeople then promised that any symptoms people were suffering should soon resolve. *That's a bold statement*, I thought. And it defied logic. If Catacarb wasn't the cause of these symptoms, they couldn't possibly predict when the symptoms would resolve. Moreover, the panel members were saying that Catacarb's connections to illnesses had never been studied, so how could they predict anything? *Were these just irresponsible medical predictions, or will they really just say anything to downplay the event?*

Apparently, the audience had the same questions, and these pacifications, dare I say outright dismissals of the audience's experience, were not well-received. I left the tape recorder running, just in case anything juicy slipped out, but my attention from the speakers was wandering; I was becoming less interested in what was being said and more focused on the townspeople's reactions.

Clearly, the company had come to appease what it expected to be just a few townspeople, maybe even avoid litigation. The company wanted to foster just enough doubt in the residents' minds so they would do what most seemingly powerless people do—go away. And how do you do that, at least ordinarily? Well, you make them doubt their own experiences. You make them doubt the causal connections. Unocal tried, but it wasn't working this time.

Indeed, it might have worked in the past, even with these people, but the worm had turned, and there was no turning it back. And the crowd was too large, meaning that the residents just had to look around to see their sickness was collective, that they weren't alone. People at the prior town meeting didn't enjoy this solidarity. That audience felt lost, disconnected, and few of them were ready to take steps to change that.

Tonight, however, was special. Each remark about the alleged health benefits of Catacarb exposure or, worse, that people were making up their illnesses was coalescing the community, in turn, angering many residents who came for information but might have never filed lawsuits. Not that I could have controlled it at this point anyway, I just stood back and let Unocal throw lit match after lit match onto this powder keg.

With tensions and distrust so extremely high, the speakers taking such a dismissive approach was patently insane—at least from a public relations perspective. Even a novice like I was could see that. Unocal's staffers should have just said they were looking into the matter and would report back soon. They might even have sweetened the message by saying the company had assembled some sort of All-Star science team to figure it all out. Damage-control, not damage-production, should have been the objective.

At least with that approach, no matter how angry some audience members already were, Unocal wouldn't be fanning the flame. It wouldn't have challenged the townspeople's credibility and their intellect. With the correct approach, the less-contentious or -impacted residents—the ones who had come just for information, not litigation—might have gone home a little unsatisfied, but not felt insulted and labeled liars.

Some of the calmer townspeople might have even felt some sympathy for the panel members being attacked as was now the case. Unocal's ridiculous message and insensitive approach virtually foreclosed that.

And garnering some sympathy wouldn't have been so unlikely. You see, these speakers weren't the people who released the Catacarb and doused these residents' homes. Nor were they truly representative of the group of people who did. The horrible decision to keep operating the faulty tower came out of Unocal's headquarters in Los Angeles, and no one from that corporate office was on stage tonight. In fact, the representatives who did come this night probably wouldn't even have been there, absent being ordered by their bosses to take the heat for the real cowards. All of us could tell they didn't want to be here. Someone else made them come. That's who I really wanted to see.

From what I could tell, they were also ordered about what to say. *This stuff is safe. You're not that sick and, if you are, it's something else. Our insurance adjusters will take care of any loose ends. Oh, and don't forget about the free car wash.* No, taking an even mildly respectful approach tonight just wasn't part of the company's plan. And, for that decision, these speakers bore the brunt of a lot of misdirected rage, and the company ultimately paid a very high price by inducing many more townspeople to join our case.

Nevertheless, these company representatives had come to the meeting thinking their canned speeches and answers would cut it, but the crowd wasn't practicing patience and didn't care about the agenda. The audience laid into them within the first minute, leaving the panel surprised and adopting a deer-in-the-headlights look that lasted for two hours. *Why are you so surprised?* I wondered. *Can't you see what you're doing?* Residents were furious, and the speakers were giving them no reason not to be. For the entirety of the meeting, increasingly uncomfortable panel members, completely unprepared for this degree of backlash, struggled to be heard, even when they had good answers.

I was also quite uncomfortable at times, wondering if this pandemonium—a scene for which I felt some responsibility, having so widely advertised it—was going to get completely out of control. Was I supposed to feel shame for being an integral part of what might devolve into a riotous situation? Logic said "no." Logic said this was an inevitable showdown that needed, maybe was even destined, to happen sooner or later. This town had been dumped on for decades, polluted from all sides. They'd hold their resentment and put up with that for only so long.

This push-back was long overdue, cathartic and important for everyone to see, myself included. While passing out flyers, I'd met with people from all across the town and, while all of them had been touched in some manner by this release, I still didn't fully believe it. Now, directing their stories so loudly and so publicly at the company substantiated their suffering, making it, at least for me, very real.

I saw a lot of familiar faces that night and it gave me pride that they cared, listened, and showed up. They were the homeowners and business owners we'd met, frustrated by their financial losses, teary-eyed parents, with frightened and confused children on their laps, burly construction workers, furious, cursing, sometimes leaping up, almost toppling their own chairs, all to amplify their voices, to point fingers at the spokespeople. In the beginning, the panel members stumbled over their own words, trying to stay poised but answering rapidly before the next indictment came. They soon gave that up, electing to sit quietly and submissively, saying as little as possible in the face of tremendous abuse.

A few times, mothers or fathers stood up to address the stage, determined to stay composed while telling anecdotes of their sick family and disbelief that the company didn't afford them the right to know what was happening, to let them get out of town with their kids while it was still safe. Generally, those stories would end awkwardly and abruptly, with the parents too distraught and defeated to finish, choking on their own words, unsure where to go next, and then slowly, self-consciously sitting back down.

For others, their impatience was sometimes too much even for them to bear, audience members frequently yelling over each other, or at each other, in competition over who had more cause for outrage. They were relentless, hurling insults, seemingly more interested in just being heard than really listening to any answers—with one exception. It was the question for which I'd waited all evening. It was whether the speakers had a response to the class action lawsuit filed that day. Predictably, they didn't. They didn't even know about it and, once learning the situation had elevated, they knew they'd better be careful. The room was already electric from the scrutiny of hundreds, but, now, they were under an even bigger microscope. The panel members looked uncomfortably at each other and kept quiet.

If you haven't experienced this sort of thing before, I can tell you it's both thrilling and horrifying to be trapped at the back wall of a packed room of hundreds, watching people going out of their minds, launching the most vicious attacks, and getting either no response at all from the panel or more false assurances that their fears are unwarranted, that everything is just fine. But, that night, everybody knew damn well it wasn't fine, and that it might never be.

The overwhelming wall of sound made my breathing labored. I wanted to get out of there fast. This wasn't safe. As I saw it, if any of these people had brought a pitchfork or torch or, worse yet, a gun, no one would have been in any position to stop what was bound to happen next. There was no security detail for the speakers, and no way for any of us to get out before the emotional freight train slowed down, save for forcibly breaking through the dense pack of onlookers now blocking the only two exits, some 60 feet from where I stood.

My eyes turned often to those doors, but my astonishment at how wild this got so fast compelled me to ride it out. And ride it out we did.

As the meeting concluded, however, Doug and I hustled out, finding a safe spot in the cool air outside. Finally, I could breathe. We stood there quietly for a bit, wanting to remain visible to anyone who needed to talk about what had just happened, yet not intrude into the space of people still rattled by it.

At first, I expected a reception line of people needing to let off more steam but, instead, everyone just wanted to go home. They seemed to feel as I did—spent. No one stopped by. The audience was in recovery from hitting a high that was tremendously uncomfortable, even for those who had perpetuated the aggression. You can't operate forever on a plateau of rage, and they needed to come down.

People poured out of the hall and just kept walking—all the way home in the dark, or to their cars, too lost in their own thoughts to socialize. I understood. I wanted my freedom too. Twenty minutes later, Doug and I were back in my car, somber and silently driving south. I can't speak for him, but I was feeling profoundly sad, and, at least for the remainder of that evening, I just wanted to forget about Crockett.

CHAPTER 9
IS THAT WITH A B?

Ironically, I woke up the next morning in a sunny mood for what turned out to be a landmark day. I wasn't thinking much about the prior evening's debacle or about the interview at the County Clerk's office, but, apparently, that reporter had been busy at work. Overnight, he changed my career.

When you're a young professional in any job, it's exciting when a news reporter wants to interview you. And, sure, I was excited when he interviewed me, but my hopes for a big media splash were diminished by the lack of media interest in the event to date. Whether that was due to their ignorance about the event or just a lack of enthusiasm, I couldn't tell, but I was certain of one thing: if this reporter ran the story—and that was still a big "if" in my mind—it wouldn't be front-page news.

When I walked into my office early that morning, the flashing number on my answering machine was already in the double digits. I glanced at it curiously as I threw my jacket over a chair and grabbed the stack of documents waiting on the fax machine. Sorting through the pages, it became obvious why I was getting all this attention. One of the documents was a snapshot—a photograph of the front page of that morning's *Contra Costa County Times*. In big bold letters, it announced:

Residents Sue Unocal for $1 Billion over Leaks

Now, I know why I'm so popular, I thought. I also thought it was a nice touch that the reporter had added up the different kinds of damages I'd included in the Complaint, just like Doug had done as we were driving to the meeting. I stopped for a moment, staring at the headline, wondering where this was all going to go.

Granted, this wasn't the *Wall Street Journal* or the *New York Times*, but this publication was an important news source for an area of more than a million people and, until then, it was the only news source that seemed to know about the event. I briefly contemplated this and then spent the next half hour cycling through faxes and telephone messages.

Within minutes of my assistant's arrival, we began answering the phones that had been ringing all morning. I beamed with pride as I was transferred a call from Ralph. He'd seen the headline too, and was happy, and that made me happy. There was an undeniable smugness in his voice suggesting he thought we'd already won—not the case, of course, but in exposing the company. We were in agreement on that. Unocal certainly couldn't hide any longer. In a very short amount of time, we'd blown the event wide open.

Whether that would likely have any long-term impact on its pattern of carelessness, we didn't know, but this wasn't our focus at the time. It was enough that we'd planted that seed and that it would now grow organically, without us needing to pass out more flyers, without us initiating phone calls or attending meetings. That headline was going to change everything, we already knew. I thanked Ralph for helping to make this happen, hung up, and then spent the morning treading water while the phones rang and rang.

While the notoriety was fantastic, the callers were uniformly people who wanted something *from* me—information, representation—whereas

I'd hoped some would be able to fill in some gaps in my understanding of the event. In fact, I'd been eager for some time to get off this hamster wheel of exclusively processing new clients. A front-page news story wasn't calculated to give me that break, but maybe it would also draw out someone with an interest in sharing his secrets, someone who knew about oil refining. I needed to understand how Unocal could benefit from doing something that hurt people. I needed an Insider.

Shortly after lunchtime, I got what I needed in a call from a guy named "Ben."

"Mr. Cole. A neighbor of mine saw the article about your case and said I should call you. I was working at the Wickland oil facility just north of Unocal when that Catacarb release was going on. I was calling to figure out what you guys were planning on doing about this."

I listened to his intro, thinking it was odd he'd ask such a question *after* hearing about our lawsuit. In my mind, the lawsuit *was* the plan, but I figured I should start with the basics.

"Well, we filed the case against Unocal on behalf of—well, right now it's just a couple dozen people who were pretty badly affected by the release, but that number is going to grow significantly," I explained. "What we're planning on doing is, basically, trying to make this right. That refinery has been there for a hundred years but doesn't seem to care that it has twenty thousand neighbors." It felt like a sales pitch, like I was practicing again for the media, but it was the right script.

Ben, however, was more interested in showing off his knowledge and connections than hearing my bravado and that was perfectly fine with me.

He went on to explain how he'd been within a half-mile of Unocal's facility during the entire two-week period. "I also live right there in Tormey," he said, which I already knew to be nothing more than a one-block road with about a dozen houses and a rusted cattle gate at the end, right across from the Wickland facility.

"A lot of us have been sick ever since the release," he explained. "In fact, I was one of the guys who called over to Unocal around Labor Day to find out what was going on. I know a lot of guys that work there. I may actually have been the person that ended the leak." I told him I was glad he did.

He said that, about a week into the release, a lot of his fellow workers started getting really sick and couldn't stand for long. He said his company set up some Army cots for those employees. After a couple of days of this, he called a buddy over at Unocal and asked if his company was releasing anything.

When his buddy acknowledged it was, Ben told him to make it stop since brown goop was hitting and dripping off Wickland's equipment and workers' cars and had been making his co-workers nauseous. I told Ben I'd heard before it was a Wickland worker's call that motivated Unocal to shut down the tower and that I appreciated the confirmation. According to Ben, ending the release was more a favor to Unocal's business neighbor than due to any community health concerns. *Why was I not surprised?*

I'd been itching to talk to someone in local refining who could speak to Unocal's motives, and I was getting it. As he went on, it was clear he knew several of the Unocal workers assigned to or around the leaking tower and that he knew all about their health and safety complaints to management. He also knew pieces of the chronology leading up to this event.

For example, according to his sources, Unocal was supposed to conduct regular equipment inspections, generally every one to two years. In fact, earlier in the year, an inspection of tower D-409 had been set. Once set, however, its inspection was postponed for several months, apparently to maximize profits. Gas prices were up. People tend to use their cars a lot in the summer for taking long trips and such, so revenues were also up. Unocal had also been examining whether the time interval between plant inspections, in general, could be increased—the idea being that less down time meant higher production levels. Although management was told it was a dangerous plan, they delayed the inspection anyway.

Finally, and most maddening, was to learn that the plant had particular production quotas and that, if those quotas had been met, Unocal's upper management would have received sizeable bonuses. Shutting down and inspecting the plant as scheduled that spring, or shutting down the tower in a disjointed, emergency manner, when it began leaking in August, would've jeopardized meeting those quotas. These, Ben said, were the real reasons why company management let it go for 16 days. It all made sense, but I couldn't help but feel stunned.

Ben was a gold mine. I thought, *If he knows about this much, maybe he'll also know if this kind of release was as unusual as I suspected. He might even be familiar with Catacarb.*

"Well," Ben said, "I don't know how much you know about Catacarb, but it's a scrubber they use in one of their hydrocrackers. I don't know which Catacarb they used, but they all have a really high pH. I mean, it'll eat the paint off your car if you leave it on there for long." I didn't know there were different iterations of Catacarb, but I was feeling lucky I'd spent that time in the library since I could now understand what he was saying. Scrubbers. Hydrocrackers. Got it.

We talked about the composition of Catacarb and its handling requirements, and I asked if he knew what it could do to people. He wasn't well-versed on that but recounted that Wickland had paved its parking lot just before the release. When the Catacarb landed there, the chemical turned the black pavement white. *Good enough for me!* I thought as my eyebrows raised. Frankly, I hadn't spent much time thinking about the property impacts since most of my clients were focused on their health issues, but it really made me think, *If this stuff can alter a parking lot, what else can it do?*

Ben was sure his work crew and his little neighborhood were the hardest hit, given their proximity to the refinery, although he cautioned me about focusing too much on that or on Crockett. He said the wind patterns off the Bay were unpredictable and that, especially at night, those patterns would've blown toxins south into towns like Rodeo and Hercules too. He thought I should check those out.

As cut off as Crockett was, I hadn't heard much talk about Rodeo or other surrounding cities, but I thought it was time I looked into how widespread the impact might be. In fact, amidst the flurry of calls those next several days, I found myself thinking a lot about Rodeo. Despite being twice the size of Crockett, Rodeo was even poorer and, thus, even less likely to be militant in its response to an event like this. Even if the citizens of Rodeo were sick, they might not know why, much less have the confidence to address it.

The lawsuit wasn't on file more than a week when I heard about yet another community meeting, this one in Rodeo at its Hillcrest Elementary School. Rodeo now being on my radar, I suited up and went—a red tie this time. Clearly, I was feeling my power. Although nearly 200 Rodeo residents attended, few seemed to know about the lawsuit and even fewer had contacted my office to talk to me, much less retain my services.

So long as the science supported their exposure to Catacarb, I was eager to increase my client base with this group. Going to the Hillcrest meeting would help do that. It would give me some face-time with the few people I already knew and would also show their neighbors I was on the scene. From what I gathered, this town was hungry for some-one to step up and take on Unocal. Although the Hillcrest meeting was slightly less ferocious than the one in Crockett, Rodeo families were just as scared and longing for protection, especially in light of yet another, albeit more localized, release of chemicals by Unocal just a couple of days before.

This second event lasted only hours but exposed Hillcrest's K-5 students to hydrogen sulfide, that intense rotten-egg smell we all know that, even at low exposure levels, can cause burning eyes and coughing and, at higher levels, dizziness, blackouts, even death. When I heard about this second release, I could hardly believe it.

Unocal just keeps screwing up, I thought. What's more, the company clearly hadn't learned its lesson from the Crockett meeting. That night at the Hillcrest in Rodeo, it approached hostile questioning with the same evasive, dismissive and contradicting lines it had spit out the week before and, once again, it was an approach that moved scores of townspeople to contact my office for representation over the following weeks.

Just like I'd done after the Crockett meeting, as soon as the speakers finished, I dragged my body out into the parking lot for fresh air and conversations with whomever wanted more information. Also as had happened after the Crockett meeting, everyone filing out of the auditorium seemed friendly enough, but emotionally taxed. A few handshakes and short exchanges later, I was ready to head home.

As I prepared to leave, Cindy Buchanan, a long-time Hillcrest teacher, stopped me. She thanked me for coming and asked if she could speak to me for a few minutes. Apparently, one of the parents had pointed me out to her during the meeting and she thought she could help. She wasn't interested in participating in the litigation, but, having worked at the school for years, she felt compelled to speak out about what it was like to stare at Unocal's monstrous holding tanks during recess, to smell every wisp of chemical odor that crossed the fence they shared, and wonder when the next big one was going to hit.

I'd heard some people refer to Hillcrest as bordering or sharing a fence-line with Unocal, but I thought it was hyperbole. No, it was real. There was, literally, a chain fence that separated Hillcrest's grassy field, where the grade school children played, from the deadly toxins that flowed through, and often escaped, Unocal's 1,100-acre system. Cindy said this proximity greatly concerned her. It concerned me too.

She said she was worried about her health, but more worried for the well-being of her students—a fear that made her seem even more credible. I tried to sympathize, saying, "You know, I'll be honest. I'm not a chemical expert, or that knowledgeable about Rodeo, but I did grow up in Richmond, not far from refineries like this. Still, I can't imagine how it would be if I was one of these parents, knowing my kids were playing next to this thing all day."

Undeterred by my own story, she continued, likening her work at Hillcrest to being in a "chemical war zone." She said that the smells from the refinery were almost constant but that you got used to it. You had to. The school and the refinery had shared that chain fence for four decades. I explained that, even as a kid, I'd heard my dad refer to this area as "Cancer Alley" and that, more recently, I'd done some reading on the connection between the heavy industry around Rodeo and the disproportionate number of health problems.

I said, "Our case is just about the Catacarb release, but I think that people in Rodeo, having become so susceptible over the years, means I shouldn't be focusing just on Crockett." Of course, she liked hearing that and said she'd happily be a resource in any way we needed her.

Having also grown up in the area, she was convinced the steady stream of toxins from Unocal and its commercial neighbors was slowly poisoning her students, but pointed out that these families were poor and had little say in where the school district sent their kids. Whatever the cause, she explained that these students' pre-existing conditions alone made them more vulnerable to chemical releases. When I asked her to elaborate, she pointed out that, of the hundreds of students attending Hillcrest, roughly one-half of them suffered from asthma, making more chemical releases particularly dangerous.

What? I've never heard of such a thing, I thought, yet she offered the statistic almost without emotion. *Does she realize how wild that statement sounds?* I wondered. I guess she was right when she said you get used to it, which apparently includes becoming numb to how anomalous this community really was.

Caught up in my own thoughts about what researchers had been saying for decades, her words left me nearly speechless. Apparently, those researchers were right—this area was a hotbed of disease. One-half of the kids had asthma? Wow. When I was young, maybe one kid out of fifty at my school had asthma. In Rodeo, it was 25 times that! *What,* I wondered, *will that number be in the years to come if Unocal keeps doing this?*

Right then, I knew Rodeo needed to be a big part of this case, but, before I left, I wanted to hear about the recent hydrogen sulfide release. She said she'd been there that Thursday when it happened and explained that her students experienced the same litany of symptoms reported by people across Rodeo and beyond. She was at the chalkboard when the pungent rotten-egg smell hit her class suddenly and hard, and it was overwhelming.

Hillcrest had been built in 1951 and had the disadvantage of few major upgrades over the decades, making entry of gases into its class-rooms easy. Being heavier than air, hydrogen sulfide slipped under doorways all around the school, including her room, trapping her frightened third-graders, burning their eyes until they cried, causing shortness of breath and vomiting. An emergency school announcement directed teachers to "shelter in place," a common response to such events, leaving Cindy trapped and powerless to do anything except witness this horrible scene while trying to convince her group of ter-rified eight-year-olds they were going to survive.

To her, this was just something you dealt with at Hillcrest from time to time. To me, living that way was outrageous. Imagining little boys and girls locked in a room, flipping out, while the gas kept pouring in was enough to make me sick too.

I promised her I'd do whatever I legally could do to make this better, but, other than compensating these families financially, I really wasn't sure what that would look like. I wasn't an environmental activist, or a member of the school board, or a carpenter that could reinforce classroom doors. I was motivated to do whatever I could, but I don't think I've felt as disappointed in the limits of my career choice as I did following that conversation.

Maybe for that reason, other than perhaps to Doug, I never talked again about what Ms. Buchanan said to me, or about the hostility at the Hillcrest meeting—until now. Back then, I didn't need to; information about how poorly Unocal had treated the people of Rodeo would undoubtedly spread without any help from me. Rodeo's population was twice that of Crockett, and that meant news of an angry town-hall meeting, and the nasty chemical releases that prompted it, would travel quickly—without flyers, knocking on doors or asking residents for five minutes of their time.

Surely, these events would spread like a wildfire all over town, attracting not only the attention of townspeople, but of sharks and, by sharks, I mean lawyers. I knew it would and, sure enough, like blood in the water, it did. Within a few days, I started hearing reports of other attorneys nosing around and asking questions, in Rodeo, but also in Crockett. That other lawyers might step in to file copycat lawsuits wasn't completely unexpected, although I hoped they wouldn't. But, if they did, I trusted we could work harmoniously with them. The moment I heard they were calling my clients, however, my hope for a harmonious working relationship plummeted.

In the days following the Hillcrest meeting, clients were calling me to ask if I knew about my competition, wanting to know if I'd authorized those calls, and if these other attorneys had good intentions. Beyond saying that I was surprised, especially that someone had read our Complaint but was calling our clients anyway, I confessed I had no answers. That fact alone worried me. Admitting you're surprised you even have competition doesn't exactly communicate strength and authority.

But, worst of all, no one could tell me who was making these calls. The lawyers were discreet about saying who they were, until they got a bite, I suppose. All I knew for sure was that I needed to nip this in the bud. I mean, somebody daring enough to call my clients to woo them away was somebody worthy of my concern.

Just shy of two weeks after hearing copycat lawyers had descended upon these communities, Doug and I were invited to another Crockett town-hall meeting. Ours was now a high-profile case, with many new residents joining every day. We agreed we had to go, if for no other reason than to remain visible and accessible to the community at all times. Equally important, however, I was curious what Unocal would say about the lawsuit.

And so, Doug and I suited up again and went, this time without a hint of trepidation. Unlike at the last Crockett gathering, I felt it was my *right* now to be there. I wasn't an outsider anymore. I felt like the new Sheriff in town, having been called in to keep the peace and make sure Unocal's spokespeople didn't start making up stories or otherwise get out of line.

Believing I had things under control, the last thing I welcomed was the interference of other lawyers competing for the affections of townspeople, much less my own clients. Indeed, in this town, at least for now, I thought I was still king. Everyone seemed to know my name, the company included and, soon, they'd know my face too. We arrived in downtown Crockett, this time not giving a damn about where we parked.

I stepped out of the car and walked into that Community Center like I owned the place, like I was royalty, bestowing nods and smiles upon familiar faces. After a few handshakes and quick words, Doug and I took seats right smack in the middle of the hall—among our people. As we sat and laughed and made a few new friends, I wondered how tonight's play might unfold and, beyond making another tape recording, what our role should be.

What's more, since this had become a legal matter, I wondered if the company would be sending its A-Team, the people more suited to handle hostility and not blurt out dumb things under pressure. I wondered if it'd learned anything from the last fiasco. Whatever was to happen, I was convinced that the evening would be fun.

As before, the energy before the start was high, but the speakers, a slightly different lineup, seemed cooler, more practiced. Whether the audience took cues from this or was simply pacing itself, I didn't know, but the locals seemed less activated, more receptive. I wondered if the townspeople had gotten the hostility out of their system—that is, until the show started.

And what a show it was.

Apparently, the company didn't share my zeal for the truth and the message was identical to the ones before. Catacarb is "safe," they promised. Just ask us, they suggested. Here is our scientist. Scientists don't lie, right? Please ignore that they're on our payroll, and just—believe.

Once again, the audience wasn't having it, and much of the fury I'd witnessed the last time was bubbling back up. The locals had insightful questions and caustic accusations. I thought they'd given it all last time, but, clearly, they had a lot more left in the tank. Oddly delighted by the conflict but somewhat bored by its predictability, my eyes started panning the room, curious if others were finding this equally tiresome. In doing so, my gaze quickly locked on a stocky elderly gentleman standing at the far end of the room who was, in turn, watching me.

Much too flashy for a Crockett resident, I immediately took him to be an outsider and a competitor. His clothing alone made that obvious—white collar and white French cuffs on a striped shirt, with an obnoxious tie. His wasn't a hometown style. This guy was from somewhere else and was trying to make a statement, maybe that he could bankroll any project that came his way, maybe that the townspeople had choices.

Supporting my judgment was his level of curiosity—too curious, but not about the speakers. His eyes went between me and various random points in the audience. He was searching for something. By my guess, he was evaluating what it would take to tap this rich vein of misery. As some resident would stand to emphatically make a point, the old man would watch him or her briefly and then switch back to me to gauge my reaction. Intuitively, he knew my connection to all this. I know first appearances can be deceiving, but, looking into his eyes, all I saw were dollar signs.

Who does this guy think he is? I thought. Nudging Doug with my elbow and nodding in this interloper's direction, I wanted Doug to see what we were dealing with. "Lawyer," I said, disdainfully.

Doug agreed, "Totally," and then added with a smirk, "Who's the blonde?" referring to a younger, taller woman next to him.

They were standing too close not to have arrived together. Doug and I each knew what the other was thinking and we laughed, silently acknowledging a range of potentially indecent answers. Nevertheless, I was anxious. I knew we had a problem.

I was confident this flamboyant old man was a rival but wasn't so sure about his colleague. *Were these the copycat lawyers we've been hearing about?* I wondered. I knew I couldn't appear concerned, but I was irritated and distracted. This was *my* case and these were *my* clients. *But be cool,* I reminded myself. *People are watching.* I stayed for the entirety of Unocal's dog-and-pony show, tape-recording everything like the last time, but watching the newcomers intently.

"What's up with these people?" I asked Doug as I again glanced in their direction. The couple just stood there with arms crossed, backs to the wall, judging the crowd more than the speakers. What were they looking for? I wondered if the rage factor tonight was some kind of litmus test for whether the situation was worthy of their attention but worked to keep my patience and irritation in check. I assumed all my questions would be answered in time.

I assumed I'd go over and talk to them when the meeting adjourned, or they'd come find me and we'd figure all this out—unless I saw them hitting on my clients again. Then, it'd be all-out war. And, yet, I didn't see them talk to anyone, even each other. Then, when the meeting was over, I completely lost track of them. I even poked my head outside briefly and looked in all directions. No trace.

That's lame, I thought. So much for being friendly. No exchange of business cards or talk of how we might work together on the case. Just gone. Maybe this was strategic, maybe they wanted to hide.

While surprised by their detachment, I can't say I was surprised they showed up. Although frowned upon, copycat lawsuits are common in situations where a large number of people are injured. I knew there was the potential for other lawyers to come along and piggyback the work we'd already done, although I'd hoped bringing this case on behalf of the entire community would serve as a "keep out" sign to other players. Sure, victims are free to choose whatever representation they want; it's just that, so far, they'd been only choosing us. However, it was probably time for me to start accepting that, especially after another enthusiastic crowd display like we saw tonight, and with thousands of claimants still up for grabs, to put it crudely, we were likely to have company.

As for these newcomers, could we work with them? Did their prickly demeanor signal a power-play was coming? And, if their intention was, in fact, to steal our clients, then what? Would they try to take over my case entirely? Would they then settle out cheaply? Unocal and its insurance adjusters would sure have loved that. Whatever was coming, I sensed it was going to get nasty. When a case is this good and this big, it usually does.

Walking outside, I thought our work for the evening was done. I assumed everyone was, once again, emotionally drained and eager to get home. Just as tired and digging in my pocket for my keys, I was taken aback when a reporter, identifying herself as representing the Associated Press, cornered me for an interview. Not seeing the old man or his partner, I figured I should make the time.

Confirming which service she represented, I knew how helpful an interview with her would be to my notoriety and, yet, I wondered, *Was that necessarily a good thing?* The recent *Times* article already had my phone ringing off the hook, keeping us running at full capacity. Without money, more help or hours in the day, I had misgivings about promoting another big jump in my client base. But this was the Associated Press, the nation's largest news service, and I just couldn't resist.

Just in case I'd been living in a cave, she explained what the Associated Press agency did, that the interview would be shared with numerous bureaus and subscribers nationwide. She thought readers of her article would be fascinated by the longevity of the Catacarb release and my allegations of a cover-up by Unocal. I agreed and told her to ask away.

Doug graciously flicked his hand in my direction, signaling I was free to go solo on this one. As I elaborated on our claims, I couldn't help thinking about Unocal's reaction to the increased publicity this might generate, including whether the added attention might provoke a bold response. Many people who read the *Times* already knew about Unocal's track record in the area. Readers elsewhere might be a little more surprised though. I liked the idea of it—that access to this information would make distant readers question this company's values, about whether consumers should buy its gasoline, about whether they could mimic what Crockett had done and take on bad businesses in their own areas.

I was also intrigued by the specter of other companies seeing a little town stand up for itself against a big business enterprise, but let's face it—to a 28-year-old, just the magnitude of this type of publicity was intoxicating. It's one thing to get media attention at home. It's another when the report is cast on national television news stations and in newspapers thousands of miles away, like this one ultimately was. As someone who loves to stir the pot to begin with, I was completely open to whatever questions she had.

While I thought the courthouse reporter was good, this woman was far better. She understood the claims intimately as well as the legal barriers we'd need to overcome, but her skills drawing out the good stuff, the stories that would make people care about this town, were terrific. She knew about the absence of studies regarding Catacarb, and *that must terrify people*, she'd suggest. "Definitely," I'd respond. "Some people are now afraid to leave their homes. Some will suffer PTSD over this. Some lost their jobs." We carried on for a good five to ten minutes, her grilling me masterfully, me keeping my responses punchy. I was learning.

After covering the basics, I promised to connect her with any clients who I thought might open up. I then gave her a few stories to tide her over before I left. She liked the emotional ones, such as where children were doing childlike things—playing outside with toys, swimming at the pool, running track at the high school—and then getting wickedly ill. Animal stories were a big hit too, for obvious reasons. Sick dogs and cats are usually an excellent draw. I doled out anecdotes like a pro, as she scribbled furiously.

To questions about our potential competition, however, I was a little more tongue-tied. The reporter was naturally curious how large the case could get and whether we'd be working closely with other law firms. Other than the few stories I'd heard about lawyers snooping around, and the couple we saw that night, I tried not to think much about that. Clearly, I was in denial.

For every other curiosity, I'd prepare a response. I needed to. I wasn't going to be caught off guard again like we were at the courthouse. But, for the possibility that we may be in for a battle over client retention, maybe even control of the litigation, I had no sound bites. And for the battle that was coming, I had no strategy. Witnessing the intensity of that sharply dressed old man tonight, I realized I'd better figure one out.

CHAPTER 10
THE FIGHT IN THE DOG

Growing up in Northern California in the 1970s, I was taught to dislike Southern California. It started with rumors of Los Angeleans taking our water during our droughts and using it for frivolous things like filling swimming pools and fountains and watering excessively large lawns. Then, I learned that Southern California was where Hollywood was located and, while all that Hollywood glitz was enchanting, it also turned me off. I thought being fake was necessary to thrive in the entertainment industry, and so L.A. equaled "fake"—or so I thought.

These prejudices were a big deal when I was younger since authenticity was a deeply held value. My parents were authentic people. My mom was a liberal writer and an environmentalist, and my dad, while he worked for a big corporation, he wasn't your traditional big-corporation guy, meaning he willingly cashed his paycheck but secretly wished the company was more socially conscious. We were progressive, outdoorsy, mindful and, for whatever reason, I didn't see our neighbors to the south as sharing these earthy qualities.

Not long after the Associated Press article generously gave my visibility yet another spike, the sharks arrived, and the first were from Southern California. I should have known they would come, but, like any good shark attack, I didn't know they were locked onto my scent until it was too late. Maybe I should have worried more when I saw the flashy guy and his female sidekick at the town-hall meeting. Maybe I shouldn't have been swimming in such deep water to begin with. Either way, my rivals were here now and the best I could do, for now anyway, was damage control.

When they struck, my client, farmer Larry Duran, was the first casualty. From his hilltop property in Crockett, Larry could almost see the refinery and that made him a great client. Unocal may have thought itself clever in washing down all those houses and cars, but there was no way it could wipe away the tons of Catacarb deposited on hillsides and yards around Crockett and Rodeo, his included.

Larry owned a large patch of that now-adulterated land, and on that land, prior to the release, Larry had a small herd of goats. His goats would bleat and graze on those hillsides all day long. He loved those goats because, well, who doesn't love goats? After the release, however, many of his goats were found dead. I was certain Larry would be one of my best clients.

Three weeks after he retained me as his attorney, Larry was no longer my client. One autumn day, he called to let me know he was changing attorneys. He explained that he'd received a phone call from a lawyer based in Southern California asking if he'd been impacted by the Catacarb release. Larry had been impacted, of course, and for more than just his dead goats. When he re-told my competitor his sad story, he undoubtedly got the full-court press to change his legal representation, and it worked.

"You're changing lawyers? What did I do?" I pleaded with Larry, to which he uttered something about me being inexperienced, not caring about the community, about me just wanting money and other such things—at least that's what he'd heard. "Larry, that's just not true," I explained. "Will you tell me who called you?" I asked, but he wouldn't reveal more. He didn't want to create more conflict. He was moving on and that was that.

I was stunned. I wondered if this lawyer was Mr. Well-Dressed from the community meeting and if his office was contacting other community members, maybe even other clients of my office. I wondered if he might try to steal them away and, if so, how in the world he could justify doing that. According to Larry, this lawyer said he wasn't working alone and was connected with a couple other Southern Californian law firms. *Southern California, you say? I should have known, right?* I asked in silent condemnation. This was fueling a distrust I'd not considered in years.

Needless to say, I wasn't happy. Actually, I was furious. Half to vent and half to strategize, I called Doug and explained what these Southern Californian lawyers—or "SoCals," as I began calling them—had done. He was angry too and we immediately formed a few vile expletives; that was the easy part. Forming a concrete defensive plan wasn't quite as simple. We'd need more time and more data before we struck back, if this even warranted a strike back. *Let's not get ahead of ourselves here,* I thought. *For now, it's just one client lost.*

But then it was another client, Jackie Patterson. And then Patricia Nance. And then others fell. Within days, I was receiving all kinds of calls from clients all over Crockett indicating they had been contacted and encouraged to change law firms. These clients said the new lawyers told them they didn't need to tell me what firm was taking over yet; the new lawyers would handle that part, the transition, the mechanics of it. But, when they did say who called them, it was always some SoCal lawyer.

I was getting desperate. While a lot of people said they were happy with us, and ultimately stayed, we lost Larry and Jackie and Pat and, in the weeks that followed, we lost many others. And, with those departing clients, we lost all the costs for medical records and our photocopies, and the postage and telephone charges and everything else we'd spent on them so far—money we didn't have to waste. Sure, we could file a lien on what the new lawyers might get, but that reimbursement, if any, would be years away and there would surely be a fight over that too. I didn't have much money to start, and I'd gone into a hole financially for every one of these people, not to mention all my time and energy.

Damn it, I thought. *Our clients are getting poached!*

I asked these clients what was being said to them, and they told me it wasn't nice—not nice at all. They were told we were too small and reckless and that we didn't know how to handle such a case. But they were also told that our filing this as a class action meant that we didn't have our clients' best interests in mind, that we were just out for money, that we'd screw them in the end. These clients were already scared, and now these lawyers were whipping up a fear culture among them for their own gain. Like I said, I was livid.

If anyone had asked, I would have been truthful and conceded our offices were small, but no one ever asked. Plus, I knew we could handle this case just fine. I just knew it. I'd already lined up a dream team of experts, and Doug and I would find a way of bankrolling it; I was sure of that too. I'd always found a way of coming out on top in any situation. I'd sell everything I owned if need be. I'd be very efficient. I'd find free labor if need be. That didn't make me reckless. It made me scrappy and confident and that's invaluable as an attorney. Finally, the suggestion that I didn't care about the victims' interests and would screw them over in the end was completely unfounded.

While I didn't have the obvious resources of these other firms, there were more important things to consider. As I'd always said, "It's not the size of the dog in the fight; it's the size of the fight in the dog." I'd always liked that expression, since I was usually the little dog. Here, I was young and inexperienced, but, of all the people that would take on this case, I was the one with biggest chip on his shoulder, the guy who had something to prove, and who was incensed by what Unocal had done. That meant I was ready to fight.

And I'd already proved I was fighting. Come on—did we see any SoCal lawyers passing out flyers all over town so as to rally community interest and stop the company's whitewashing of this event? No. Did they do my investigation, my research? Did they clean their plates of virtually all other cases to make room for this giant? Not likely. They probably just read about some incident 400 miles north of where their offices were located and then showed up at a random town-hall meeting. How is that *fighting*?

Unfortunately, even the best efforts can still lead to sad results and, here, mine came in second to aggressive marketing. Over the next couple of months, a flood of calls came in, announcing that the SoCals were calling them, coming to their homes, hanging out at a downtown pizza parlor and holding pancake breakfasts for residents and would-be clients. The stories were making me sick. My moral compass just points a different direction. But, I have to give it to them—it worked.

I continued doing everything I could to crystallize my remaining client relationships, sending newsletters, making telephone calls, even designing a makeshift medical and exposure survey for them to complete. However, over those next couple of months, many of our clients jumped ship, and I still didn't know exactly where to. *How do you battle a phantom?*

Indeed, it wasn't until the start of the holiday season that I even knew our competitor's names and, even then, only by reading the Complaint they just filed—a Complaint which, by the way, looked an awful lot like mine, including many familiar residents' names. As frustrated as it made me to see our clients' name in that Complaint, and as distasteful as it was knowing how they got there, at least the phantom had taken human form. And that meant, at least now, I had a target.

Having gone to a poor high school in a rather dangerous city, it was ingrained in me at a young age that, if a known bully approached you, sometimes it was best to swing first. The SoCals were moving in on my turf, telling my clients that I was a cheat and too small-time and inexperienced to represent them, breaking up relationships that I had spent a lot of time forming. It was really getting to me and, so, I figured that, if there ever was a time to swing first, this was it.

I got the contact details for Adlin Katz, the top lawyer from the SoCal's group of firms—a guy with a reputation for handling big cases like this—and I took my complaint about him to the State Bar, the organization that licenses us and can, therefore, de-license us. I said he and his crew were calling my clients, and that I had proof. And then I wrote Adlin a letter telling him so, making sure to courtesy copy each of my newly poached clients in the process.

After a few boastful remarks, my letter to Adlin explained that any poached clients were interested in changing attorneys only in reaction to his team's misinformation. It said that I'd heard about his team's promise to pay clients' expenses whether related to the case or not. I told Adlin I had called the State Bar about this, that the SoCals conduct was an "embarrassment" to the profession. I told him I'd said the same to my clients and that I'd sue him and make his conduct widely known to the community if it continued.

I dropped the letter in the mailbox and, then, I waited. *You guys don't want to even say "hi" at the town-hall meeting? OK, well, you'll have to acknowledge me now.* No one with any healthy ego—and lawyers generally have healthy egos—could let accusations like mine just sit, and Adlin was no exception. A few days later, he wrote back. I excitedly opened his letter, eager to see who had won.

Adlin's response made excellent use of a thesaurus, and his tone was dismissive and haughty. After explaining that my "impudent" behavior smacked of "bravado," he claimed he had "never heard [my] name before," suggesting he mis-equated notoriety with good work quality and, basically, calling me a nobody. I felt very much like we were squaring off on a grade-school playground. But he didn't back down. To prevail in this skirmish, I needed to ratchet this up.

Lest I allowed myself time to consider if he might actually be right about me, I immediately fired back another letter, calling his tone "arrogant" and promising that his own bravado didn't impress me. I reiterated my confidence that I could aggressively and successfully litigate the case, that I didn't need him for anything, and so on and so on. Nothing like a good old-fashioned legal temper tantrum to stir the pot, right? I did that a lot in those days, assuming a fiery approach would cast me as aggressive, maybe even unpredictable, in my competitors' eyes. It seemed like a good defense mechanism.

To this second letter, Adlin didn't write back, but I didn't need him to. I just wanted the poaching to end, but I wasn't bluffing. I swear that, after this letter campaign, if I had heard one more report from a client about the SoCals calling them, I would've filed a lawsuit in a heartbeat. I had resigned myself to this before I wrote the first letter to Adlin. I am almost certain I would have lost that lawsuit, but I would have filed—no doubt about it.

Luckily, a lawsuit was unnecessary. My letters worked, and that was the end of that. I heard no more client reports of poaching. At least for the time being, I thought, maybe I could focus my energy on the company who brought us to this point of contention. Indeed, I hoped, before other plaintiffs' lawyers took all of my clients, maybe I could do some damage to Unocal. With a very minor success under my belt, I naively thought my trouble with competitors was over.

CHAPTER 11
TIT FOR TAT

While the Complaint may be the document that broadcasts your indictment—like the medieval practice of a knight throwing down a gauntlet to signal his desire to do combat—when we talk about litigation, we're really talking about "Discovery." The Discovery process is the demanding and obtaining of facts supporting your opponent's position and getting information that supports yours. It's requesting the production of documents, sending written questions and subpoenas, taking oral depositions, conducting property site inspections. It's vast and it's complicated. It's where you get to turn over all the stones to see what's lurking underneath, talk to witnesses, spend time with your client and piece it all together. In legal lingo, the word "discovery" can refer to the process, the facts themselves, or even the stage of litigation during which you're allowed to collect them.

Many procedural steps occur between filing the Complaint and trial, but, in my humble opinion, discovery is where it's at. Other practitioners believe writing legal briefs and making complex oral arguments are the loftier, more exciting side of the practice of law. That's fine for them, but, as someone who hates to lose more than he enjoys winning, taking a scorched-earth approach in discovery virtually guarantees I won't miss anything, and that feeds something in me. Plus, developing strategies to get the information nobody else wants you to have taps my creative side.

In California state court cases, like this case was, the attorneys are allowed to serve discovery as early as the tenth day after serving the Complaint. In the simplest cases, particularly ones with a single party on each side, there is rarely a good reason to wait longer than that to start exchanging information. In fact, if you wait too long to start, or your trial is set early, you might run out of time.

In 1994, judges were often setting trials in cases within a year of their filing date. That's what the guidelines told them to do and, frankly, they were happy to oblige since they wanted the cases off their dockets. What's more, a fast-approaching trial date motivated the attorneys to get moving. It provided a great stick. When I filed our case, I knew we'd get some slack and not get pushed too fast to get our discovery work done, given the stakes and all, but I didn't know how much slack. I had to be ready for anything and so I started considering what we'd need.

In most cases, a year is more than ample time to assemble what is needed, but only if you know how to avoid common lawyer games. A clever adversary can put up roadblocks that make the simplest steps take months, leaving the unwary wishing he'd started earlier. No matter how straightforward your case may be, if you don't take discovery seriously, you can be left unprepared for trial and frantic in the final hours.

While the same rules applied to serving discovery in class actions, judges in those kinds of cases did not, even back then, stick to the goal of setting trials within a year, although I didn't fully grasp that at the time. Judges managing class actions—and only some judges within a county would be assigned to handle them—understood the complexity of the issues presented in such cases and gave the lawyers a lot of leeway. They knew about the potential number of parties and the volume of information that was possible. Discovery of that scope takes time.

Judges also knew class action cases could result in handsome payouts, meaning the parties tended to self-regulate and get things done without unnecessary delay. Indeed, with a possible payout in the millions, plaintiffs' lawyers usually didn't need much outside incentive—like an early trial date—to get them to push the case quickly. The same went for the defendants. While notorious for preferring and manufacturing delays in ordinary cases, companies being sued in class actions were often incentivized to step up the pace of litigation and bring it to resolution, given their desire to avoid astronomically high legal fees.

Hoping for a healthy amount of breathing room from our judge, I hadn't felt the urgency to serve our first round of discovery on Unocal, but my attitude was changing. If I intended to ward off poachers, my clients needed to see me being aggressive, getting the data, being the only one mixing it up with Unocal. I needed to prove to them that I actually wanted to litigate, not just collect signatures to score a fast deal.

At first, every time I heard about lawyers calling my clients, it was the SoCals. By late fall, however, that had changed. By that point, there was a feeding frenzy going on in Crockett, with many firms busily rounding up new bodies to file new cases. My clients were watching all this activity and, rightfully, finding it distasteful. I shared their disdain for it and did what I could to fend off the effort, yet I couldn't spend the rest of the litigation focused on my competitors. I had so many questions for Unocal. It was high time I put them to paper.

Indeed, we'd done a lot to move the litigation forward, but Unocal wouldn't have known it. Ours had been behind-the-scenes work—talking with hundreds of potential new clients, interviewing potential experts, acquiring medical records, mapping out a litigation plan. From Unocal's perspective, all we'd done was serve the Complaint, including amending it once to add a truckload of new clients and recorded some town-hall meetings. In return, the company had filed its denial to all aspects of our Complaint but, beyond that, didn't feel inclined to do much else, save for picking one of the best defense firms available and waiting for our next move.

I saw the face of our new adversaries when Unocal's response to the Complaint showed up. As most big companies do, Unocal picked a big-name law firm to defend it: Kenecke, Peters and Wade. I hadn't crossed paths with Kenecke's lawyers before but knew they handled a lot of environmental litigation and I knew they were aggressive. I asked around to get the scoop on them and everything I'd feared was corroborated. They were brilliant and well-respected, and promised to be tough opponents.

It was time to get on with the discovery process but, not wanting to be outmatched by Kenecke's work quality, our requests for it needed to be perfect. My questions, however, sought very technical answers, and digesting what information the company might produce in response to them was still way beyond my expertise. In that way, the discovery process can be a bit of a paradox—you don't know exactly what to request until you know what they might produce, and they'll never offer it until you ask. Given that, seasoned practitioners will tend to duplicate what they sought in the last similar case, but, here, for me, there had been no last *similar* case. In fact, given how unique this release had been, I doubt anyone could say they had a last "similar" case.

Without any meaningful scientific training, I'd be asking questions about engineering, toxicology/medicine, refining processes and chemical reactions, topics that eluded me. That damn chemistry! I hated it in high school and I was sure I'd hate it again now. I never saw the long-term benefit of knowing about things I couldn't touch or see. In school, I just wanted to blow things up.

Clearly, I needed help. To do this right, I needed to find somebody with a hard sciences background to join our little team, and I had a plan. Since I started my law practice, I routinely posted announcements at local schools about openings at my office for secretarial help or legal support. Sometimes, these led to great arrangements—that is, free arrangements. For short stints, I worked out symbiotic relationships whereby the students got some experience and academic credit, and I got free labor with the need for minimal supervision. Maybe I could do that again here.

I'd need significant education or experience from this intern though and obtaining that would be a long shot. Anyone with higher credentials was likely unmotivated to work for free, the potential for some school credit notwithstanding. Then there was the issue of availability. My previous assistants rarely committed to more than 15 hours each week and were often flaky about keeping even that schedule. I figured I could deal with scheduling limitations, but I really needed someone sharp, someone with enough relevant background that I wouldn't end up feeling embarrassed.

Undeterred by these admittedly unreasonable expectations, I reached out to the Career Services offices at nearly every local campus and the ads went up:

"Boutique Plaintiff-side law office has immediate opening for an administrative, paralegal or law student intern interested in supporting our environmental class action litigation team. Candidate will help draft pleadings, discovery, memoranda and motions, conduct investigative research, and participate in team strategy meetings. Law firm experience helpful, but not required. Must have excellent organizational and proofreading skills and the ability to multi-task and prioritize effectively in a team environment. Professional attitude and appearance required. Students with background in chemistry, medicine or toxicology particularly encouraged to apply."

Proudly, I showed Doug the ad.

"So, wait—you're not going to pay them anything?" he asked.

"No. They'll work for credit. We can do that," responding to what I knew was Doug's concern about violating minimum wage laws. "The school is their employer and we don't have to pay them anything so long as we're giving them experience relevant to their academic area. And, look, if they don't want to work here, they won't apply," I responded defensively. Still, Doug wasn't convinced.

"I don't know, man. I don't think anyone is going to want to work for free," he explained.

Still, I saw no downside to throwing a line out there and seeing what bit. I would have bitten. I remembered being in college and thinking that I'd do just about *anything* to avoid sitting in certain classes each week. If given the chance to work for a company applying my skills, I would've jumped at the practical experience, regardless of what grunt work they asked me to do. The same goes for law school. In fact, there, I may have paid *them* to let me pitch in or just watch. I explained all this to Doug, who was still doubtful but, nonetheless, agreed to help interview and work with whomever we might find.

Luckily, Doug didn't have to conduct interviews, except for one, and only because, with this one, I was already fairly sure. That candidate was Brian, a student at a local university, over-achieving his way toward yet another graduate degree, the first one being a PhD in Chemistry. Jackpot. As he expressed at his interview, he was thrilled by the prospect of working on this particular case.

Similarly, we were thrilled to have him, knowing that any supervision would be light because of his particular background and since, honestly, we weren't at all qualified to manage him. Whether we used him for anything related to his then-current studies, well, I'd rather not say, but none of us seemed to care. We needed a chemist, and Brian needed the school credit and experience. We got lucky.

With the addition of Brian, our team was taking shape, meaning we were poised to make Unocal really get to work. Our plan was simple: Bombard the company's lawyers with a comprehensive battery of discovery requests. Ask questions and make requests for documents about the release itself, plant maintenance, chemical concentrations at various times, safeguards for Catacarb handling, and Unocal's profit motives. We'd ask the company to identify witnesses, its investigation and, most of all, how it could justify saying Catacarb was safe. We wanted this to seem like an onslaught to Unocal, like our second act of war and another proclamation that we meant business. Basically, we wanted to get in Unocal's face.

No matter what we asked from this defendant, we knew its lawyers would fight us aggressively. They wouldn't want to turn over anything and, if they thought they could get away with it, they simply wouldn't comply. What's more, we would be demanding a library of information that would take us weeks or months to digest. Given that volume, if these initial requests weren't drafted perfectly, the debate over exactly what we were seeking, what information should remain confidential, and who'd pay for all that photocopying could bottleneck this process for six months. With poachers on the prowl already, we didn't have six months. We needed to show our clients we were making progress now.

I pulled Brian in and we got to work. In most cases like this, attorneys might ask a couple dozen questions in the first round—same for the number of document categories. We drafted a couple hundred, carefully worded to avoid most objections, yet exhaustive enough to miss nothing. Brian was a tremendous asset to the process, providing invaluable technical expertise, levels beyond what I could have picked up alone. We poured over each request with the precision of a watch-maker, formatted them for delivery and dropped them in the mail. California law gives a defendant 30 days to respond to requests like these. We marked their due date on our wall calendar, and we waited.

The suggestion to "let sleeping dogs lie" is not a motto I ever lived by and, so, poking the company with such an enormous discovery stick felt quite natural. Apparently, however, it felt natural to Kenecke's team too. As soon as we sent Unocal's lawyers our requests, they sent us theirs—significantly amplified. Clearly, this timing was more than a coincidence. They didn't need all this discovery from my clients right now, particularly when more plaintiffs were joining every day.

But, I shouldn't have been surprised. In the context of big-ticket litigation brought by a little operation like mine, sometimes the company's best defense is not to attack the merits of your case but, instead, to demotivate and wear you down. It's war, pure and simple. Defense lawyers will throw up roadblocks, delay the litigation to disrupt your momentum, make you spin your wheels on unnecessary projects, and force you to spend far more money than you ever imagined. They'll tell you all this is necessary to "protect the due process rights" of their clients. That's hogwash. They want to break you down, and it's one of the reasons why people hate lawyers.

Unocal already knew I was inexperienced or, at least, it should have known. All decent lawyers investigate their opposing counsel. Kenecke, Peters and Wade was full of decent lawyers, and they could easily have checked my bar admission date to see how seasoned I was. In fact, I'm positive they did. And why not? I checked theirs.

They could also have figured out I was litigating on a shoestring budget just by checking my office address, the one right alongside those noisy train tracks. It would know that I was purporting to manage hundreds of very sick clients, possibly entire towns of them, with minimal resources and that this would be a risky undertaking. Do you really think big businesses don't do their homework?

No, the company saw a cheeky young man looking to ruffle some feathers and so it was going to have some fun with me. Specifically, Unocal's idea of fun was to deliver to my office several banker boxes full of written questions and requests for documents, just like the ones I'd sent them. The only difference was Unocal delivered to me a set of questions and document requests for every one of my roughly 250 clients. Not only did I have to read all this—and I prayed they were the same—but all our responses had to be carefully considered, prepared and formatted, verified in writing by the clients and delivered back to Unocal within 30 days of receipt. This was obviously an effort to "paper me under," a common litigation strategy whereby the more powerful party so inundates the little guy with discovery that the little guy folds under the volume.

I knew what Unocal's lawyers were up to, but I could hardly fault them. Actually, I respected it in a sick sort of way. I mean, I chose to represent so many people. No one forced me to do that. Moreover, there was no turning back now. If I was unable to deliver responses to this mountain of paper on time, for everyone, I could be in really big trouble. Kenecke's team could file a brief with the judge arguing that each plaintiff who failed to respond should now be ordered to respond—immediately. That's bad enough, but what's worse is that Kenecke would then go on to claim I should be ordered to pay their fees for drafting that brief and making a court appearance over the issue. And those fees would be really high. These lawyers were good—really good—and their rates would surely reflect that.

Considering the worst-case scenario, I wondered how I could pay, potentially, thousands of dollars when I had almost no assets from which to draw. If I sold my car, maybe I could barely afford it. But then I'd have no car. And, then, if the judge was gracious enough to give each plaintiff a second bite at the apple, and they failed again, those plaintiffs' claims would be dismissed altogether. Then, once again, I'd be ordered to pay Kenecke's high fees for making the second request, and I'd be done, no assets, out of business.

Looking back now, I recognize I had other options. At the time though, I thought I needed to achieve a perfect return rate or figure out a really good reason why not. And to achieve a perfect return rate, I'd need the cooperation of everyone, and that would require motivational skills I wasn't sure I possessed. I presumed I already had the support of most of my clients—I mean, just remember those town-hall meetings. But those were a couple of months past, and I had clients who were now feeling a little better and some who realized they weren't as sick as others to begin with. These were my biggest concern. Were those people really in it for the long haul or just hangers-on because it sounded good at first to jump in and no one had yet given them much reason to reconsider?

If anyone was having buyers' remorse, I questioned if I should cut them loose and, if so, how? Would it motivate them more if I frightened them by claiming they could be liable for Unocal's fees, or would it just enrage them? That seemed like a heavy-handed scare tactic, but it was a true statement. I worked for my clients on a contingency fee basis, meaning they didn't pay me anything unless we won, but our contracts were less clear regarding penalties in situations like this. All I knew for certain was, if I couldn't get a full response rate, I might appear inept to the judge and to the lawyers, and I could lose a lot of hard-earned clients, maybe even the case, maybe my business. My competitors would have loved that.

Already knowing this, the day I received Unocal's boxes of discovery, my stomach dropped. I was sitting at that old metal desk when a courier walked in, asking if I was "Scott." When I told him he had the right guy, he announced he had a delivery of some documents from Kenecke's office and that he'd be right back. I thought it odd he didn't just hand whatever he had to me, but all he was carrying was a clipboard. Alone, that was cause for concern.

A few minutes later, he returned with a hand truck stacked with three banker boxes, and then a few minutes later with three more. "Have a nice day," he said, as he raised his eyebrows, smirked and then turned and left. I had no witty retort, forcing me to realize I was clearly on the defensive now.

Once he was out of range, I advanced on the six ominous cartons tentatively, cut the packing tape on the first box, removed its lid and stuck my nose in. Removing the first of the hundreds of stapled sets inside, I read the front page "Defendant Unocal Corporation's Request for Production of Documents to Plaintiff Teresa Abrams, Set One." Alphabetically, Ms. Abrams was the first of my roughly 250 clients. The paper war had begun.

For a low-tech office with minimal experience and support staff, responding to this much discovery on schedule was going to be an Herculean effort. Wasting no time, I grabbed a calendar, determined the due date one month out and got to work organizing the sets, two for each of the 250 clients (i.e., one set of document requests and one set of questions). I would have to photocopy each of those 500 sets, each more than a dozen pages in length, collate, staple and stuff those 6,000-plus pages of photocopies into big envelopes. I'd have to draft a long client cover letter explaining exactly what to do, blowing through another ream of paper, just in copying that. Then, I'd meter each envelope with postage—*thank God I just started leasing that metering machine*, I thought—prepare and affix mailing labels and mail them out to each household. That was just Day One. Luckily, I had family and friends I hadn't completely abandoned since I had to now call in some big favors.

Days Two through Five would be calling every household, re-explaining the process already explained in the cover letter, and urging them to get back their responses fast. *Hopefully*, I thought, *they won't have too many questions*. Since that's a couple hundred phone calls right there, I figured I should write a short, tight script.

I wrote the script, and then made the calls, and then flipped out. No one was answering, but I left detailed messages and hoped for the best. By Day Five, I'd made a huge dent in my call list but still couldn't determine if as many as one quarter of my clients even got the package. I called and called. My assistant called. Brian called. We asked neighbors to spread the word. We then left more messages. In the meantime, I had given Doug part of the list to handle at his office. His success rate wasn't much better.

The plan for Day Six forward—although we were already way behind schedule—was to start processing the responses. As the answers came in, I would digest the information and decide what was relevant to produce and what should be withheld. I would take the good parts, type those into an electronic template I created for each client, format that, print it out, and then have each person review and sign the 15-plus-page formal responses. If all went according to plan, I'd copy and pack all those formal responses into boxes and get them back to Unocal's lawyers by month's end.

But, believe it or not, those were just the easy logistical pieces. I had to get the information itself from each client and it had to make sense. To do that, I first had to reach the people, but people leave on vacation, or they move, or they throw away the package thinking it's junk mail. If they do answer, they may not answer all the questions, or they just send right back the same documents I sent them, without a single mark on them, as if in protest. *What?* Sometimes responses would come back with such minimal information I had no idea who even sent them. Other times, their penned-in responses were illegible, or they misunderstood the question altogether. It was a nightmare.

But could I really blame them? I doubt more than a few of them had been involved in litigation before and our means of communication were limited in those days. If they sent anything, it had to be deciphered and retyped, with no other mode of communication available to me than the postal service or the telephone. Adobe Systems had developed the .pdf format just one year earlier, but I had never heard of it, much less used it. Nor did e-mail services exist—at least for little shops like mine—for another few years. I wasn't quite doing the project by type-writer, but it was pretty darned close.

So, I worked every day and night for a month on that project, with-out a complaint, staying focused on the prize. I knew what Unocal was doing, wasn't giving in to it, and, in the end, mission accomplished. On the date due, we hauled a truck bed of boxes of our clients' responses to San Francisco in Doug's vehicle and, literally, dumped them at the Reception desk of Unocal's surprised legal team. Were these responses thorough for every one of our 250 clients? No—not exactly. There were a few utter no-shows and incomplete responses where the client just couldn't be reached again; in those situations, our responses contained only my legal objections, but we delivered something for everyone.

Whatever was in there, our production of responses was enor-mous—box after box, filled to the brim, and vastly overshadowing what Kenecke had dumped on us. We worried about our few deficient responses but, being the exception to the rule, Kenecke cut us a break, filed no motions for dismissal or requests for us to pay their fees. I kept my car, my business and my false sense of invincibility.

For the clients with deficient responses, I hinted to Kenecke's attorneys that I might dismiss those clients voluntarily. But, it was just a hint. Without a firm agreement, I had no intention of dismiss-ing anyone, at least without a better reason, and a better reason never came. In the pandemonium of new cases and new law firms, and with Kenecke's focus now turning toward the discovery requests I had served, my nonresponsive clients simply got lost in the shuffle.

The extension Kenecke had given me to produce information for these stragglers came and went and, still, no serious response from the company's lawyers. Had I not demonstrated I could handle the mag-nitude of this project, I'd probably have gotten no favors in the first place. Even now, having blown the extended deadline, Unocal realized its heavy-handed strategy wouldn't work, and so it just stopped trying.

Good thing too because I'm not sure we could have done this a second time. At least for now, however, we were still in the game.

The day we closed out that project, we turned our attention to the information Unocal owed us. Given the advent of .pdf transfers and document "drop boxes," it now seems crazy that we spent days reviewing a seemingly-endless quantity of documents in a conference room at Kenecke's San Francisco office. Today, documents would be organized much differently and completely electronically. Back then, we flipped through every page, by hand, and not in the comfort of our own offices. Sure, we were told they could be copied and delivered to us, but, frankly, we just couldn't afford it.

According to Kenecke's estimate, the photocopying price tag was upwards of ten thousand dollars. That's a hefty price tag as it is, but then consider that my monthly office rent in those days was $500, a bargain-basement price, even for 1994. My monthly phone and fax services were another $200; office supplies and random expenses ate up another few hundred bucks, and forget about paying for any support staff. Mostly, I recruited volunteers.

And, even at those levels, I was barely covering my overhead. The Unocal case was all-encompassing, leaving me little time to help other clients who might provide me an income. There was no way I was spending thousands to have documents shipped a short 15 miles to my door. That was wasteful. Plus, I didn't want to wait one day longer than necessary to get my hands on that evidence, so we'd go there.

Terri Armstrong was one of Kenecke's lead lawyers and my primary contact at their firm. From what I could tell, she was one of these people who'd smile while slowly inserting a knife into your abdomen. Smart, but shrewd, and relentless. I contacted her and made arrangements for her'to put the documents we requested in one of her conference rooms. When she asked if I just wanted to send a check to have them shipped, I exaggerated my entitlement to view the originals of everything, but it was really just a ploy to obfuscate my financial vulnerability.

After some negotiation, she said that we could come by the next week, at which time she'd have a paralegal on standby to address questions or in the event we wanted to flag pages for photocopying. She was vague about the number of boxes we'd be reviewing, except to say the production was "voluminous." The company was still gathering documents; it was impossible to say how many pages would be ready by the time we arrived, or so she claimed.

The logistics were straightforward—we'd start the following Tuesday morning, flagging documents as we saw fit. Terri explained that, when we arrived, her paralegal would set us up in their conference room and provide as many post-it stickers and legal pads as needed. At first, that seemed generous. Usually, when you go to the offices of your adversary, they'll give you coffee but certainly not office supplies. Over the subsequent days, however, I began to suspect her overture probably wasn't generosity at all but, rather, to facilitate our note taking so we'd ask for fewer actual photocopies of what might end up being very damning evidence.

Tuesday rolled around before we knew it and our legal team (a.k.a. Doug, me and Brian) met early to discuss our goals for the day. Not only were we getting our first peek at important information, this was the first time we'd meet our opposing counsel, and that always demands good acting skills. We needed to appear seasoned and confident, when we were anything but. We presumed Terri would check in on us from time to time, so we rehearsed some technical questions we'd ask her, which we figured would flaunt our insight and expertise. As it turns out, we were wasting our time. Neither Terri nor anyone else of any significance to the case ever stopped by.

As we disembarked the train in San Francisco, we hurriedly walked the few long blocks to Kenecke's office on the Embarcadero, recognizing we'd have to calm our nerves significantly before we arrived. How appropriate, I thought, that the Kenecke firm would be located in the once-famous Hills Brothers Coffee plant. The plant was built in 1926 and long since out of business, but the building still stood, now a San Francisco historical landmark with a tall red sign still visible from across the Bay. It just seemed fitting that both Unocal's refinery and the coffee building were relics, yet had both played an integral role in the development of the surrounding communities. By contrast, the fragrant coffee manufacturing facility had been since repurposed into interestingly configured office spaces to support companies like Kenecke, Peters and Wade, whereas Unocal was still Unocal and still smelled as foul as ever.

Upon our arrival, we introduced ourselves to the receptionist and then we waited. And then we waited some more. That's a game many defense law firms play—not with their clients, of course—just with you, at least if you're a plaintiffs' lawyer. They make you wait. They want you to know they're in demand, and you are not. And, if you are there to review documents they never wanted you to see in the first place, as we were, they'll make you wait even longer.

Over half an hour later, a bubbly assistant escorted us to the conference room where Unocal's documents were temporarily being stored, at least the ones Unocal wanted us to see. As we walked through the labyrinth of hallways which was Kenecke's main floor, we struggled to remain calm behind our guide, not push past her, and not telegraph we were in any rush. None of us knew what was waiting for us, just that it was, as Terri had warned, "voluminous."

Arriving at the conference room, I paused at the open doorway to witness our future stacked before us—within scores of 12×15 inch bankers' boxes. The sight was far greater than we expected, a large conference room with two long walls wallpapered with cartons over half way to the ceiling. Sure, Terri warned me about the size, but this was a dizzying sight, and I immediately realized why she'd been so cagey about the quantity. This was an onslaught.

My God, I thought, as the company's plan for me became evident. *Unocal is trying to bury me in paper...again.* But, this time it was by producing such a mountain of probably-trivial information that it assumed I couldn't reasonably digest any of it. The company was taunting us, asking us, "So you want to try to hurt us? Here you go. Good luck finding what you need to do that." Just like Terri had done by delivering sets of discovery to each of our hundreds of clients several weeks earlier, this was another warning that we weren't ready for this kind of war, a not-so-subtle suggestion that we should have stayed in our safe little offices with our other safe little cases.

Indeed, we would need luck digesting this and finding something incriminating. To the untrained eye, much of what it gave us appeared like garbage—like the tons of garbage Unocal had dumped on my clients. Tens of thousands of pages of dot-matrix printouts of chemical compound concentration levels, articles regarding the toxicology of Catacarb's breakdown products, memoranda between researchers and management concerning general refinery maintenance. This information was extremely remote to what we had requested. If Unocal got its way, this mountain of information would leave me feeling overwhelmed, view most of this as useless and, by rushing through its review, overlook something important.

Where the company got it wrong though was, as a new lawyer, I was already familiar with this kind of treatment and, therefore, content to play along. This wasn't the first time some defense lawyer had seen me, the new lawyer, come along and decided to try this game, thinking my lack of help and experience would compel me to just give up. In fact, Unocal itself may have done this before, maybe even on more seasoned attorneys, thinking the veteran attorney would just send down his lowly first-year associates to do the review instead. Maybe those kids, instructed to work fast, would have rushed through the review and missed some really juicy evidence.

Whether this was Unocal's custom, the unethical dumping of just-barely relevant information on one's adversaries is more common than you think, but it's hard to prove; the test for what is relevant is just so squishy. Usually, the documents produced are, at least technically, responsive, but they don't really fall within the obvious *spirit* of what you're seeking. As long as they can prove you asked for it, you can't really complain to your judge that you got it.

Kenecke's team could probably prove that here. But, if they were willing to play this game, what others might they play? I'd seen defense attorneys employ others schemes to throw me off the scent. Sometimes they'd copy documents so poorly, I almost couldn't tell if they were helpful at all. Other times, they'd bury a critical page within a stack of unimportant ones, knowing I'd be fanning quickly through the bundle. I'd seen those tricks.

Not having worked with Kenecke's attorneys before, I didn't know what to expect. I had to be careful. What's more, most of the information was so hyper-technical that only Brian could decipher it, so we had science questions for him often. Clearly, setting aside only one day for this project, as we had, wasn't going to cut it.

After the initial shock wore off, we cracked a few box lids to get our bearings, but the priority of where to begin eluded us. There was no rhyme or reason to how the documents were organized or what we might find in any particular box. This was going to be a torturous exercise of plucking off the stack one box at a time, going page by page through it, and making notes along the way.

After a few silent, dejected glances, we took our positions at the conference table and each of us grabbed a container. Taking deep breaths almost in unison, we pulled off the lids and dove in. Whether we thought we had the time and endurance to do this wasn't important. We had committed to this, no matter how long the project took us—in the end, over two weeks. And it was one of the most exciting and the most boring two weeks of my legal career. But we did it, we got through the boxes, and, in doing so, the real tale of what had happened at the refinery those 16 days finally came to light.

For most lawyers, document review is not sexy. Actually, most document review is pure tedium, and that's often how it was for us. But, once in a while, finding some gem reminded us why we were there, why we started down this road. Once in a while, as we sat hunched over in our chairs, turning pages, scribbling down notes between sips of the nasty coffee that big law firms always seem to serve, one of us would encounter something really provocative—maybe an important memo or handwritten note describing what was dripping down D-409. In those rare cases, we'd become animated about what we saw and stand up, and the others would rush over to huddle around the document, eager to see if it might be our key to success. We'd stand shoulder to shoulder, reading together as frantically as we could, pointing at passages and raising eyebrows and grunting, like cavemen who'd just discovered fire.

CHAPTER 12
BIG MONEY VS. LITTLE PEOPLE

Whenever prospective clients call me for help, it's always the same. No matter the type of case, they want to tell me a story—their story—about how someone harmed them, and how I should fix it. That shouldn't be a surprise to anyone—they have an experience which ended badly, in which they think they were mistreated. They want to focus on the "what." It is, more commonly, my job to figure out the "why."

Since most legal claims require proof of intent, recklessness or neglect (the law rarely punishes simple mistakes), plaintiffs' attorneys are hard-wired to seek out the defendant's mind-set early on. I was also hard-wired that way and, yet, why Unocal let hundreds of tons of toxins rain down on these towns for weeks had been eluding me. Even following the massive document review, the company's reasons still seemed speculative, although our work uncovered a few viable theories.

To me, the most likely rationale was that the potential profits associated with Unocal's continued oil production at the Rodeo plant were simply too intoxicating. Coming in a close second was that Unocal's management just didn't care and, in a distant third place was that this organization's decision-makers were just too lazy or uninformed to react responsibly. I'd also assumed, at least before our document review, that this behavior was an anomaly for Unocal. Apparently, I was ignorant about its history. Our review of documents at Kenecke's office, coupled with a bit of independent research, quickly opened my eyes. Once opened, it became clear that Unocal's greed and indifference toward both the environment and neighboring communities went back months before August 22, 1994, the day the Catacarb release started. Actually, it went back years.

Most people who recognize the Unocal name do so only because they've seen Unocal's "76" gas stations, or because they've seen the company's commercials encouraging consumers to "Go with the Spirit..." For some people, however, particularly those attentive to environmental issues and/or who have lived on the West Coast, Unocal is also known as a major polluter, partly arising out of its ownership of a six-square-mile oil field 30 miles south of San Luis Obispo, along the coast of Central California.

If you follow such things, you might have heard that Unocal, over a period of 38 years, contaminated the area around that oil field, known as Guadalupe Dunes, with somewhere between eight and twenty million gallons of petroleum thinner. It was an event that threatened human health and caused the death of countless seals and sea lions and, as of the printing date of this book, remains the largest petroleum spill in United States history.

At Guadalupe Dunes, just like at its Rodeo refinery, workers knew of the spillage, yet their complaints about it were ignored. In fact, to this day, I wonder how long the Guadalupe Dunes event would have continued had California Fish and Game wardens not raided Unocal's offices and found substantial evidence of unreported spills and maps already tracking the plume for years. Something tells me that, but for the Fish and Game Department's eventual response, the cover-up might continue today.

There can no doubt that Guadalupe Dunes was a horrible event or that the time interval between that event and the Catacarb release was so great as to allow Unocal to forget. It was March 15, 1994, just five months before the beginning of the Catacarb release, when Unocal entered a plea of "No contest" to criminal charges of failing to report the Guadalupe Dunes spill, forcing the company was forced to pay tens of millions to settle the resulting lawsuit and to fund cleanup efforts that continued for decades.

The Guadalupe Dunes event was tragic, but was hardly an isolated event—at least not according to the Sierra Club. In fact, in Northern California, just a few years before the Catacarb incident, Unocal settled a multi-million-dollar lawsuit brought by that environmental organization alleging that, between 1977 and 1989, the oil company committed 2,300 discharge violations at its Rodeo, California, refinery (yes, the same refinery that released Catacarb in 1994). That litigation charged Unocal with dumping hundreds of millions of gallons of toxic waste into San Francisco Bay. In that case, Unocal was again accused of silencing a foreman who wanted to report the practices.

So, Unocal learned its lesson that time…right?

No. Not even close to right.

By February 1994, the part of Unocal's Rodeo facility where the D-409 tower stood was due for a routine shutdown, and it badly needed it. In an oil refinery like Unocal's, many of the inspections and minor maintenance work can be done while various plants in the refinery are still in operation, or "on line." However, there are also times when outages are scheduled for more substantial maintenance work. These are often referred to as "plant shutdowns" or "turnarounds." The turnaround process is a continuous cycle—from one major planned outage to the next, them oftentimes being scheduled months before each particular plant is taken off-line.

Scheduled plant shutdowns often last only a few weeks, and are highly efficient, high-intensity events. To perform them inefficiently would be extremely expensive, due to the additional loss of fuel production and elevated worker payroll costs.

When the D-409 unit had been inspected during the last plant turnaround in February 1992, heavy pitting and corrosion was noted inside the tower's hull. Yet, despite the instability of the unit, an early 1994 Unocal memorandum asked if the maintenance of this tower and hydrogen plant around it, tentatively set for that February, could be delayed until that October. "If it ain't broke, don't fix it," right? And so, sure enough, the timing of the inspection was bumped to October, and the heavily corroded tower kept on running.

Now, let us fast-forward a few months:

Sunrise was at 6:19 am on August 22, 1994, and Unocal's Rodeo management team was starting its day feeling pretty smug. A few years earlier, the refinery had claimed the longest safety record in the country: six million hours without an accident serious enough to cause anyone to miss work. But let's be honest here; given its other record—the long one of silencing workers who dared to raise safety concerns—Unocal's so-called "record" was dubious at best.

The management team was also excited. In 1994, executives there operated under a "Pay for Performance" program, an incentive structure that included enormous cash bonuses if the plant hit its production goals, but highly discouraged such simple procedures as routine equipment overhauls. With hefty financial incentives hanging in the balance, Unocal's management team was holding its breath, praying there would be no surprises.

So far, it had been a great year—the refinery being on a record production run—meaning that, while it could tolerate the D-409 plant going off-line in October, any unexpected hiccups before that would threaten their paychecks. Indeed, as Unocal explained in an August 1,

1994 memorandum to its workforce (received just three weeks before the release), "with [maintenance] scheduled for October, 1994, we will need to stay above the year-end [pay for performance] target going into [the October shutdown], since gasoline, jet fuel and diesel fuel production will greatly drop off during this 37-day turnaround." Going into late summer, management was almost giddy.

And then came August 22nd:

Half an hour into the sunny new day, the D-409 tower's lead operator called an emergency. He'd received a report of something "unusual," a stream of colored mist emanating from a hole 140 feet up the tower wall, and a brown stain on the side of the unit. Workers mobilized instantly, contacted the General Manager of the facility and a refinery-wide emergency was declared.

Refinery protocols dictated that, in an emergency situation, the County Health Services Department be notified, but did not specify the level of detail to be conveyed. Also consistent with the refinery's safety protocols, the tower operators were then told by Unocal management to reduce the flow rates into and out of the D-409 tower and shut down the facility. So far so good. Dutifully, they got right to work.

Within the hour, however, those same operators received another call from Unocal management, this time ordering them to bring the tower's rates back up and continue operating D-409 at full force. The workers were shocked. Operating a tower with a hole in it was clearly against protocol, but they assumed the directive was the product of informed decision-making. But it wasn't. In fact, nobody with any meaningful health or safety background was consulted, just the executives and the money-men. This meant management could only have focused on three things: whether the leaking tower could explode (costing more money), the price of an early shutdown, and the loss of their bonuses.

According to upper management's analysis, there was a slim chance of explosion, but a shutdown *prior to* its next scheduled maintenance, then set for October 8, would have cost Unocal—a multi-billion-dollar operation—a whopping $1 million. And that was the big choice Unocal had to make on August 22nd: protect one million dollars (and the executives' bonuses) or protect the health of tens of thousands of people in the neighboring towns, maybe even their lives.

To the workers, especially those who had been on the job for decades, keeping a leaking tower operational was an absolutely unprecedented, jaw-dropping decision. What's more, it was contrary to numerous refinery regulations, not to mention a dangerous violation of state and federal law, and everyone knew it. But the workers followed their orders. Their jobs were on the line and so, as directed, they brought the levels in the D-409 tower back up for what was expected to be another six weeks.

While Unocal did report the incident immediately to the Health Services Department, the message was that the emergency was under control, and no other agencies were notified. The county jotted down the information and, then, what did it do? Nothing. Accepting refinery management at its word, the Health Services Department never questioned the decision.

The very next day, just to ensure the county didn't go and do something crazy like investigate the emergency, Unocal called again, this time telling the county officer who answered that the previously reported leak posed no further problem. Knowing a half-truth is, generally, more effective that an outright denial, Unocal claimed that any chemicals that either were or might be released in the future could pose no danger to human health or the environment. Just like in response to the first report, the county took no action.

And, yet, at every moment between August 22, 1994 and September 6, 1994, Unocal knew that the Catacarb leak was not only continuing but was becoming larger and/or more dangerous. Documents Unocal produced to us and witness interviews conducted clearly showed it.

For example, on August 25, Unocal employees reported that the leak was "steadily worsening," and yet Unocal continued to operate the tower.

On August 26, Catacarb and its breakdown components were observed on the ground surrounding the leaking tower, according to documents produced.

Then, on August 29, Unocal management was told by its own workers at a plant safety meeting of the dangers of the continuing chemical releases. Management rejected these comments, said it was safe, and that the workers should just do their jobs.

On August 31, Unocal employees reported that the hole in the tower was "enlarged." On both September 1 and 2, "increased" discharges were also noticed. Nevertheless, Unocal continued to operate the tower.

On September 2, Unocal management was informed of streaks of Catacarb and its breakdown components on some of its refinery tanks.

Around September 3, 1994, workers observed the Catacarb "fallout" sticking to other refinery equipment. On the same day, an employee reported, "Catacarb on the ground. Hole seems bigger."

Despite all this, Unocal continued to operate the tower, knowing full well what Catacarb could do its neighbors. Meanwhile, in the town of Crockett and beyond, unsuspecting people went about their business.

September 3 fell on a Saturday, and, in Crockett, it was turning out to be a beautiful day. The mean temperature that week had been in the high 70s and this Saturday was the first day of what promised to be a fantastic Labor Day weekend. The day was looking like every other sunny day the townspeople had enjoyed recently, but something felt different. Actually, for the past couple of days, something felt different. There had been a rough taste in the air, gritty and metallic, and no one could figure out why.

And it had been warm, with recent highs in the 90s, leaving locals unsure if the sticky droplets on their skin were anything more than perspiration. Even when attempts to wipe it off left undeniable brown smears, residents chalked it up to dirt, pollen or pollution from the nearby interstate. The smears were odd, but no one was assuming the worst. Instead, hoping the dirty air would pass, Crockett residents went on to enjoy their holiday weekend, oblivious to the carcinogenic material that was, literally, showering their city.

By September 4, Unocal's community hotline had received complaints of chemical fallout in Crockett. Someone had put two and two together. Also on the 4th, Unocal's own employees complained of eye irritation and nasal congestion when they worked on or near the leaking tower. A company employee reported that day that there was "Very little steam in the cloud. Looks mainly like vaporized Catacarb. Hole looks bigger." By that time, the hole had indeed grown and was emitting a high-pressure stream of toxins. Even with this report, Unocal continued to operate the tower, all day, all night.

Just another five weeks to go, must have been the general thinking of Unocal's management team, but that's not to say all managers were complicit in these decisions. In fact, one of the most offensive details of this event was how upper management responded to personnel charged with refinery safety—the same workers who were, by now, begging that the plant be shut down. Utter rejection. No discussion. No consideration at all. One worker pleaded for the authority to shut down the unit, yet was told this was "not an option." Another worker even considered sabotaging the unit to force a stoppage. Yet another operator later explained that he was shocked to learn that management planned to operate with the leak until October and that never, in his several decades of experience, had he seen a leaking system allowed to operate, particularly without any repair effort whatsoever.

In the meantime, workers noticed a massive loss of Catacarb—no big surprise since as much as 225 tons of it was ultimately released through the gaping hole. To account for this, Unocal management did what any bonus-minded executives would do—*it pumped even higher levels and concentrations of the toxin into the tower* in order to compensate for the loss. And then it continued to operate the unit, knowing the now-higher concentrations were venting to the air.

On September 5, Unocal received more calls complaining about fallout in Crockett. On that date, Unocal's own employees, including a health and safety worker, told the company the unit should be shut down because of the air condition complaints. Another Unocal employee reported that "because of a complaint from a Crockett resident, they are attempting to knock down the vaporized Catacarb with a fog of water. Hopefully, this will minimize the distance the vaporized Catacarb will travel."

At the same time, refinery workers were noticing and complaining of sticky brown spots on their cars and on refinery equipment. Many of these operators were becoming increasingly worried about their health, and they voiced those concerns. Others, however, were afraid to say anything for fear of retribution. As a memorandum signed by more than a dozen Unocal employees explained, "[W]e were not willing to jeopardize our jobs by individually insisting on shutdown of a unit making a quarter-million dollars daily when the company and all their experts said it was safe to keep going."

To all the complaints and pleas, management reiterated, "We can make it," assured workers that the toxic compound was safe, and permitted the tower to continuing venting to the atmosphere. Management repeated this message, despite numerous worker reports of illness due to Catacarb exposure. It repeated this message, knowing it was seriously risking human life.

At around 8:15 on the morning of September 6, 1994, employees at the nearby Wickland oil terminal called Unocal to report skin and lung irritation suffered by their operators. Apparently tired of hearing all the fuss, three hours later, Unocal finally notified the Health

Services Department that the leaking unit was being shut down. In reality, however, the tower continued to leak Catacarb until almost midnight and the toxic contaminants continued to drift downwind into the community until the early morning hours of the next day. Even after the shutdown was complete, locals continued to smell unusual odors from the refinery and feel sticky residue on their skin for days.

The suffering came later.

According to a CNN newscast on December 13, 1994, an unidentified Unocal worker stated that Unocal failed to shut down the leaking tower in order to continue a "so-called record run," which produced more gasoline than the equipment was suited for. In December 1994, another Unocal employee stated during a KRON-TV (San Francisco) interview that Unocal's failure to report or stop the Catacarb leak was a case of "big money versus little people." Seeing the harm this event did to so many people, I would have to agree.

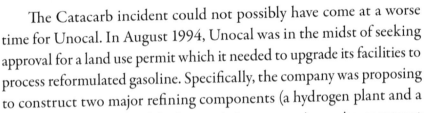

The Catacarb incident could not possibly have come at a worse time for Unocal. In August 1994, Unocal was in the midst of seeking approval for a land use permit which it needed to upgrade its facilities to process reformulated gasoline. Specifically, the company was proposing to construct two major refining components (a hydrogen plant and a steam boiler plant), modify three existing processing units, construct up to ten new storage tanks, and add pipeline and drainage systems on 25 of its 1,100 acres. For that, it needed a lot more land.

Permission to engage in such development, however, required that Unocal make the neighboring communities feel safe—hence, the town-hall meetings. Indeed, had it not been for the public comment period required before such permits can be issued, those town-hall meetings would probably never have occurred. Prior to the Catacarb incident, only a handful of citizens knew, much less had expressed concern over Unocal's application to develop more land.

Now, however, in light of the release, Unocal's open dismissal of residents' suffering and trivialization of the event in its so-called Fact Sheet, the locals were taking a much closer look at that permit application. When Unocal allowed the second toxic release—the one exposing people to dangerous hydrogen sulfide on September 15—residents hit their breaking point.

And, so, they took action.

There's no question filing our lawsuit was a major event in shaping the next few years of life in Crockett and Rodeo, but it wasn't the community's first official step toward taking back its power. In fact, just a few days prior to the filing of (and all the publicity around) our lawsuit, a few residents approached Unocal and made demands on the company for long-term changes that even a lawsuit like ours wouldn't likely address. Among other things, those few residents were calling for funding for immediate local health care and community warning protocols for notifying residents in the event of future refinery emergencies. Those few residents were determined not to be ignored—not this time.

To appease these early complaints, Unocal claimed a willingness to negotiate, but would put nothing in writing and refused to recognize the authority of any citizen as representative of the demands of a larger group. If the community was going to see meaningful long-term change, it would need legal action, but it would also need grassroots collective bargaining, which Unocal would view as a threat to its operations. Without that organization, preferably through both litigation *and* neighbors working together, broader community demands would be ineffectual. Unocal knew of its bad deeds, but wasn't ready to own them. Indeed, even the County Supervisor's office had trouble getting Unocal's attention, as one community negotiator later explained:

> *"The County Supervisor call[ed] up the president of Unocal down in southern California shortly after the incident occurs, and he says I'd like you to come up and address the Board of Supervisors, which had been the precedent established by other companies in the aftermath of an incident. The President of Unocal said to him why the hell should I come up there? You can't force me. [T]hat antipathy [was] Unocal's demise within the community and ultimately their economic demise within the United States."*

With that kind of repugnance toward the towns and local governance, the question for proactive citizens became how the community would achieve change, and I mean the kind of change which would last long after our litigation was over. Our lawsuit sought money, maybe even a fund for monitoring illnesses—but that was it. And, even if we achieved an impressive judgment or settlement, that alone probably wouldn't stop Unocal from doing this again. It would just throw money at its lawyers again, and then at the victims. Corporations aren't quite like the Treasury Department—they can't just print currency—but, if you see how exhaustively they can litigate sometimes, you'd think they had money to burn.

These towns needed more than just lawsuits and payouts. They needed assurances. But, how, with no established spokesperson, an ineffectual county, and a recalcitrant polluter, would they obtain such assurances, especially ones with real teeth? Well, there were already countless examples of communities throughout the United States ravaged environmentally and socially by neighboring polluters, most commonly in areas dominated by petrochemical, manufacturing, and mining industries. Maybe they didn't need to re-invent the wheel. Maybe Crockett could mirror what those communities had done.

In prior situations, even where government agencies had stepped in to protect those communities and issue notices of violation and monetary fines for bad behavior, the governmental efforts were frequently viewed by citizens as inadequate, particularly when they failed to recognize the full range of local concerns. Compounding the problem was public awareness that those agencies possessed limited financial and human resources, and access to limited remedies. This left citizens doubtful of the efficacy of the government's remedial efforts.

As a result, community organizations—sometimes in association with those government agencies—were increasingly electing to address their conflicts with local industry through deals negotiated directly with the polluters. These so-called "Good Neighbor Agreements" were documents promising company concessions and behavioral changes to reduce adverse community impacts, but, despite the positive sentiments evoked by the "Good Neighbor" terminology, they were typically the product of hard-fought negotiations. Even when such Good Neighbor Agreements were achieved, they were commonly offered in exchange for a community pledge to stop litigation, withdrawal of a land use permit challenge, or ending some other form of activism against the company.

Feeling community pressure in the wake of, now, two recent Unocal chemical releases in quick succession, and the commencement of our litigation, the local Planning Commission, in early October 1994, was persuaded to delay approval of Unocal's permit application, so as to give the company and community representatives a chance to work toward one of these Good Neighbor Agreements. In fact, the Planning Commission made Unocal's good faith negotiations toward such an agreement an absolute prerequisite for approval of its land use permit.

At the same time, the County Board of Supervisors authorized creation of a Citizen's Advisory Panel to serve as a refinery oversight committee. The Panel could report back to the county as needed, with updates about the authenticity and course of the good neighbor negotiations. As a result, in order to get its permit, Unocal had no choice but to negotiate with residents—not necessarily agree to anything, but negotiate.

This wasn't just a speed bump for Unocal. It'd be like a cinder block wall if the company couldn't work out a deal with the locals or at least pretend to try. Unocal had already started late in pursuing its land use permit. Construction was ready to begin and deals had been made. Being forced to negotiate with the community to get its permit was bad enough—now it had to negotiate quickly. The resident groups assembling to deal with Unocal knew this too, recognizing that Unocal simply couldn't afford the kind of delays that protracted discussions would cause.

Empowered by this leverage and realizing that the communities wanted measures that our civil suit for monetary compensation couldn't realistically achieve, the residents' demands were numerous. For this part, I just sat back and observed, not wanting to interfere with this grassroots endeavor, but cautious to ensure nothing in our lawsuit was being horse-traded without my blessing. As momentum in these negotiations increased, residents organized into nearly a dozen subcommittees and solicited help from specialists and environmental justice groups. While Unocal stayed strong in the talks, it soon recognized the need to deal.

For months, citizens from Crockett, Rodeo, Tormey, and Bayo Vista (ultimately forming a Crockett/Rodeo coalition) continued their intense negotiation directly with Unocal—in all, 14 formal meetings with refinery management, not to mention numerous calls and informal gatherings. Many of these citizens were clients of my office and saw their work as picking up where our lawsuit left off, and I was thrilled to hear it. What's more, the citizens of these respective communities were building alliances that would never have otherwise existed, and that was inspiring too. If the proverb suggesting that "the enemy of my enemy is my friend" is true, Unocal must have noted the kinships forming between these towns in the wake of the Catacarb release and hated it.

You see, Rodeo and Crockett had traditionally been rivals. Both being small unincorporated towns with already relatively weak positions from which to negotiate with government agencies, they routinely fought over allocation of money from the county's coffers. Moreover, Rodeo's Bayo Vista project was a government housing complex situated on Unocal's fence-line. Its concentration of low-income people traditionally disenfranchised them from surrounding areas, leaving them relatively invisible in political decision-making. Not surprisingly, the people most vulnerable to Unocal had the least clout.

But now, however, joined against what they saw as a common adversary, the budding Crockett-Rodeo alliance pushed a comprehensive agenda with Unocal and it worked. Impressively, within just three months, a Good Neighbor Agreement was reached in principle (pending only Unocal's legal review) in late December.

The 21-page agreement (ultimately signed in April 1995) was unquestionably an amazing result for the affected communities, in all, establishing a $15 million commitment by Unocal, with highlights including the payment of $2.5 million for fence-line monitoring, early detection and notification, up to $600,000 for improvements to the Hillcrest Elementary School in Rodeo, a half-million dollar set-aside to fund a health risk/epidemiological study, and the establishment of a "Good Neighbor Clinic" to treat the health impacts of Catacarb exposure.

Indeed, even Unocal's competitors were complimentary of the result. According to its November 1996 press release, the Chevron Corporation applauded the new fence-line monitoring system, acknowledging that it would "generate enormous amounts of data," utilize three different technologies, and share that information with "Contra Costa County, the Bay Area Air Quality Management District, the Unocal Community Advisory Panel and the Good Neighbor Agreement signatories." A Tosco Corporation's General Manager echoed that endorsement, claiming "the completed system will be unlike anything in use at any other industrial site...."

And they were right. The fence-line monitoring program was revolutionary. It could track refinery emissions as they crossed refinery property by gathering "fingerprints" of the chemicals that passed by its light beam and then comparing the fingerprints in the monitor's internal library. By doing so, it could determine the precise composition, and threat level, of any chemical release immediately.

Unocal's concessions also included a community warning system capable of linking directly to all major local TV, radio, and cable stations, activating sirens audible to residents within a mile of each major industrial facility in the county, including Unocal. The system would then activate a computerized telephone system which would deliver messages to businesses and residents during an emergency. High-tech stuff for little unincorporated towns like these.

Like most victories, however, achieving the Good Neighbor Agreement required some concessions by the community. Sadly, the most expensive outlay by Unocal under the contract was seen, at least by townspeople, as doing nothing for the health and welfare of people affected by the Catacarb release. This outlay was the $4.5 million Unocal agreed to contribute to Contra Costa County for improvements to the local transportation infrastructure, all within a mile and a half of its facility and on "routes of regional significance." In oil company vernacular, that means the trucking routes necessary to get goods in and out of the refinery itself and little else.

I disagreed with the residents on this one though. Whether these funds were intended as mere window dressing, I still saw the payment as a win-win for the parties; it's true that this near one-third of the overall $15 million commitment wasn't earmarked directly for the people of Crockett or Rodeo but, if better roads someday prevented a petroleum tanker truck from pitching its lethal cargo across the highway, or if clearer road signs prevented a driver's death, well, that seemed like a victory for everyone.

CHAPTER 13

CONFIDENCE IS KING

I've always understood that your perception is your reality. When it comes to power, if you think you have none, then you have none. *Confidence is king* and, if you don't naturally have it, fake it.

With their marble, glass and wood-inlaid fortresses, big law firms are often masters at shaping perceptions that they have a monopoly on power. Just go and visit any one of the nation's largest law firms—those hired to protect, at great expense, the legal interests of our country's most profitable corporations—and you'll see what I mean. They'll put on a dazzling show for you, not unlike the puffer fish that blows itself up like a balloon to ward off predators. It's all intended to convince you that their firm is the best, if for no other reason than the ample resources they have at their disposal.

These large firms have disproportionately large reception areas and conference rooms as a display of their grandeur, yet provide tiny working spaces for their employees. They'll commission gorgeous web sites, but serve cheap coffee. Their post-modern décor, disdainful attitudes, and Ivy League accomplishments, often displayed behind their desks in oversized frames scream "leave us alone" or, more accurately, "leave our clients alone." For new lawyers and seasoned practitioners alike, at least those unfamiliar with puffer-fish trickery, it's natural to presume that this opulence and ornamentation must be the product of superior lawyering. Indeed, inculcating the belief that skill and financial prosperity are inextricably intertwined is at the core of big-firm marketing.

Common indoctrination protocol for new lawyers at large defense firms paints plaintiff-side attorneys as under-funded, under-educated and eager to settle cheaply. Once preconditioned this way to the maximum degree of ideological absorption, budding defense lawyers are released onto plaintiffs' lawyers to flaunt their alleged superiority.

And so it goes, not just for large defense firms, but for many plaintiff-side practitioners too, particularly those who face off with big law firms on a regular basis. Plaintiff-side practitioners, at least the seasoned ones, know how many of these defense-side attorneys were trained, and they counter it by puffing themselves up too. Some counter it by appearing wealthy and, thus, in no rush to settle. They'll do it through their dress, their cars, their offices and other trappings of their financial status. They desperately want their defense counterparts to know they can handle whatever is thrown at them.

And, yet, for other plaintiff-side attorneys, the display of wealth is secondary to that of their skill and experience. Many plaintiffs' lawyers show that through specialization, becoming the "go-to" practitioners in their particular fields of law. Oftentimes, they'll go as far as founding their own "boutique" firms—generally, niche firms that build great reputations for being big fish in small ponds, or just fish in unique ponds, dedicating themselves exclusively to a particular field and doing it really well.

The plaintiff's class action firm is a breed of the boutique firm, the attorneys there being specialists in large-volume case management. Although their focus is often limited to just one or two substantive areas, it's their expertise in procedures not well-understood by most other lawyers that makes them dangerous. If they're also well-funded, perhaps by achieving enough sizable fee awards and stockpiling their winnings, their threat to companies is doubled.

But, whether financial, intellectual or both, having one of these assets is crucial. No Fortune 500 executive is going to lose sleep over a lawsuit where the plaintiffs' lawyers lack the resources or know-how to take it to trial. And, if the plaintiffs' lawyers can't survive until trial, why would the company ever offer a meaningful settlement?

With an office the size of a two-car garage, no big company executives would have taken me seriously had I ever let them see my work space. In fact, that's why I utilized a large communal conference room in a separate wing of my office building to conduct important meetings. It's also why I devoted the majority of my already-tiny floor plan to a Reception area. I was forced to master the smoke-and-mirrors approach to small firm practice. And, so far, it was working, like that same approach had worked all my life. Starting as a little kid, I got good at bluffing my way through situations, even really threatening ones. I figured that, if it worked so far, why stop now?

By the time I received the telephone message from Jeremy Abbot, I was already having mixed emotions about working with anyone else on this case. Jeremy was an attorney working for a well-known plaintiffs' firm in San Francisco that handled only class actions. I'd never met him, but I knew his office by reputation. Among other things, I knew his firm was experienced in environmental litigation like this, and that meant he probably had little use for me. His message said it was just a courtesy call, to give me a heads-up that his firm intended to pursue a case of its own against Unocal. But then he said he thought we should meet and talk.

A call like this wasn't a surprise; in fact, it was inevitable. It had been a couple of months since I learned Doug and I weren't the only ones with clients. By December 1994, the SoCals had filed their copycat lawsuit and, by that month's end, at least four other firms, with hundreds of plaintiffs between them, had filed theirs too. The filings were coming fast and furious. By the end of January 1995, two more cases, and word on the street was that Crockett was host to a legal feeding frenzy.

By then, our numbers had grown too, to nearly 400, leaving me remembering with fondness the late-September guessing game when Doug and I made predictions about how large our client list could get. Recalling our naive estimates, I was ecstatic that we both lost.

With this much action in just one season, I was certain many more firms would emerge, probably to a point where we'd have to find a way to work together, at least most of us. We'd be forced to. Wanting to promote delay and keep its money as long as possible, Unocal would have complained to the judge about the expense and inefficiencies of it responding to the same demands from different law firms. The judge would have agreed, as judges usually do to that argument. To force a work-sharing agreement, he would have put our case on hold until we did. I hated the idea of sharing my case, but I wasn't going to have any choice.

In light of this, receiving Jeremy Abbot's message wasn't a shock, but it was still unnerving. I'd heard his office commonly took control of cases like this and, by control, I mean they ran them and other lawyers just tagged along or got pushed completely out—kind of like what Adlin tried to do. I wasn't giving in to that.

Whether Jeremy was going to mimic Adlin's approach, I couldn't discern from just one phone message, but I hoped for the best. It did give me some security, though, that his firm was local. That meant they'd likely be more collegial. Maybe it was just my provincialism, but I was convinced a Bay Area firm would more likely care about helping a Bay Area community, not just its percentage of a settlement or judgment. Second, I assumed a local firm would be less cavalier about burning bridges with nearby practitioners.

I also liked how Jeremy wasn't working in the shadows, trying to take my clients, piggybacking my efforts and then filing his own case before even shaking my hand. That's what the SoCals did and it felt dirty. By contrast, Jeremy was reaching out to me—like professionals should. I just needed to figure out his angle before calling him back. He claimed he just wanted to give me a heads-up, yet he also wanted a meeting. Recognizing those goals were slightly inconsistent, I guessed he was looking to deal—about what is the thing I couldn't understand.

Given the number of high-profile cases Jeremy's office handled, I suspected he would insist on a prominent role in the case. That much seemed obvious and, frankly, I was warming to the idea. There were just too many experienced lawyers by this point for the judge to realistically put me—the youngest guy around—in charge of everyone's cases. Plus, the aggregate number of clients, more than a thousand now between roughly ten offices, was a group greater than I could possibly bankroll. Jeremy must have known that about me as well.

By contrast, Jeremy's firm could bankroll nearly anything, and that's important if you're going to be doing the heavy lifting—taking the depositions, obtaining the important documents, trying the case if necessary. Unlike the remaining firms, Jeremy's office had a tradition of accepting just a few *representative* victims and then getting paid by asking the judge for a special award for its legal work. Most other firms focused on amassing and hand-holding as many clients as they could tolerate, and then collecting one third of each person's recovery. But all that client management and interpersonal stuff wasn't in Jeremy's interest. It would just slow him down.

After some telephone tag, Jeremy and I found time for a lengthy conversation, during which he labored through a scripted set of questions. He wanted to know how I got involved, the number of clients I had, my interactions with the company's lawyers and my investigation, generally. I felt like I was being interrogated and it felt weird. He first acted intrigued but then dismissive of the discovery I sent to Unocal, explaining that, once all the law firms got organized, we should send out a new series of requests for Unocal's files anyway. Was he already signaling that we'd be working together *and* that my discovery—information requests that he couldn't possibly have seen yet—unquestionably needed an upgrade?

That's a little insulting, I thought, but then I checked myself. Perhaps it was merely a form of psychological warfare calculated to make me distrust my work quality—or he was just plain arrogant. He explained his firm had been retained by some vague number of residents and that Doug and I should come to his San Francisco office to meet him and one of his partners to discuss these issues. I hesitantly thanked him for the overture, spoke with Doug, and then circled back to Jeremy to set a meeting for the next week.

I spent just as much time selecting my necktie for the meeting with Jeremy as I'd done before the town-hall meetings. Red won out again. Red is the power color, and I wanted him to know I felt in charge, at least for now. I wasn't sure what to expect that day but recognized we probably weren't on equal footing. *Confidence is king*, I silently chanted as Doug and I exited the subway station and approached the massive tower where Jeremy worked. I was jittery, like I was heading into an important job interview. I was about to visit one of the best-known class action firms in the nation. I had to convince them I could compete.

"So, what's the play here?" I asked Doug. "Are they going to try to serve us with something? Maybe they'll give us money to take over the case entirely and then show us the door. Maybe we fouled something up and they're going to call us out for it. Maybe they'll poison our coffee." I was praying Doug would dismiss my worries as ludicrous. But he didn't. All he said was "I don't know," which just worried more me more. *Not satisfying, Doug!* I thought as we speedily moved along the busy downtown sidewalk. *Not satisfying at all.*

But for the coffee comment, mine weren't unreasonable concerns. Was it crazy to think we may have made mistakes? And buying our clients? Well, Adlin tried that. Plus, I'd read stories in the legal newspapers about lawyers paying others to take over their clientele, but, usually, those stories concerned some unscrupulous attorney who signed up a bunch of people and then, effectively, abandoned them, making a few bucks on his way out of the case by asking a bigger firm to take on their representation. Usually, this was news since the unscrupulous lawyer was getting his law license revoked as a result. I didn't recall the bigger firm getting in trouble for it, but I still sensed it was wrong all around. I didn't want to get anywhere near that sort of activity. I'd worked way too hard to risk losing my career—particularly so soon into it.

Then again, I told Doug, maybe they wanted to join forces, fifty-fifty. Maybe they'd immediately sense our ambition and genius and, upon that revelation, they'd ask if they could work with us—as partners, of sorts. Maybe Doug and I would agree to all that, and we'd all toast with champagne to our new alliance. Doug found this fantasy even less humorous. Indeed, it wasn't until I announced my conviction that they'd bully us with scare tactics to make us feel small that Doug agreed with me about anything on that walk.

For good reason, the bullying approach did appear the most likely. Think about it: when a host invites you to his office, when he could as easily have come to yours, it might mean he's lazy or busy, but it usually means he wants to put on a show. I braced myself for the latter.

We walked into Jeremy's high-rise building and sauntered up to the security desk. Several people hurried confidently past without checking in, but the guards intuitively knew we didn't belong and stopped us. *Great, even they can tell,* I thought. No worries though. We showed our identification and got the green light to pass. I was oddly pleased by the detention. It felt symbolic, as if signing our names in their log memorialized our commitment to boldly face whatever was coming. No turning back now. On the elevator, I hit the button for their floor and the car shot up, with me straightening my tie for the third time.

Upon our arrival at their chic offices, the receptionist summoned Jeremy who, after some small talk, introduced us to Walter Pierce, one of the firm's partners. Like Jeremy, Walter seemed to be a likable-enough guy. Walter and Jeremy were quite different, but, maybe for that reason, I could see why they were teamed up for this project. Jeremy was the nerdy research guy. He'd write the briefs, figure out the legal arguments, memorize all the data points that no one else could keep straight. Walter was the more affable, fatherly, soft-spoken, Big-picture guy. Walter would be the architect of whatever claims they brought and, if his firm took a dominant role in the litigation, Walter would be its spokesperson and leader.

They walked us to their main conference room and we sat at their huge meeting table. Oddly, I almost couldn't take my eyes off it—long and layered brushed gray steel, and cold, very cold—not just its temperature, but its personality and what its personality conveyed about the culture of their office. Most lawyers in those days adorned their spaces with dark, rich wood paneling and floors, and cushy, home-style furniture—all hallmarks of a place and people you can trust, that has been and will be around for a very long time. Conversely, this table was designed to communicate counter-establishment, that these people didn't need or want to fit into old-school corporate culture, that they gave the middle finger to conformity. I thought that was excellent. It was an unorthodox direction to go within a profession that can be really stuffy, and I loved the symbolism.

Jeremy explained that his firm was getting involved in the case and would be filing a lawsuit shortly for an unidentified number of clients.

He made the number of residents who'd retained him sound unwieldy, but I knew his interest was less about managing clients and more on managing other lawyers. First, Jeremy talked, briefly, and then Walter took over. Walter presented as the guy in charge—more direct, not exactly curt, but impatient. No fluff. "So, do you know what you are going to do with your case?" Walter wanted to know, as if to suggest we hadn't considered this, or might even abandon the lawsuit, now that he was on the scene.

Without waiting for an answer, he launched into a recitation of his background with other cases with similar issues and how his firm had led those and how the other lesser firms were, generally, okay with it. But, as he talked, I got the distinct impression this was more than just fact-finding, or fact-sharing, or even good ole posturing on his part. He seemed to be urging us to step out altogether, to move on to other things.

But, finally, he just came out with it. Suggesting we work out some kind of an "arrangement," such that Doug and I could get paid for the work done so far and then, presumably, be off the hook, I was stunned. *Am I hearing this right? Is he saying he is willing to buy these people?* I wondered. *How do you even do that?*

Presuming I was catching his drift, I wanted no part of it and, yet, I didn't flinch, not wanting to reveal my irritation or confusion. I pretended not to have heard what sounded like an affront and blandly explained that we were going to litigate, just like we told our clients, and the court, and Unocal's lawyers, and the newspapers that we would. I explained that we'd already served discovery on Unocal and had reviewed countless boxes of documents at its lawyers' office.

I was turned off by the idea that clients who trusted me to advocate for them were being viewed as commodities to be horse-traded but I stayed engaged, curious to see how far Walter might go. As he moved the conversation forward, I jumped in from time to time about the investigation I had done and said we were pretty far along in the case. It was a bluff. We had barely scratched the surface. In fact, we hadn't even met our judge. I didn't owe this guy the benefit of full disclosure though.

Jeremy and Walter seemed like good bluffers too, until I realized they genuinely didn't care about the posture of my case. They didn't care about the anecdotes about our clients' misery, or the discovery we exchanged with Unocal. They either wanted our clients or they wanted to know how we would coordinate the cases and how the lawyer management would pan out.

I, however, wasn't ready for that conversation, meaning I wasn't ready to share my clients or my work product. I kept on talking about the scientific connection I saw between the injuries and Catacarb, them listening respectfully, at first, but restlessly. Our agendas couldn't have been different. In fact, Walter's façade remained detached, at least until I mentioned Brian's chemistry background and his excitement about particular Unocal documents we'd seen. Walter seemed intrigued by that part, and I thought I was picking up steam, putting on a good show for people I thought were the gurus in this field.

But Walter's interest was fleeting. He didn't want me to pick up any steam. That wouldn't be consistent with his master plan to run everything. Not willing to let go of the reins, he interrupted and commended on the "good work" we'd done but, as Jeremy had earlier done, he explained that we'd need new document requests as soon as his firm filed. *Who the hell does this guy think he's talking to?* I thought. He hadn't even seen any of our "good work," so he was clearly just flattering us, but then boasting that he could do better. This wasn't at all the way to approach me, so I stayed wintry, but not letting on that he was irritating me. No need to. You don't learn by talking and, if you give people enough rope, they will usually find a way of hanging themselves.

Finally, he went on to explain this was going to be a big case with a lot of experts, many of whom he'd worked with before, comments which I countered with my own conversations with experts and, with that, we were at a standoff. We both knew the other wasn't going to budge or go away and that we probably needed each other, either because of sheer client volume, or to look cooperative to the judge, or merely to circle the wagons and keep out the SoCals, if he even knew about the SoCals yet. Whatever the reason, both of us could tell, finally, that we'd have to work together.

Walter suggested that if Doug and I intended to keep prosecuting our case, maybe a meeting should be scheduled between all the offices involved so far. I told Walter we'd be happy to meet with them—a lie, of course, since the prospect of sharing didn't make me happy in the slightest. And, yet, being socially appropriate and staying within the inner circle of whatever alliances were developing seemed more important now than transparency.

And with that, we took the first step toward a unified front. Doug and I left the meeting excited, but with a sense of foreboding, like the first clickety-clackety ascent on a roller coaster, where you're fairly sure you're going to be all right, but you also know you'll need to hang on very tightly.

As we walked out, Walter promised he'd let us know about the anticipated meeting and that I should let him know if other lawyers contacted me. I hadn't mentioned the SoCals, nor was I going to unless directly asked. If it was preordained that Walter would take his shot at running these cases, I'd let him learn about his competition all by himself.

CHAPTER 14
CMC

I'm not sure why it took Jeremy and Walter so long to contact us, but I'm glad they did. A standoffish approach like that of the SoCals would have doomed a good working relationship. Still, I was curious about their timing. Our case became high profile way back in September. Then, once the local news and the Associated Press picked it up, the articles were replayed across the country. Not everyone would have caught that news, but any well-connected local lawyer would have.

Given this and their firm's substantial resources to track new litigation, I have no doubt Jeremy and Walter knew about our case immediately. What's more, it was highly unlikely that their first client waited to call them for several months after the Catacarb release. No, they had clients for a while but were letting the dust settle—waiting to identify their competitors—before filing anything.

That strategy changed, however, when our judge scheduled us for our first Case Management Conference and posted the appointment for all to see. That's when they filed. When Jeremy and Walter learned, shortly after our meeting in San Francisco, that we'd soon be appearing before the judge for the first time, they simply couldn't wait any longer to make their presence known. They didn't want to get left behind. They wanted to come to our court appearance, tell the judge their firm was joining the action and look knowledgeable while doing it. It was a calculated move, at a point where I was hoping for more transparency. All these games were becoming tiresome.

A Case Management Conference (a.k.a., a Status Conference) is one of the most rudimentary and common court proceedings in the course of litigation. When you say you have an upcoming "CMC," every lawyer knows what you're talking about. At its core, a CMC is simply a meeting between the judge and each side's lawyers, sometimes in open court, other times in the judge's private office, for the purpose of giving the judge a progress update on your lawsuit. You are usually expected to file a Statement, normally a week before the conference, that identifies the parties and lawyers, your litigation time line, what sort of discovery you'll need, what motions you intend to file, what you've accomplished already. Then, you go into court and talk about these issues, your thoughts regarding discovery, settlement and trial.

Generally speaking, Case Management Conferences are not terribly exciting, because they usually aren't terribly controversial—not like trials or motion hearings anyway. Trials can be full of drama. Motion hearings—where you ask the court for some change in the status quo, like ordering your opponent to produce certain documents, compelling a witness to appear for a deposition—can also be defining moments in a case. Because the stakes are higher and because they are usually handled by more seasoned and artful advocates, motions and trials are far more interesting to watch. Eight out of ten times, CMC's are handled by newer attorneys who approach them checklist-style and they're usually quite dry.

Finally, the predictability of Case Management Conferences allows an informality and pace not often seen at trials. The parties themselves rarely appear and the entire hearing often lasts no more than five to ten minutes. During the life of most cases, the judge will conduct several CMCs, generally several months apart, the first of which being more of a meet-and-greet than anything else. That's how I presumed our first CMC would be.

While we filed our lawsuit in September, our first Case Management Conference wasn't scheduled until February—far off for a case of this magnitude and really not what I would have preferred. Had we met our judge earlier, I could have used that fact to help ward off attorneys, to prove we had everything well under control, not that it would've made much of a difference. There is an unwritten rule about not filing a copy-cat lawsuit where another case has already made significant headway, but the cut-throat firms now on the scene didn't use that rulebook.

There are also supposed to be rules about *who* can appear at a CMC, but, once in a while, attorneys who are not "of record" in a case are permitted to make an appearance at another attorney's CMC anyway. Since anyone can search court files to determine the upcoming conferences in any case, if someone has something important to contribute, he could just show up, ask to speak, and the judge will sometimes let him. Knowing all this, Doug and I worried about the circus our CMC might become. We'd heard rumors that several other firms would be attending and that alone destined this to be quite a show.

Having company was the last thing we wanted. In fact, we dreaded it. It would be a huge distraction when Doug and I wanted to keep it clean. We just wanted to meet our judge, set timetables, maybe grand-stand a little about our efforts. That predictable agenda is exactly why others wanted to come. Others didn't want us to get traction or set dates. They wanted a power-play. They wanted to frame the hearing in terms of *who* would do things, not *what* needed to be done.

Sure enough, by the morning of the Conference, rumor had become reality and it was confirmed that we'd have a lot of company. They just couldn't let us be. Conferences rarely draw an audience, but high publicity and outstanding evidence made this case very different. Everyone knew a leadership battle was coming.

To guarantee we weren't late, Doug and I showed up almost an hour early. Since it was the first conference, we wanted a guarantee we'd be on time to meet our judge, and almost no traffic made it easy. We also wanted to be early so as to watch and participate in whatever transpired in the hallway before court went into session. We were sure both the SoCals and Walter's team would show up and that there would be sparks too juicy to miss.

In the time before the courtroom's doors opened for business, Doug and I sat in the corridor talking about our morning's strategy, trying to guess which of the people milling about were there for our case. With several high-profile attorneys predicted to show up, the hearing was already shaping up to be a beauty pageant—a vehicle for each lawyer to curry favor with the judge, peacock around the courtroom, grandstand about why he should be the head honcho over all the lawsuits. Having never been in the middle of such a gunfight, we were glad for our fast commute that day and the extra time it gave us to practice our lines.

But there are also downsides to showing up too early for any hearing, one of which being that you risk looking overly eager and that you're open to having extensive conversations with the other lawyers. Plus, if your intention is to sandbag someone in court (i.e., surprise your adversary with an unwelcome request of the judge), you can't do that if you've already met and conferred in the hallway. No, the trick there is to show up at the last minute, looking rushed and, if your adversary still seeks a conversation, you pretend you don't have time.

The less shrewd attorneys tend to arrive early though, like they have nothing else to do. And, usually, they're too nice and too available. They like to hang out, converse with their opposing counsel, and maybe even reach agreements with them which, ostensibly, save time once inside the courtroom. Adlin Katz and his group, having flown up from Los Angeles just for this conference, also got there rather early, but it certainly wasn't for a lack of shrewdness. It was one of those times I wished we'd waited someplace else.

As Doug and I sat there memorizing details from our CMC Statement, my eyes rarely left the staircase or elevator door. Being so vigilant, I immediately caught sight of Adlin as he exited the elevator car and approached us. I'd never seen his picture but, somehow, I just knew it was him. He was flanked by two other older men, one being the man I'd seen at the town-hall meeting—the guy I'd already pegged as being a lawyer—and another one whose identity was a mystery to me.

I'd heard a third SoCal firm was involved. *Maybe he was from there*, I thought. Doug and I previously agreed that, if the SoCals showed up today, we'd play it cool—really cool. *Don't pick a fight or be overtly unprofessional. This is our case. We're in control*, I told myself. Inwardly, I was seething but didn't want to make a scene. Why be responsible for further souring an already acidic relationship? My letter campaign to Adlin seemed to have worked. *Let it go.* Still, I asked myself, as each of these men caught my eye and began walking in our direction, *Christ, what do they want now?*

I had nothing positive to say to them but, not to appear rude, Doug and I stood up as they approached us. Adlin asked if I was there for the "Unocal CMC," but he already knew. "We both are," I replied, as if to say "I see your team, but I have backup too." After brief introductions, Adlin explained that there was a cafeteria downstairs and asked if we could join him there for coffee to discuss the case. Trying to appear busy, I explained there were attorneys from other firms I was waiting to speak with. He dismissed my concerns, promising to just need a few minutes.

I didn't want to be anywhere near them. I felt sure it was one of these guys who'd made, or at least directed, all those calls to my clients, meaning none of them were safe. And, yet, hearing what Adlin had to say might be educational, maybe even useful information to take back to the people whom I did trust. Plus, he'd piqued my curiosity. Adlin seemed intent on telling me something important and I didn't want to be out of the loop.

I looked at Doug with raised eyebrows, as if to convey that a discussion with the SoCals might be worth our while and we both, reluctantly, stepped forward. I directed Adlin to go ahead so Doug and I could follow his group downstairs, as Doug rolled his eyes and made faces at me as if to say we were so much better than this. After rejecting Adlin's offer to pay for my coffee (I didn't want anyone thinking I was indebted to him for anything), I treated Doug to a cup and the five of us huddled around a wobbly, undersized bistro table to hear the inevitable sales pitch.

Not surprisingly, Adlin immediately launched into a harangue about how many cases he'd handled and how many attorneys worked for his firm. I supposed, in his mind, these facts entitled him to bad mouth me to my clients. Apparently, while he already had a big firm, he wanted to make it appear bigger. Apparently, he wanted to intimidate and impress me, but it wasn't working.

Instead, he kept on going, not understanding his audience, boasting about the magnitude and magnificence of his office, and digging his own grave deeper. I didn't want bragging. What I wanted was an apology, maybe even some acknowledgment that he'd been a jerk for calling my clients and telling them I couldn't handle this case, telling them that I had bad intentions. Barring that, I would've taken an outline about his plans for the case or some vague proof that he was any good at all at what he did. Maybe something in that would have impressed me. But that wasn't a conversation that interested him.

In fact, Adlin didn't want a *conversation* at all. He wanted to lecture me. He offered false sympathies about how "unfortunate" it was that, even though I'd filed the first case, I was now caught in the middle of a tug-of-war between the SoCal attorneys' offices and Jeremy and

Walter's firm. "I wasn't aware of any power struggle," I said, but Adlin didn't flinch. He had a speech to get through.

I listened to everything he said, but his tug-of-war comment was distracting. Were Jeremy and Walter holding back some information from me? I had no corroboration that local firms even knew about the SoCals, much less had reached an impasse regarding some kind of working relationship. And, assuming Walter and Adlin had been talking, did Walter consider it a power struggle? And why was Adlin telling me all this? Was this just a fiction to make Adlin appear on par with Walter, as if he was the sole potential challenger to Walter? Was Adlin trying to relegate me to non-player status in the management of my own litigation?

Adlin then pulled out a news article he said I should read carefully. It explained how Jeremy and Walter's firm had recently been fined tens of thousands of dollars by a local federal judge. According to the article, one of their partners had submitted fake documents in a case. The article went on to say that yet another ex-partner at that office was now suing the firm, claiming that he had been forced out for refusing to keep quiet about the cover-up there. Adlin asked us if Walter's was the kind of firm with which we wanted to align ourselves and warned us about getting caught in the middle when he brought these indiscretions to the attention of the judge. The implication was that Doug and I would look guilty by association if we didn't support his SoCal team's petition for case leadership.

I have to admit that it was eye-opening to hear about such a huge fine being imposed against Walter's firm, but Adlin bringing this to my attention was still presumptuous and distasteful. Apparently, this was how Adlin litigated, by ambush and dirty tricks. Apparently, he hoped I did too, but I wasn't looking to build a reputation in this business by trying to embarrass people. Walter hadn't hurt me, so why hurt him? I wanted no part of this and had no intention of taking sides. In fact, despite all these workings to divide up the kingdom, nobody had even announced there were sides to take. *Why all the games when the real villain here is Unocal?* I thought.

Dismissively, I told Adlin this was all very interesting but that whatever beef he had with Walter's office had absolutely nothing to do with me. I told him I'd considered it professional that Jeremy reached out and invited me for a meeting, whereas nobody from the SoCal group ever made that effort. I told him the only contact the SoCals ever made with us was through Adlin's abrasive letters, which just demeaned and called me names, but none of this registered with him. Zero accountability. Zero remorse. He just said he hoped we were past all that. *Well, I'm not past it.* He wasn't giving me any reason to be past it. In fact, his threats to humiliate Walter's office were just making it worse.

Adlin said his group was going to ask the judge for control of the litigation, that his attorneys had spent more than a hundred thousand dollars on experts already and that his team had been retained by hundreds of clients. He had some nerve saying this, I thought, since some of those clients used to be mine. Still, I listened, albeit skeptically, wondering where all this was going. And then he came out with it. I knew it. It was just a matter of time.

He explained this litigation was over our heads and that he was willing to take over the representation of our remaining clients so we could step out of the case altogether. He said we ought to reach some kind of an agreement about that. He wanted to buy our clients.

How magnanimous! I thought, in silent contempt. But, of course, it wasn't magnanimous at all. It was vile and offensive, and I was livid. *Why would I dream of walking away from this case?* I asked myself. *What—because I have no money and you do? Not good enough.* We had nearly four hundred of the most seriously damaged people in the region, people who his group probably advised to defect, yet they'd stayed with us. I have to assume that had something to do with more than whether we had money.

We had an engineer at the C&H Sugar plant who worked high up on scaffold rigging during the release and tasted this stuff daily, whose throat then changed color. And we had Ms. Boucher, whose previously fit husband died after the release, after he spent his days at home gardening. We had people who itched and scratched themselves almost constantly now, and asthmatics whose bronchial spasms had dramatically increased in frequency and intensity. We even had a construction worker who was assigned to work at Unocal during the release who was now fatigued daily and showed high levels of boron (a key Catacarb ingredient) in his urine and elevated enzyme levels in his liver. *These people trusted us to make this right,* I thought. *Why would we walk away from them now?*

Not only that, but this was the second time inside of a month somebody was telling us we had to make some kind of a decision about our own clients. But, I'd already made a decision. I made it within 48 hours of Ralph calling me way back in September. I didn't care about trying to impress or convince Adlin of anything. I just wanted to see if Adlin was going to do what I thought he would do—wheel and deal with us and try to cut us out—and he didn't disappoint. He asked us how many hours of work we had put into the case so far and to tell him what our hourly billing rates might be if these had been paying clients. He explained that, perhaps, his team could reimburse us for those hours if we referred to him my clients. And, with that, he simply went too far.

I was taught as a kid that it's gauche to discuss—at least beyond your family and bankers—how much money you make. I didn't come there to make deals, nor did I want his money or to step out of the case. I told Adlin it was none of his business, and Doug agreed.

Adlin seemed perplexed by this. To him, it must have been unfathomable that a young, broke, inexperienced kid wouldn't take all that money and move on to greener pastures. If he bothered to ask why I rejected the offer, I would have told him. There were several reasons:

First, he was a jerk.

Second, my hourly rate didn't reflect what I saw as the enormous risk I took. Doug's rate wouldn't either. From my perspective, I'd launched the investigation, mobilized a lot of townspeople, filed a risky class action case against a huge oil company, went to a lot of trouble uncovering what was, obviously, a big story, and put my career on hold while I did it, and without any money in reserve. I felt like an underdog in a big way, and I couldn't imagine how I'd adequately capture that risk in an hourly rate. Nor did I want to.

Third, while I had worked on this case all day, nearly every day, for many months, I hadn't kept a good record of my hours.

And, finally, I had been rejecting almost every other potential case that came my way because, whether Adlin could understand this or not, I really worried about what was happening to this community. I felt that our partnership could help not just get them compensation but, just maybe, harmonize their relationship with all the industry around them—the industry that had been poisoning them for generations. None of those goals would be met by me auctioning off my clientele to the highest bidder.

Although these values may have surprised him, nothing Adlin said surprised me. And, as I predicted, as soon as I didn't accept his offer to graciously bow out, he did what every bully does who doesn't initially get his way—he beat his chest and threatened more. Allegedly, he was going to run things. He said we'd be pushed out, right along with Walter's office. That he promised. Allegedly, we made a big mistake and shouldn't have gotten involved in the first place, and so on, and so forth. You get the picture.

What a blusterer, I thought, and I knew blusterers. I grew up seeing that kind of thing all the time, people like me getting bullied that is.

Whether it was getting pushed up against fences and cornered, having school books knocked out of my hands for no apparent reason, I knew bullies. Adlin was a bully for sure, but he wasn't getting his way this time.

As much as I knew to take the high road, it was hard not to condemn Adlin publicly right then and there, to bluster and threaten back. But I didn't. They say that just living well is the best revenge. That's what I'd do—just do my work as best I could and outperform his team in the end. This wasn't about my ego. Doug and I thanked him for the information, abruptly stood up and walked out. I couldn't get back to the courtroom fast enough.

After composing myself on the climb back upstairs, we were greeted there by several new arrivals. Jeremy, Walter and one of their younger associate attorneys were part of a small crowd waiting outside the Department. Catching their eyes, I figured I'd better say "hi." Walter immediately noticed my irritability as I approached him, and so I thought it was best to come clean about the café meeting with Adlin's crew. The meeting piqued his curiosity, and to a degree which, in turn, piqued my curiosity.

So, there is some bad blood between them, I concluded. I told Walter what I thought of the SoCals and I mentioned the deal Adlin suggested. Sadly, Walter's lack of surprise confirmed what I already suspected— buying and selling clients wasn't all that uncommon in this business. Apparently, if I wanted to play this game, I'd have to get used to it.

I explained to Walter that we'd rejected Adlin's offer and, for the first time, told him about the poaching of my clients and how we had sworn statements to that effect. I told him I'd considered sending those statements to the State Bar's office but that the SoCal's poaching had since died down. Consistent with my decision to keep those statements as an insurance policy against future poaching, Walter explained that we could bring them to the judge's attention if necessary. That was good enough for me.

I knew the Clerk would be unlocking the doors at any moment and, yet, there was much to say. I told Walter I predicted Adlin's group would be announcing their candidacy for lead counsel—as sort of a "first strike" approach. Walter didn't seem surprised by that. I told him he should probably preempt the effort by taking a dominant position today, before Adlin did. He agreed. I also explained that, if the competition between firms became obvious to the judge today, Doug and I were in favor of excluding the SoCal's from the mix. As we talked, I glanced down the foyer at Adlin's SoCal group. They were watching us, maybe even scorning us—at least I hoped.

It was important to tell Walter about the meeting with Adlin, and how to neutralize what the SoCals might do in court, but my heart wasn't in it. I was learning that building alliances—this particular one with Walter's office—was critical to survival in this practice, *but who were these friends I was making?* I wondered. I mean, what Walter had alluded to at our first meeting wasn't terribly different than what Adlin was offering me now.

And why should I trust Walter? At our first meeting, Walter made the number of people he represented sound unwieldy. Since then, he'd filed his Complaint—for just a handful of people. I was shocked. We should have been the ones absorbing Walter's clients, not the other way around. While not actually saying it, he gave the impression he had scores of them already. But one thing was clear: whether or not I could trust him, working at odds with him was no longer an option.

The Department's doors finally opened and more lawyers entered than I'd initially seen lingering about, meaning some had either showed up exactly on time or had been waiting around corners, outside my view. Maybe some had engaged in their own deal-making—maybe even with Adlin. I suddenly felt very much like an outsider in my own case as we checked in and found seats in the gallery, where the public sits to observe court proceedings.

The 15 attorneys appearing on the Unocal case that morning weren't a quiet group, many shaking hands and slapping backs and making small talk as we waited for the judge to take the bench. Everyone was social and excited to be working together—nearly everyone that is. The SoCals didn't shake any hands and didn't smile once. They wanted nothing to do with us. They sat in the jury box, some 30 feet away, an unusual but clever move. It made a bold, definitive statement of separatism, as well as a pronouncement of their ease in the courtroom. It was as if they were saying they were better than the public and better than us. It said they owned this courtroom and could sit wherever they wanted.

"All rise," cried the bailiff and everyone stood as the judge entered the courtroom, stepped up to and then sat down behind his lofty bench. That, in my mind, had to be the best part of the bailiff's job, telling the lawyers what to do, telling us when to stand and sit, not unlike a drill sergeant barking out orders.

"The Superior Court of Contra Costa County, State of California, is now in session, the Honorable Robert Monroe presiding. Please be seated and come to order," he continued.

The script changes slightly from courtroom to courtroom, but the bailiff's message is always the same—shut up and get ready. As he spoke, I quickly surveyed the courtroom again, noticing that the counsel tables flanking the podium were barely large enough for two attorneys per side to sit, meaning we'd have to stand when talking to the judge. Plus, the area between the swinging gate (the "bar") and those tables was pretty small. *How are we going to fit more than a dozen lawyers in that space?* I thought.

There's a sense of theater and urgency when the bailiff first makes his announcement, but then, unless you're first on the docket, you usually have to sit quietly and respectfully and watch other proceedings for a while, sometimes for as long as an hour or two before you're up. Sometimes, you can predict the length of your wait by viewing a printout of the morning's calendar, pinned to the wall just outside the courtroom, but there isn't always a calendar posted, and sometimes judges take the cases out of order. You just never know. You can't foretell what the judge might do; if your case is complex, or has many parties, or you've upset the judge and need a good chewing out, you might wait all morning.

Other times, as a courtesy, a quick matter may be called first so the lawyers can go home. That's nice. Other times, you just wait. Today, we didn't have to wait long until the judge's clerk was passing an unusually large file to him. That's one of the clerks' roles—to keep the judge on track, keep the hearings moving along and to handle the judge's calendar. Since all related cases traditionally get consolidated and then referenced by the name of the first filed action, half of the court's audience that morning waited for the judge to call mine.

"Calling case number C04-04141, Calli Santos, et al. versus Union Oil Company of California," the judge boomed. All 15 plaintiffs' lawyers stood, grabbed papers and briefcases and jockeyed to be first through the swinging gate. Once through, they approached the attorney's tables and engaged in the time-honored dance over who should stand where. And who stands where matters.

There are hard rules, and then there are negotiations governing the lawyers' positions during court appearances, some as subtle as head nods, foot shuffling and "Excuse me's." Lawyers for the plaintiffs sit or stand at the table closest to the jury box. That's a rule. You cannot stand in the "well" (the zone between the counsel tables and the judge) where the bailiff, clerk and court stenographer are usually working. That's a rule too. If you want to hand the judge something, you give it to the bailiff.

Beyond that, unspoken protocols abound, the primary one being that, the more important the attorney is to the proceedings, the closer he or she stands to the center podium, and therein lies the purpose of the dance: grabbing that center spot as fast as possible announces you're in charge or that, at least, you want others to think you are. The dance is to establish a pecking order. If anyone steps aside voluntarily, they've effectively been pecked, and they lose—one less challenger to worry about.

Being next to the podium also tells the judge you want to speak—sometimes because that's the only place where there's a microphone—and that the others are amenable to that. Again, the dominance-hierarchy dance is subtle, and that's why it's so interesting to watch. Having never before been joined by other plaintiffs' lawyers at a court appearance, I never imagined so much thought went into such things.

To match the SoCals' multiple attorneys, Walter brought multiple attorneys. That's important. If you're part of a large firm, you want to remind the judge of it, that you can handle a big case, and that you intend to allocate significant resources to it. That's another power-play. These two groups hadn't coordinated this display—they weren't even talking. They just intuitively knew the importance of setting the dominance hierarchy early.

To do so, the junior attorney from Walter's firm rushed to be first through the gate. Once through, he quickly took the power spot next to the podium, and then, when Walter approached, the younger lawyer gave up his ground, and Walter stepped in. Impressive choreography.

Despite my *Santos* case being the so-called "lead" one, I wasn't invited to this dance. Not being seasoned at such maneuvers, and being a little short in height already, I was forced to wedge myself into a space far to the left of the action just to see the judge. This was not going according to plan. I was ready to enjoy a leading role, but Walter was writing me out of the play. The moment I saw him step up, I knew this. He was telegraphing to everyone he expected to come out top dog, but I wasn't prepared to fight him over something as minor as where to stand. Maybe I should have. At the time, I figured I'd be called upon by the judge when it was time, I'd offer my lines and everything would be fine. Until then, I wasn't going to make this contentious.

As the judge recited what he knew about the facts and procedural posture of the litigation, I watched the SoCals with interest. Surprisingly, they stayed lined up along the rail of the jury box, physically distancing themselves from everyone else on our side, impatiently shifting their weight from side to side, calling attention to themselves frequently. This wasn't an accident; they wanted to stand out, messaging that they didn't need us, didn't like us, and that they hoped the judge would understand why. They wanted the court to see we wouldn't be working together and that a decision by him would be needed soon. Like Unocal's attorneys, who watched all this from their positions across the courtroom, I found all these manipulations distracting. I wanted us focused on the case.

After commenting on the number of attorneys present, the judge paused. Not missing a beat, Walter jumped in, capitalizing on his opening, graciously apologizing for the size of the lawyer turnout—as if he, the self-appointed representative, was ultimately responsible, maybe even that he'd made a mistake in inviting all of us. He explained, however, that the number of lawyers simply reflected the number of residents impacted by the release and that he saw a lot more cases coming. I knew his game. He wanted to minimize the stature of my *Santos* case and to worry the judge that, absent Walter's leadership, court oversight of so many cases would be impractical.

Walter's approach made obvious he was intent on sealing the deal today before this judge, convincing him that Walter's was the only voice he needed to hear. He embarked on a lengthy monologue about the extensive investigation his firm had done, that he'd spoken to

Unocal's lawyers already about certain issues but the content wasn't critical. His genius was that he spoke first and spoke globally and that he didn't flinch in doing so. And it worked. It cast him immediately as our spokesperson, our storyteller, the liaison between whatever was happening in Crockett and this court. Each time the judge nodded his head in agreement, I found myself trivialized in my own case.

I couldn't believe how smoothly this was happening. Walter's timbre and rhythm were grandfatherly and metered, refined by the experience of winning with this same shtick many times before. Watching him operate was like being in one of those dream states where you're seeing events unfold in slow motion toward some horrible outcome, but you're helpless to do a single thing about it.

I wanted to act, but what Walter was saying wasn't controversial; he wasn't saying *his* case or *his* clients deserved special treatment. That would have given me grounds to argue with him. Instead, he talked about his experiences in prior cases, and some of the information we'd be gathering for trial. Who could disagree with any of that? He left me with nothing to contribute except a "Yeah. What he said." and I was, at least, smart enough to know not to say that. I was mad. This was supposed to be my narrative, and Walter was stealing it.

Not satisfied with just reducing me—all of us really—he wrapped up by noting the presence in court of representatives of a few other firms. He said he'd worked with them before on similar cases. The implication was obvious. He was trying to deal them and cut us out. He couldn't do it at his office, so he'd do it here, for all to see. Walter conveyed how discussions were ongoing with these other firms toward assembling a litigation management team but that they'd need a little more time to finish talking. It was perfection. He told the judge exactly what he wanted to hear.

Alas, I had been sandbagged by the same people who'd welcomed me into their office, seemingly an overture toward developing a friendly working relationship. I had no idea what a *litigation management team* even looked like, but it sure sounded good, and the judge didn't bother to push for details. Why would he? Nothing had happened yet, but I knew what Walter was doing—not actually announcing that I was out—but certainly letting the judge assume it, softening him to the idea, maybe just enough so that I'd look like a sniveling, over-reactive kid if I suddenly became combative.

No, Walter didn't say any actual deals had been made—just that the lawyers were *talking*—but, to a judge, lawyers working things out for themselves is like heaven. A judge will postpone almost any decision if it appears the lawyers might work things out for themselves. Walter knew this and gambled on the court not making any decisions that would benefit me so long as balls were still in the air. And, yet, for that same reason, I wanted decisions today—any decision. I wanted to take steps to move my lawsuit forward. My lawsuit moving forward would make my clients happy. Plus, it'd give me leverage to secure a place within whatever inner circle Walter might be forming.

Liking what he was hearing, the judge directed us to figure out the management structure before more work was done on the case and, with that, I knew I was in trouble. I struggled to stay relevant, uttering a few lines about how it was only Unocal that would benefit from more delays, how we had momentum that shouldn't be disrupted, but I wasn't enough of a statesman in those days to perform this level of damage control. The judge was just listening now to be polite. His mind was made up. The lawyers were getting organized—that's the only message he could hear. This went exactly how Walter wanted it to.

Ironically, through all of it, I found myself wanting the SoCals to rescue me, by saying something—anything—that would upset what Walter was doing. And they did talk, but they didn't say much, probably thinking it better to pick a later time to fight than cast themselves now as contrarians. I knew Walter was on a roll, and the SoCals knew it too. When Adlin spoke, he explained that the SoCal firms were *already* organized and that he hadn't been privy to Walter's negotiations.

And the judge listened but, I suspect, tuned out much of what Adlin had to say as well. He was simply too focused on what Walter had offered, and, as hope springs eternal, once hearing about the prospect of lawyers interacting productively, he was happy to close out this meeting. Judge Monroe didn't want infighting and didn't want to make any unnecessary orders. He preferred to wait and let the dust settle on these talks before he stuck his neck out like that.

Advising us to report on these issues at the next Conference, the judge asked if Kenecke's office took any position on what we'd discussed. Like Adlin, their comments were relatively inconsequential, and, with that, we were done. We thanked the judge for his time, picked up our papers, and walked out of the courtroom, Walter quite content with himself, and me seething.

As we spilled out into the corridor, Walter and Jeremy approached me as if we were best buddies, but my trust for them was shot, and my icy demeanor showed it. Noticing the change in my attitude—and the other lawyers now crowded around us—Walter's smile disappeared and he said was sorry for not notifying me beforehand about their management team talks. Feeling a modicum of power from our onlookers, I decided not to let him off the hook so easily. This was dirty pool, and we both knew it. I told him I thought everyone's voice was important and that working at odds with each other just played into Unocal's hand. I assumed the others would agree.

Whether not realizing how well he'd performed in court, or concerned about appearing autocratic, he decided it was wise to back-pedal. He explained that nothing had been set in stone, that we could work together, but I doubted the sincerity of the sudden reversal. Recognizing more was needed here, he said that, if I was interested, we could set another meeting, this time including lawyers from a few additional firms to discuss the cases more. One of the attorneys he referenced practiced in Walnut Creek, a suburban town about 25 miles east of San Francisco. Walter said we could meet there.

Too little, too late, I thought, but it was the best I was going to get. Plus, time before another meeting would give me the chance to strategize. I knew my options were rapidly shrinking and, if I had any chance of staying relevant in this litigation, I needed to accept the invitation. I knew Walter and his friends had a history and that I was the young outsider. Maybe I could change their perception of me. I was game to try. We set a date for the meeting and left the courthouse, me feeling a lot less smug than I did an hour before.

CHAPTER 15
CIRCLING THE WAGONS

The term "Steering Committee" is well-known within legal circles to signify a group of attorneys from different firms appointed to manage complex cases. These are the massive, high-profile class actions addressing the claims of thousands or even millions of people, which, given their size, need special management. We've all heard of major lawsuits like the ones against Enron for investor fraud, or against Exxon Mobil for its Valdez oil spill in Alaska or against Big Tobacco for pushing its drugs on adults and kids. What you probably haven't heard, though, is that a group—generally, an executive committee—of plaintiffs' law firms was organized to lead each of those cases, and a thousand others just like them.

To occupy a Steering Committee position in a class action case, you must be appointed by the judge, either after waging a vigorous battle to prove your superior qualifications or, more harmoniously, by agreement between the plaintiffs' firms having already filed lawsuits. Appointment methodology aside, once the management group—which can range from a few firms to more than a dozen—is formed, its members regularly meet, assign work among group members, and make the strategic decisions that govern not only each of their own firm's cases but every other lawsuit filed thereafter. Depending on the impact and reach of the event, some Steering Committees manage only a handful of additional cases, while others coordinate and serve hundreds or even thousands of related matters.

Not every amalgamation of cases requires a formal Steering Committee—some have just one lead lawyer or sometimes a lead lawyer and then another advocate to serve as a liaison between the leader and the remaining firms. When a more elaborate Committee is needed, a lead attorney is also appointed, but that person may have limited authority without the consensus of Committee members. In each of these scenarios, you have lawyers who are in the loop and those who are out.

In my humble opinion, if you're not going to be part of the management group, you might as well not file a lawsuit in the first place. There's really nothing exciting for you to do. When a Committee exists, it takes over and runs the litigation, for everyone. If you're not part of that, you'll be largely in the dark about what's happening. It also means your clients will be in the dark, and why would any client stick around for that? Frankly, if I was a client, and my lawyer couldn't detail for me the prospects for my case, I'd move on and find representation elsewhere.

If you're an outsider to the management group, and some of your clients stick around anyway, you might get them some money in the end, but you'll probably have no say in how much or when. In short, about your only purpose will have been to file a Complaint and then cash a check for some modest amount of fees some years later—not a bad gig if you're just looking for a handout, but not the kind of thing that motivates me. From Unocal, I didn't want a handout. If a management team was being assembled to run this litigation, I was determined to be on it.

When Walter first invited me to the Walnut Creek meeting, I couldn't tell if it was out of guilt for having just sandbagged me in open court or because he wanted to circle the wagons against the SoCals. When I arrived and saw no sign of Adlin and his SoCal crew, yet observed the presence of several partners who'd recently filed cases,

I knew it was the latter. This wasn't a meeting to talk about the merits of the case; this was conspiratorial partisanship. Walter knew Adlin had tried to befriend me before the CMC and that I was now mad at Walter for building alliances aimed at carving me out. Walter wanted me at this meeting to keep me close or, if that was impossible, to deal with the conflict sooner than later.

All this meant the meeting was pivotal for me. Being here, I had a chance to push my way onto this budding management team—my first ever—and help run this case, not just for my clients but for everyone within the affected communities. Had I not shown up, or if I couldn't prove my value to this group, Walter would just solidify his relationships with the other Northern California firms, and my participation in the litigation would have effectively ended.

Not knowing what to expect when I arrived, the legal firepower I saw when I entered their conference room was eye-opening. If there wasn't already a question, I was now positive that my role in this case was far from secure. This wasn't going to be about who had more clients or who'd done the heavy lifting so far. I was wrong to think it was, just as I was wrong to assume other lawyers would never call my clients, bad-mouth me and steal my business.

From the moment I walked in, I felt my presence there was more a privilege than a right. I was seriously out-matched. Even the least experienced of the partners there had been practicing five times as long as I had. Even their younger associates who tagged along to watch their bosses at work were senior to me. And every one of them had litigated these issues before, albeit in response to corporations which had engaged in behavior less egregious than that of Unocal. A couple of these partners I had met briefly at the CMC, and, of course, I brought Doug. Doug had to be there. Now, more than ever, I needed backup.

As we took our seats, Walter was pacing around but trying to look relaxed. He was making perfunctory small talk but really just getting warmed up to tell us how this was all going to go. *Why did he really invite us here?* I thought. *Hadn't he already picked his so-called litigation team?* I guessed he was looking for support, unanimity perhaps, such that the SoCals—his only real competition—would be compelled to play along, lest they risk being completely shut out, but he wasn't about to spell out his concerns.

He began by talking about the necessities of case management and how, without skill and organization on the plaintiffs' side, Kenecke's lawyers would take a divide-and-conquer approach that would put us all at odds, delay the litigation, and exponentially compound our work load. Ostensibly, he was merely advocating cooperation and efficiency, but I interpreted his presentation as more of a campaign for our vote—and that, if we supported him, some of us might be invited along for the ride. If I was right, this was our opening.

Clearly, Walter's end-game was to assume the lead role; yet he was also signaling that he needed us, at least some of us. I was already resigned to not being top dog since—let's face it—Walter's resources and reputation for handling these kinds of cases meant the lead role was probably his for the taking. There was more than a hundred years of collective experience, just in that room alone; the judge wasn't about to put me, a second-year attorney, in the position of telling these guys what to do, controlling their lawsuits, collecting fees on their cases, when people as experienced as Walter or these others were already willing and available.

Walter was not only ideal for this, he was motivated. If you remember, he had only a handful of clients. Without this lead appointment, he wouldn't be relevant at all. With it, he'd be at the helm to litigate for everyone hurt, including the tens of thousands of victims still unrepresented across several affected towns—and get a fat paycheck for doing so. Without that, his paycheck would be, at best, one-third of the settlement or judgments of his few clients, and he'd have a small voice in the decisions over whether they'd get paid at all. For him, that was simply unacceptable.

But while Walter's role on the team, maybe as its leader, seemed preordained, my application was still under review. In fact, as I listened to Walter's speech, I wasn't sure I was being offered any role at all. To cement my place, I needed to get creative fast. Being in a key role within the management circle meant I'd keep all my clients and, at the same time, I'd help call the shots for every case that came along later, and I suspected there would be many. Also, by helping call those shots, I could effectively position my clients for an excellent payout, maybe even get wealthy myself in the process. How was I going to convince all of these seasoned attorneys to trust my skill and judgment enough to help run their affairs? And what leverage did I have to compel them, ultimately, to share potentially tens of millions in fees with me when they probably didn't need my help to begin with?

By the time Walter finished his introductory comments, I knew that a group would be formed today. It had to happen now. Judge Monroe wasn't going to allow multiple cases to proceed on parallel tracks, each with its own representatives, costly exchanges of information, and perhaps even multiple jury trials. That's completely inefficient, a waste of the parties' and the court's resources, and it can lead to inconsistent results. To avoid that, it was obvious Walter had already tapped his colleagues for key roles. I could hear hints of it in his presentation. Doug and I were being handed our hats.

If Walter was carving us out gently enough so we wouldn't run into court and make him look heavy-handed, then I wasn't putting up with it. At the first break in his speech, I jumped in. I took my days in the library, our review of Unocal's documents, and the numerous interviews I'd conducted and I proclaimed us subject matter experts. I suggested we were indispensable to the team when I knew we weren't. We told the group about the town-hall meetings, the impact on Rodeo, the Wickland oil worker's call, and all the stories from our clients. But, mostly, we told the group we were determined, hard workers which, I explained, we'd proven by going solo against Unocal for six months at great personal and professional risk. Indeed, whatever we lacked in experience, we made up for in exuberance, and we wanted them to know it.

Walter wasn't happy with our grandstanding, but everyone else seemed glued to the information and stories we offered. They knew we didn't offer vast litigation experience, but they liked our spunk, that we'd not been sitting on our hands. I'd take someone with guts over practical experience any day of the week. Hoping this group saw it the same way, I played our only card repeatedly.

I also mentioned the SoCals and how they'd approached us. It was fear-mongering and a not-so-subtle threat that we had options, but I was also pointing out that whatever agreements we made that day were tentative and could be challenged by the SoCals later. I had no intention of aligning myself with Adlin, but it was unlikely that Walter wanted to test the bluff.

Finally, I talked about justice, and how determined I was for it. It was a little trite, but talking about justice always sells well. I knew Walter and his friends wanted to create a coalition that would exclude us, but that would be difficult if it meant they were excluding the true believers—those in it for the people, the cause—not for the money. Judges don't like lawyers focusing on profits, especially those from victims. They especially don't like lawyers who form teams that carve out people willing to work hard for the right reasons. Carving us out would require Walter to show the judge his goals were nobler than mine. I wanted to show him that would be a tough sell.

Apparently, my speech was working. At the risk of appearing dictatorial, asking us to leave, and losing almost everyone's support in the process, Walter was softening. I could see it. As long as we didn't budge, I knew he'd come around. The others sensed it too and they, in turn, capitalized on the opportunity, occasionally jumping in to explain how they were also qualified to participate, how they were also upset, and how everyone in attendance that day should play a role. Walter had promised a few people a role on his litigation team, but his vision for limiting it to that was crumbling fast. Apparently, I'd started a mini-revolt.

This, of course, was not the meeting Walter had mapped out. He expected to tell us what to do and how this was going down, not listen to our demands. At best, he wanted soldiers. He certainly didn't want dissenters. One of Walter's friends meekly cut in and said a decision on Steering Committee membership might be premature, that maybe we should postpone selections until a later date (perhaps at a meeting to which some of us wouldn't be invited), but I knew all too well what punting today on this decision would mean: a sweetheart deal between just a couple of firms that would cut us out, requiring us to go on the offensive to win back any control. That was too risky.

We were on a roll, and I wasn't letting up. Another participant asked for a vote right then. Doug and I echoed the request, and so a vote was taken. Despite the initial reluctance by Walter and his friends, all hands went up to form a Committee which included each of the half-dozen firms represented there that day. Doug and I were in. It was virtually unprecedented that a second-year attorney would be included on the management team for a major class action. And I was equally thrilled that, for now, the politicking was over.

As expected, we all agreed that Walter could be the lead lawyer, at least with regard to appearances in court and most day-to-day communication with Kenecke's team. Walter would also be the person primarily responsible for victims who decided not to retain any particular lawyer. Each Committee lawyer would stay in charge of his own clients and make tactical decisions for his own case, but the Committee would also vote on strategies of common concern. It was a loose structure with a lot of overlap but a road map that left almost no opening for SoCal participation.

To ensure this, Walter volunteered to draft the court Order. He said it would consolidate all our cases under my *Santos* case name, identify all of us as the Steering Committee members, and list the outside professionals who would facilitate settlement talks as appropriate. Settlement was way down the road, but we agreed we'd all participate in that decision-making too, if it ever came to that. With the SoCals looming out there, poised to challenge our group's self-appointments, Walter wanted as much detail about our team and its duties as possible in the Order. We wanted it nearly impossible to unravel by the SoCals or other meddlers.

Disturbingly, it was only after nine-tenths of this meeting had passed did we ever say much about the case itself and, even then, not in the way I'd hoped. Sure, there were a few productive comments about next steps and proposals for how we'd approach discovery requests, but several attorneys' apparent elation that we'd just unearthed a pirate's chest of gold disturbed me. People who expect rewards without effort or sacrifice always annoy me and, so, the last thing I wanted to hear was predictions about the profits this case could generate.

But I bit my tongue, and so did a couple of others, and we got the conversation back on its right track, but it was clear that our agendas weren't necessarily aligned, that some members would be less involved in the heavy lifting, and that I was not going to make as many friends here as I'd hoped.

As our meeting closed, we made plans to meet again and said our good-byes. As I made my way to the door, my egress was blocked by the partner who'd been most vocal about the potential payout from this tragedy. As his associate packed documents back into their briefcases, the partner suggested we speak privately.

"Maybe we could get a cup of coffee," he volunteered as he placed his hand on my shoulder and ushered me quickly into the empty hallway.

I asked him why, given that we'd just spent two hours talking about what I thought was our only common ground and that his almost-singular focus on money had already left me antagonistic.

Once out of earshot of the others, he explained how we ought to work together to bring in more clients. "And just how do you suggest we do that?" I asked.

Well, as he explained, we could go into cities further outside what I thought to be the exposed area and, once there, we'd allegedly find a wealth of people ready to retain our services. Apparently, he'd been working for a while on another case involving those neighboring cities, a case close to settlement, and his clients there were excited about the prospect of some quick money. According to him, those residents would sign up for virtually anything. My skin was starting to crawl.

I couldn't believe what I was hearing and was bothered that, perhaps, I'd signaled a kinship that made this conversation seem appropriate. It was as if sharing a fight to get on the Committee, over Walter's gamesmanship to keep us out, meant we were now friends, that I'd be tolerant of this unethical scheme. I couldn't figure out how I'd suggested I might be open to this.

The reality, of course, was that I hadn't signaled it. My goals were obvious to everyone. Residents had put their trust in Unocal to keep them safe. That trust had been betrayed, and my case was meant to address that. While it would be nice to get paid for my work, I saw that as a byproduct. This guy should already have figured out that I was not likely to set up shop with him in faraway towns just because his clients there got some quick money before, but I suppose he had to try. Everyone in this case seemed bent on trying to convince me to do things I felt were dirty.

I listened to him, but I just wanted to go home; so I faked an excuse to get away, offering some vague promise about us talking later. Needless to say, we never had coffee. We talked at times later, as all the Committee members were required to do, but the topic of chasing new clients never came up again. He did, in fact, go into those communities to carry out his plan without me, but I didn't care. At least he was leaving Crockett alone.

CHAPTER 16
THE GOOD NEIGHBOR CLINIC

The expression "three times meds" describes a benchmark often used among insurance adjusters and attorneys for assessing the settlement value of personal injury claims. In short, it suggests insurance companies aim for settlement payouts of three times the amount of victims' medical expenses. It's a crude expression for its unabashed monetization of pain and suffering, and, equally bad, it's an extremely unhelpful model in special situations, such as where the victim's body or appearance *is* his career (e.g., for sports or entertainment personalities). Insurance carriers may tell you its usage is just an urban myth, but they'd be lying. Alternatively, they might say it's merely a starting place for settlement valuation, and, while that may sometimes be true, it's also the conclusion to an uncanny number of negotiations.

For the personal injury lawyer, knowing this settlement formula exists is critical. It provides a realistic target, and it helps you advise your clients if they want to maximize their financial recovery. For example, armed with this knowledge, you can explain to a victim that, if he wants to achieve a better settlement or trial result, he needs to see a doctor. After all, if it's not serious enough that you'd seek medical help, it's probably not going to look serious to a judge or jury. That many personal injury victims can't afford the time off or the insurance coverage to pay for medical help doesn't usually matter; you need to see a doctor. As a result, when the Steering Committee first heard Unocal was to fund a so-called "Good Neighbor Clinic," I'm sure everyone had "three times meds" on his mind.

Formation of a Good Neighbor Clinic wasn't the lawyers' success, although our case did heavily motivate Unocal to come to the bargaining table. I gave this victory to the community since establishing the Clinic was a term agreed upon relatively early in Community-Unocal negotiations. Unocal claimed it was calculated to achieve a better long-term relationship with the residents, but we all knew the motivation was to get that land use permit. But, what did it matter? With so many residents still sick, the community wanted a medical facility that could be operational quickly, pushed hard and got it.

This new medical office would be funded by Unocal for six months and operated in the town of Crockett. Its charter was to address and, to a lesser extent, study the health effects of Catacarb exposure. The Clinic would be run by a committee composed of a community representative, a physician/operator of the Clinic, a University-affiliated independent physician selected by Unocal, a Unocal representative, and a local physician selected by local resident coalitions but also approved by Unocal.

Regardless of which side selected them, these allegedly independent medical experts were required to have specializations in toxicology/ environmental medicine and be available for the full six-month term and, in some circumstances, beyond that. Under the terms of the Good Neighbor Agreement, Unocal would pay their salaries as well as the laboratory-test costs of anyone wanting treatment there for Catacarb-related symptoms. Unocal would also pay for medical treatment beyond the six-month operational period of the Clinic, so long as the Clinic's

Committee agreed the particular patient's condition was "related or most probably related" to the incident. None of this was in Unocal's best interest, but the company was desperate.

Even before the Good Neighbor Agreement was fully signed in April 1995, the Clinic's doors had opened and the patients were pouring in but not without some degree of trepidation. My clients didn't trust anything associated with Unocal, much less the doctors it paid. These locals wanted to know what forms of testing would be provided and how intrusive they would be. They worried whether they'd be charged for treatment if their symptoms weren't found to be associated with Catacarb exposure, who could view their examination and test results, and the biases and agendas of the company-paid doctors.

These were all good questions and, yet, I had few answers. Having a defendant, in the midst of class action litigation, funding a medical facility to study the health effects of what it had done was almost unprecedented. But, then again, the circumstances of this release were also relatively unprecedented. My clients didn't trust the Clinic or even the idea of the Clinic and, yet, if they wanted to get better, they'd have to take a leap of faith and go.

Sure enough, as soon as the Clinic opened, I was overwhelmed with questions regarding what services it would offer and whether I trusted its doctors. I wondered if I should be giving this kind of advice and whether I believed the clinicians would take an unbiased approach. If I didn't take a firm position, however, I knew some of my clients might find another lawyer who would.

"Well, I've never met them," I'd say to those who asked. But my ignorance didn't seem like sufficient cause to worry anyone and, so, I still suggested they go. Or don't go—I didn't have a strong opinion either way. And, whatever answer I gave would leave me stuck in a no-win situation anyway. While the Clinic was the only solution for most people, I'd undoubtedly be to blame if their experience was poor. Conversely, if I appeared too cautious, and they didn't go, I might be blamed for them still feeling sick later.

But there was a bigger picture to consider. Remember that the Clinic was established, in part, to study the health effects of Catacarb exposure at a time when there were no studies. That meant each visit would help educate the clinicians and better prepare them to treat the next patient. Each visit would also provide treatment records necessary for our court case and could provide the basis for some fantastic expert testimony about the chemicals' health effects.

As long as our clients were receiving reasonable care, using the Clinic seemed like a net win but that presupposed that our clients could even get in. Getting an appointment was easy for those residents who called early, but its "first-come first-served" basis meant others waited for months. Then, once rumor of this delay spread around town, and even greater flood of requests for medical care came in, just adding to the feverish pace at which the Good Neighbor doctors were already working. In fact, by the time the Clinic closed for good, insufficient Clinic resources and Unocal's funding left more than 100 people on the waiting list—for first visits.

The Good Neighbor Agreement required that the Clinic be "fully staffed," which meant three physicians on duty at a time, seeing an average of 36 patients per day. Even on days when it was fully staffed, however, they couldn't keep up. Other days, physicians were absent. This wasn't their only job, you know. On the upside, these absences, coupled with the high percentage of patients who insisted on multiple visits, generated so much pressure from community groups and Clinic physicians alike that Unocal extended the Clinic's operations by five weeks (albeit on the condition that no more extensions be requested). On the downside, physician absences and too many patients meant a lot of people didn't get the care they desperately needed.

Altogether, throughout that summer and fall, hundreds of locals visited the Clinic and amassed voluminous documentation of their injuries, all on the company's dime. For those who got in, I thought the arrangement was wonderful since they got free care. And we got free records, which was great for my clients as long as the records kept showing a Catacarb connection. Since the records did show that connection, I kept an open mind, kept sending my clients there, and kept ordering their files. By the time the Clinic closed for good on November 15, 1995, it had served somewhere between 800 and 1,400 residents (with one estimate of an even higher number), not bad for a town of only 3,000 people.

The diagnoses were staggering: a whopping 63.3% of patients were diagnosed with ophthalmological (eye) symptoms, 42.7% with short- or long-term lower-respiratory problems, 33.1% with psychological disorders, 29.3% with psychiatric/neuropsychological disorders, and 18.2% with autoimmune diseases, to name just a few of the dozens of related conditions.

Reports generated after it closed found that roughly half of the patients were in need of continued care, but very few got it. Under the Good Neighbor Agreement, residents with symptoms found to be "more likely than not related to Catacarb exposure" were promised continued treatment, to be paid by Unocal, but disbanding of the Clinic's health Committee left patients confused about where to go, how to secure payment for medical services and without referrals to specialists. In spite of the promises, victims were left with many unanswered questions but not much health improvement. As one Crockett interviewee explained:

It should have been continued longer because so many people were still being treated. And a lot of it may have been just placebo because they just really didn't find any cure for it. They were able to get all kinds of neurological testing done and saw aberrations and a lot of commonality of a lot of strange symptoms but they never came up with any way to treat it other than just time...."

In some cases, victims got relief from their suffering, at least temporarily, but many others were just given vitamin supplements and other placebos. That was, at least, the story for victims in Crockett. For the town of Rodeo, Crockett's poorer neighbor, the story was even worse. In fact, Rodeo's benefit from the Good Neighbor Clinic was almost nonexistent, although its residents negotiated for the facility just as aggressively.

One reason for this was placement of the Clinic in Crockett; this made it less convenient for Rodeo residents. Moreover, Unocal had misrepresented to Rodeo citizens that their symptoms could not be Catacarb-related. Unocal said the wind did not blow toward Rodeo, but it did, and that lie made Rodeo locals not want to chance it; they knew that medical treatment and laboratory tests were free only so long as the symptoms were, in a doctor's opinion, connected to Catacarb. These poverty-stricken residents simply couldn't afford to be wrong.

It was predictable that Rodeo residents would be worried. Being unexpectedly charged for medical care if company-paid doctors found their symptoms disassociated with the release would be devastating, especially to people who were already missing work *due to* the release. Rodeo folks were already poor, with a per capita income 30% less than Crockett, and Rodeo's Bayo Vista government housing project, at Unocal's fence-line, was tragically poor. These people couldn't reimburse fancy doctors. The majority couldn't even afford health insurance, which is why they were the ones most in need of a free clinic in the first place. Not knowing which direction to go, only a small fraction of Rodeo and Bayo Vista victims utilized Clinic services. Instead, they suffered quietly, while lawyers sent their Crockett clients to the Good Neighbor Clinic in droves.

While the Clinic was met with mixed reactions by members of the community, a separate but related provision of the Good Neighbor Agreement was an unqualified success. By mid-February 1995, researchers at a local university, led by Joan Eisenberg, had mapped out an epidemiological study they intended to conduct of Crockett (but not Rodeo or Bayo Vista) residents exposed to Catacarb. Although its findings were not published until March 1996, a full year and a half after the release, this Unocal-funded health risk/epidemiological study became the best evidence of a connection between the Catacarb leak and every one of the community's common ailments.

Like the Clinic itself, the Joan Eisenberg study was not without initial skepticism and hiccups. In late-February 1995, area residents were asked to attend a community forum to hear from a panel of scientists and health professionals about the proposal. While attending residents expressed great interest in and support for the study, the county's Health Services Department couldn't leave well enough alone.

First, the Department meddled in the planning of the study but, when its intervention efforts were rebuked by community negotiators, the county retreated altogether. Then, once it retreated, it withheld needed assistance and information from Ms. Eisenberg and residents, acting more like a spoiled child than an entity motivated to protect the public's health and well-being. Undeterred by the temper tantrum, Ms. Eisenberg's team found workaround solutions, and the study moved forward.

Not surprisingly, Unocal also put up obstacles, such as hiring a second researcher to examine residents' complaints. Unocal touted this research as merely a *cross-check* to the Eisenberg study, but I knew better. In classic company-speak, Unocal explained it wanted this review due to a "risk of over-interpretation" and to "perform advanced statistical analysis of correlation structure of the data and determine if substantial internal correlation of the data is present."

If you don't know what that means, you're not alone. Most others couldn't decipher it either.

But, to people who understood the legal significance of correlating chemical exposure to symptoms, it was clear. Unocal meant to debunk Ms. Eisenberg's work if it ultimately proved Catacarb was worse than soap. It didn't matter that Unocal was funding Ms. Eisenberg's work. Unocal wasn't about to sit idly by and let an independent researcher tell the community that its chemical release was the reason for this mass sickness. Hiring a second researcher was Unocal's ace in the hole.

But, in the end, Unocal's backup plan was inconsequential. When Ms. Eisenberg's work was done, her methodology was unimpeachable, and the results were shocking. After controlling for gender, educational and racial factors, the study's findings proved consistent with reports of the thousands of victims and the opinions of Good Neighbor Clinic physicians. The report tied a litany of health problems stemming to the release—headaches, respiratory, visual, gastrointestinal, memory loss, and dermatologic problems. These were ailments predictable after Catacarb exposure—but Ms. Eisenberg found them at more than *twice the level* of the control group she selected in nearby Marin County. In fact, for those Crockett residents reporting the sticky brown deposits on their property, the odds were *three times* greater they would experience dermatological, headache, visual, cardiac, gastro-intestinal and chemical-sensitivity symptoms. And this was almost a year after the event.

Sadly, it was the residents who least expected it, namely, those who spent significant time outdoors, walking, gardening or engaging in other activities during the peak Labor Day weekend, who had the greatest visual, dermatological and respiratory disorders. But we knew that already. It didn't take a study to prove that residents showered by Catacarb had been heavily impacted, but judges and juries need expert testimony, even about the obvious. Now, we had it. This neutral third-party study, funded by our own defendant, all but made our case.

Unocal had to know this would be the study's conclusion. With our lawsuit, and more than a thousand residents flooding the Good Neighbor Clinic, there could be no reasonable doubt that the company's toxins had seriously hurt people. The only question left was how badly they were hurt. Ms. Eisenberg's study gave us that. And, as soon as it appeared that her findings would be sufficiently damaging to Unocal's reputation or litigation position, the company knew the findings had to be discredited—sharply and immediately. And, so, it hired Becker Peabody.

Becker Peabody was a global construction and engineering firm, with significant experience addressing environmental catastrophes. Unocal first hired Becker's team within hours of the end of the release itself. Back then, it was just to initiate environmental sampling and evaluate the scope of the Catacarb release. Now, however, concerned over what Ms. Eisenberg's independent and more comprehensive investigation might reveal, Unocal had to step up its game. This time, Becker Peabody was asked to conduct a human health risk assessment to challenge Ms. Eisenberg's work.

Unocal claimed Becker Peabody's effort would be completed in time for the opening of the Good Neighbor Clinic. Clearly, Unocal hoped Becker Peabody's work would downplay the community's health symptoms and their connection to Catacarb. If that could be accomplished before it opened, the Clinic's doctors might trust Becker Peabody's findings and downplay the cause of the symptoms they observed.

The plan might have worked, but for significant delays. Becker Peabody's report wasn't finished until November 1995, whereas the Good Neighbor Clinic was closed by then. That meant its doctors never saw the study, much less could be influenced by it. The company's gamble failed.

What's more, when the report did come out, it was a mess, at least according to California's Office of Environmental Health Hazard Assessment (OEHHA). The OEHHA complained that, as to the rare parts it could decipher were "extremely difficult to understand," made inappropriate use of wind modeling and ignored available evidence of the amount of Catacarb deposited in the community. When it was finally concluded that Becker Peabody's methodology was inconsistent with State protocols, it was largely disavowed.

Viewed in this light, the Becker Peabody effort seemed like a waste of time for everyone—Unocal, the community and doctors who were waiting for good intelligence to come from it. It seemed to leave myriad unanswered questions for people who were still struggling. And, yet, as poor as this study was, I saw it as useful to our case for another reason.

You see, in legal parlance, there is a type of evidence known as an "admission against interest." The precept is that statements made by a party against its self-interest are deemed tremendously reliable in court proceedings, even serving as an exception to what might otherwise be inadmissible hearsay testimony. It's a fairly intuitive concept since we all know people don't usually say things that are embarrassing or may financially ruin them, unless they are virtually undeniable. People usually don't manufacture lies concerning things that will hurt them.

The "admission against interest" proposition can extend to experts hired by a party in litigation. Thus, if the experts you cherry-picked and handsomely paid publicly acknowledge your own liability, there is almost no turning back from it. Knowing this, I scoured Becker

Peabody's report for any hint of its client's wrongdoing or a Catacarb-symptom connection.

I wasn't hopeful. "Smoking gun"-evidence is rare, and I knew it would be unlikely I'd find anything particularly helpful. I'd read some of Becker Peabody's marketing material and learned that it was a defendant-friendly company—and that usually translates to bias. Most individuals and small businesses simply can't spend hundreds of thousands of dollars to commission an environmental or human health study, and global engineering firms like being paid. What's more, Unocal represented repeat business to Becker Peabody. It wouldn't want to lose that.

So, against the backdrop of those realities, the stage was set for a marginal estimation of the amount of Catacarb released and a denial of any health connection. Then, I read the report and I was shocked. Becker Peabody could not, with any degree of credibility, downplay the health impacts, at least not to the extent Unocal would have hoped. It wasn't as condemning as Ms. Eisenberg's work, but it was bad. In fact, to get an idea of the magnitude of the health hazards conceded by Becker Peabody's assessment, one merely had to look at data like the report's own Hazard Index—an industry term for the relative severity of health effects.

As the Becker Peabody study explained, a Hazard Index greater than one indicates a potential for adverse health effects; the greater the Hazard Index, the greater the likelihood of adverse health effects. While still heavily downplaying the long-term health problems, the short-term exposure Hazard Index that Becker Peabody assigned to Crockett was nearly 11. For workers like Ben at the Wickland Oil terminal, that index was 20! A severity of 20 is a major health threat. And, given the California Department of Health Services' conclusions that Becker Peabody's (flawed) methodology served to significantly *reduce* the true exposure Hazard Index, it is likely the impact on these towns was far worse.

Upon completion of the Becker Peabody study, the community's success rate with the Good Neighbor Agreement was three-for-three. Crockett residents had received months of free medical care, the public now had a trustworthy Catacarb health study, thanks to Ms. Eisenberg's team, and Unocal had all but conceded liability through the concessions of its own vendor, Becker Peabody. I was thrilled. Unocal's backup plan in hiring an engineering firm to disparage Ms. Eisenberg's work had failed, and we were collecting all the evidence we needed, at the company's expense. I was starting to believe our case was unbeatable.

CHAPTER 17
... AND ONE FOR ALL

B y the start of summer 1995, there was a general feeling of cohesion between the Northern California attorneys. Of the various
lawsuits filed to date, our Steering Committee was still counsel for the
majority of them. Collectively, a few thousand clients were now represented, and the number was growing. Luckily, nobody was poaching
my clients anymore.

Willing to consider their behavior water under the bridge, when
the SoCals asked to join our Committee, I voiced only fleeting objections. *Why contest it? We'll only have to see them every couple of months
at Committee meetings anyway*, I thought. Also, regardless of how they
procured them, the SoCals now had the interests of several hundred
of their own clients to protect (only a small fraction of whom had ever
been mine), and including their group would avoid an expensive and
distracting court battle. I agreed to let them in, but I didn't intend to
be friendly.

Summertime, for those working in the legal industry, is notoriously
slow, but not for our team, not in this case. As the one-year anniversary
of the Catacarb release approached, dozens of new law firms emerged,
each with their own new lawsuit, and the litigation had all the hallmarks
of becoming an administrative mess. We needed to find an efficient way
to respond to the infusion of new lawyers and their clients. Without

that efficiency, Unocal would be forced to answer each case separately, sometimes by filing motions to dismiss any novel legal claims, and our Committee would be compelled to fight off each new lawyer who wanted to serve his own new set of discovery. Our Committee was finally enjoying some cohesion, but the numerous case filings by these newcomers was threatening it.

Our Committee was formed around the idea of sharing the work and building our now-consolidated cases toward one common trial; we couldn't do that if the new lawsuits brought vastly different claims. We'd need to normalize our claims into one document—a Model Complaint—a document that would govern all cases, even the future ones. It needed to be so all-encompassing that each subsequent Complaint could adopt it without question. That's not simple to achieve. Reasonable minds can differ on which claims and parties should stay in and which should hit the editing-room floor.

But it had to be done. A defendant can't be expected to fight on multiple fronts over the same issues, defend the same depositions and produce identical documents in multiple cases. And, if we didn't volunteer one Complaint that addressed it all, the judge would order it anyway, and who knew what power he might give new attorneys on the scene to meddle in and muck up the work our Committee had already done. Our Model Complaint would need to please everyone, or they wouldn't adopt it, and I'd be back to where I was at the first Steering Committee meeting, fighting for my seat at the table.

The decision-making in drafting a Model Complaint is twofold: which claims, and which plaintiffs. For us, the "which claims" part was fairly simple. Most of the Complaints already on file brought the same charges: a release occurred, Unocal was reckless in a host of different ways, the chemical traveled downwind into certain communities, people got sick, property was damaged, and the Unocal officers should be strung up. The charges were presented with big words and long-winded passages, but the story was straightforward.

We tried to be thorough in alleging the various ways in which Unocal broke the law. Those were the claims, the causes of action, the myriad violations. We said Unocal was negligent in releasing Catacarb, but also claimed that it trespassed on residents' property since Catacarb landed on their homes and in their yards. Same underlying conduct, different claims. We spun the same thread in a dozen different ways.

Unusual claims—allegations such as the company not adequately marking the drums containing Catacarb solution with warning stickers, or not making MSDSs available to all workers were cut. Those seemed superfluous. One lawyer had pled those in his Complaint. Too bad. The group didn't like it. We took the best from the various Complaints, refined the language and put to rest that project.

Picking the plaintiffs to lead the case would, however, be a bigger challenge. Thousands of victims would adopt this document as their story, but not every person's story was representative of the thousands. That means we'd need to select just a few people who could, effectively, speak for everyone. That's required. A class action cannot proceed without representative plaintiffs. The judge would never allow the entire community to get up and testify at trial. These representative plaintiffs would testify for everyone else and so we needed to pick them carefully.

There are numerous considerations in choosing representative plaintiffs to lead a class action. You want people with very good claims, but you want it to appear as if you've chosen a *random* cross-section of the population. Being a cross-section is what makes them representative. If the judge concludes your plaintiff choices are anomalies, he won't extrapolate their testimony to bind anybody else. That's a death-knell; that extrapolation is what a class action is all about—representatives speaking for a larger population of people. The lead plaintiffs' testimony has to be common to everyone so it can support a single common trial, and a single common result.

Knowing this, the Committee had to determine how many plaintiffs would be enough and how we'd pick them. There was no formula for it, no clear margin of error for this kind of choice. Even the attorneys who use statisticians to guide them aren't guaranteed to get it right. Hiring a statistician just encourages the other side to hire one too, and the battle continues.

We knew Unocal didn't want this to stay a class action and, therefore, would claim there was no person or group of people who could represent everyone. If it convinced the judge of that, the members of our Committee might be ordered to go our separate ways to each fight Unocal on our own. And yet, if we selected too many people, just to play it safe, we'd be inviting trouble. We'd be giving Unocal more targets to shoot at, to call in for questioning at depositions, to point fingers at and argue they have circumstances that were unique. We'd need to strike a balance.

Finally, we'd need representatives who were ready, willing and able to stick their necks out, to not crack under the pressure of tough depositions or trial cross-examinations. We'd need people who were motivated and sympathetic but not snarky or vindictive. They'd be heavily involved in the litigation, meeting frequently with their own attorneys as well as members of the management group to rehearse their testimony. As the stewards of the litigation, they need to be pleasant, non-combative, articulate and unwavering in their stories. Among this community of really pissed off people, these really would be the unicorns.

Determining which model plaintiffs would drive the case was a stressful topic at Committee meetings at a time when we were just hitting our stride. Every Committee member knew that having any one of his clients listed on page one of the Model Complaint meant that lawyer would be promised a lot more work—appearing at the client's deposition, preparing the client for trial, and that meant more fees. Conversely, representing no model plaintiffs meant you'd be benched for most of the game, and what's the fun in that?

Ultimately, our Committee agreed that roughly ten representative plaintiffs should be sufficient to address all of the known symptoms and a cross-section of exposure scenarios. It seemed like a low number, but what did I know? To pick them, the Committee would conduct interviews of anyone willing to serve, anyone agreeable to being put under the microscope. Their records would be scoured and their testimony would be taken, perhaps repeatedly. That part, alone, could last for days.

What's more, much of their personal lives, including prior medical conditions, employment circumstances, family and home life, and other private details, would be on display. Knowing what I knew, even back then, I thought anybody who'd submit to that level of scrutiny was nuts, and, yet, the requests for the role poured in. Once the decision was made to recruit these leaders, my office got to work looking for able bodies and, if the work of other Committee firms to select candidates was anything like mine, their efforts were intense. I carefully reviewed hundreds of files, thousands upon thousands of documents over the course of weeks. The case would start and end with the people we put up as the leaders and, so, I took my role as a referee of that process very seriously.

With a large number of my clients having been exposed to high Catacarb concentrations, I was lucky to have many good choices. Each Committee member tagged several clients for consideration, examined their charts to make sure nothing negative stood out, and we then formed a small subcommittee to conduct in-person interviews with each candidate. This subcommittee would work independently and then report back to the larger group when we'd made our selections.

I volunteered to be on the four-lawyer subcommittee. Almost everyone volunteered, including a younger lawyer working for the

SoCal team. He objected to my participation and I objected to his, so the Committee picked us both. Making the best of an uncomfortable situation, the four of us immediately began reviewing extensive medical records, wage statements, property appraisals, veterinarian bills, expert reports, and repair invoices for what seemed like an endless number of people. We'd need to weed out the obviously unsupportable claims and people with credibility problems. We'd then take that reduced list and personally interview them.

Given the number of candidates and the pleas of their lawyers not to cut their clients, the work was laborious and political. But, we got it done with minimal bad feelings. With our list now down to just a few dozen people, we set a date for the interviews. Each candidate had to be available on the date picked, or had little chance of being a spokesperson.

The symbolism wasn't intentional, but we picked August 22, 1995, as the date for our meetings—exactly one year after the hole in tower D-409 first appeared. On this anniversary, our small group spent eleven hours in a hotel conference room, challenging plaintiff after plaintiff, judging the consistency of their stories, gauging their tenacity to endure the interrogation to which Unocal lawyers would subject them. If they couldn't hold up to our off-putting questions that day, they certainly weren't getting my vote.

We meant to keep it an informal process meaning that, although each of our subcommittee members represented at least one model plaintiff candidate being interviewed, we ignored the obvious appearance of impropriety. To avoid bias and reduce the competition with one another, whenever a subcommittee member's client appeared, that member probably should have stepped out of the conversation. Being more parliamentary in that way would have helped, not so much me but the SoCal lawyer since I was blatantly intolerant of his questions and his candidates, several of whom his team put up. Having his team or his clients anywhere near our model Complaint wasn't part of my agenda.

The young SoCal associate was miffed by this; he clearly didn't know the full story. He seemed desperate to be on the subcommittee, but I suspected only because his bosses had directed him to get involved. The SoCals had nominated several of their clients, at least two of whom they'd poached from me and, presumably, they wanted an inside man to bias the process. This young associate wasn't privy to all that and had no idea how much some of us disliked his bosses. He'd know I didn't care for his team after these interviews though. I'd make sure of that.

I tried to stay objective about the people I put up as candidates, questioning them just like anyone else's clients, and I tried to be fair with most of the others, but not the SoCals' selections. I didn't trust the SoCals' choices, or what records they allowed us to see, or why they chose these people in particular. And the young SoCal lawyer there that day, representing their candidates, got the brunt of it. I challenged him at every turn and was openly hostile in front of his clients about his judgment, his preparation, the questions he asked the candidates, the connections he made between his clients' symptoms and Catacarb exposure.

I wanted my defecting clients to see they didn't choose well. It didn't matter that the young associate had never done anything to harm me. He was guilty by association, and I wanted him to know it. I wanted him to know that, every time an opportunity for success arose for his team, I'd be there to threaten it. It's a message I hoped he would take back to his employers.

Despite the drama I manufactured, we got our plaintiff group. And, of the dozens of people we interviewed, of the many firms who'd put forth seriously injured victims, a disproportionate one-quarter of the representative plaintiffs were my clients. Thankfully, I'd secured my relevance to the future of this litigation since, with settlement nowhere in sight, my mind was on trial. Having some of my clients identified as leaders of the litigation meant I'd play a big role when trial came.

When our team presented its choices to the Committee, the reaction was very positive. We'd picked victims that Unocal had tremendous reason to fear. Theirs were sad stories. These were people with flawless medical support for a Catacarb connection, people who could make a jury cry, people to whom the everyday man could relate, and at least one person to speak to every one of the major injuries Unocal had caused. These victims' exposure circumstances were varied, and their symptoms read like the legal fine print of a prescription drug advertisement.

Among our selections was Keith Pitt from Crockett. Keith was a young man with a downtown dental practice. To save money, like a lot of small-business and property owners, he performed many necessary office repairs himself. During the Catacarb release, he spent significant time repairing the roof of his building, putting him directly in the wind path. At the tail end of the release, his skin and eyes burned often, he started losing sleep and developed a fever. Then, the breathing difficulties began, leading to significant sleep loss and an ultimate diagnosis of pneumonia and reactive airways dysfunction syndrome. While Keith was in great health before the release, he hadn't felt healthy since.

His neighbor, Ava Wilder, was also still suffering. Ava was eight months pregnant during the release. Her stage of pregnancy made working difficult and, so, she spent her time at her Crockett home nearly every day and night, taking it easy but remaining very excited about motherhood. The severe headaches, blood-pressure spikes and diarrhea she suffered during the release paled in comparison to the terror she felt the moment she learned that Catacarb could affect her baby *in utero*. Luckily, her baby was fine, but Ms. Wilder developed an abnormal thyroid, an autoimmune condition and decreased tear production, devastating results in their own right, but particularly bad for a mother with little energy for anything beyond caring for her newborn child. Fed up with Crockett, she and her husband put their house up for sale, but they received no offers and were forced to stay.

Nick Martin was a dedicated Wickland oil terminal worker, pulling 12-hour shifts during the Catacarb discharge. Like countless others, nosebleeds, shortness of breath, disorientation and sleep loss came quickly following the release. For Mr. Martin, the brain dysfunction, memory loss, and nightmares set in later. He took time off from work to address his symptoms and was allowed to return to his job after the incident only on the condition he be shadowed by another employee while at work. Prior to the Catacarb event, Nick was proud of his experience, skill and self-starter attitude. Now, being baby-sat by a subordinate left him humiliated and depressed.

Yet another model plaintiff, also from Crockett, learned from a sonogram that one of the twin babies she was still carrying had died and, yet, she held it, with full knowledge of its condition, inside her for months. A different resident couldn't walk through supermarkets without having an extreme reaction—what is known as "multiple chemical sensitivity"—to many of the cleaning products sold there. Another man reported that the Catacarb ate the paint off his car. We picked all of these people but turned away so many others that it was heartbreaking. They all wanted to be central to the case and I wanted them to be heard but we had limited room in the Model Complaint.

Most people not chosen as representatives were very disappointed and yet, if they'd known what I knew, they'd probably have been relieved they hadn't been chosen. While the selection interviews were rigorous, appearing for multiple, relentless days of deposition and trial would be worse. Their personal circumstances, including their sex lives, stressors in their relationships, alcohol and drug use, prior medical and psychological conditions, and a host of other personal circumstances would be open to tremendous scrutiny. We touched upon these things in our interviews, but couldn't replicate the intensity of what they'd be in for.

Still, I fielded angry calls from people who were considered but not picked. *Why didn't you fight for me?* Or, the one that always made me cringe: *But I thought you guys said I had a good case.* Of course they had good cases; the model plaintiffs' cases were just better.

Just before the release's first anniversary, we witnessed a daunting number of new lawsuits. Some people were unsure, until recently, if their symptoms were actually related to Catacarb. These were the outliers though; information about Catacarb and its effects was abundant. Others were just in denial. Some people hoped their symptoms would have dissipated already or didn't want to admit defeat. These were blue-collar townspeople, the construction workers, the refinery and other trades people, the guys who went to work even when they felt they were on death's doorstep, the mothers too busy to let sickness stop them from raising their kids and tending to their duties at home, and the elderly who just didn't believe in litigation.

For every new civil Complaint, there exists a "statute of limitations," a time window within which you must file your case in court. Prior to 2001, California law required most legal actions for personal injuries be brought within 12 months of the triggering event. Here, that meant new plaintiffs, whether they found counsel or not, had to file by September 6, 1995, one year after the end of the Catacarb release. Missing that deadline, at least as to the Catacarb incident (you'll remember there was a subsequent incident as well), was irreparable—what they'd call "jurisdictional." It wouldn't matter why you delayed. If you didn't file your case by the one-year mark, you waived your claim forever.

As word about the event's anniversary made its way around town, interest in the case exploded, again. In July and August of 1995, my phones rang off the hook. Even existing clients were calling us—to warn me about the emergence of new lawyers trying to drum up business in Crockett, even calling my clients directly. The poaching had resumed.

But, this time, it wasn't the SoCals who were misbehaving. It was people I'd never heard of, but who were engaging in tactics as bad as I'd ever heard—passing out business cards at supermarkets, knocking on doors, leaving letters in mailboxes. Some were brazen, making no apologies for trying to woo away clients of Steering Committee members. Others, like the guy who pulled me into the hallway at the first Steering Committee meeting, were tilling fertile ground far away, where competition was scarce. I even heard of one lawyer who signed up people in Monterey, a town 100 miles south of Crockett. It sounded absurd, but I wasn't terribly surprised. People just wanted to be a part of something important.

Ironically, I couldn't wait for the one-year filing window to close. The poaching was a constant reminder of my conflicts with Adlin Katz and his SoCal gang earlier in the year. Moreover, many lawyers now on the scene were signing up clients so marginally affected and/or so far away from the refinery that they were destined to dilute the quality and credibility of what was otherwise a solid base of very damaged people. I wanted everyone injured to get a fair remedy, but the feeding frenzy left me wondering about their lawyers' motives, whether these new plaintiffs were getting the best assistance, and how the management of the now-dozens of new cases would be handled.

Finally, and further complicating things, pinpointing the filing deadline for each new plaintiff had gotten messy in light of two more recent chemical releases from the Unocal plant, both of which our Committee elected to fold into the Model Complaint. Indeed, Unocal was having a horrible year. After the Catacarb release, Rodeo suffered the hydrogen sulfide release that hit Hillcrest School on September 15, 1994. That was the one I spoke about with the Hillcrest teacher, Ms. Buchanan. But then, Unocal had another hydrogen sulfide release, this one on March 28, 1995. And then it had another release on June 16, 1995, wherein it allowed burning naphtha solvent to escape during a huge tank fire.

Collectively, these more recent events blew poisonous gases and suffocating smoke into Crockett, Rodeo and several neighboring communities, sickening tens of thousands. In the case of the June tank fire, which burned off and on for nearly a week, residents were at first prompted to shelter in place from the smoke, but then, as the danger grew, many of them sought refuge outside the danger zone in motels ultimately paid for by Unocal, until the exposed area was secured.

Each of these more recent events was devastating in its own right, but each occurred on a different date. The victims now bringing lawsuits were affected by any one of them, sometimes all of them, making it an administrative nightmare to determine when each new person was required to file. More injuries and more damages weren't the worst problems to have, but they were still problems.

Despite these challenges, just like at sea, where a school of feeder fish routinely draws the attention of predatory animals, these altogether-new victims meant more attorneys and more lawsuits. By the filing date of the first Model Complaint in September 1995, my office alone had more than 500 plaintiffs ready to adopt it. Collectively, among all the firms, the number then was more than 4,000. By December 1995, there were 33 lawsuits in total, with roughly 5,000 victims represented. By the June 1996 anniversary of the tank fire (the last of the four events), and the last chance to bring new claims of any kind, Doug and I directly represented 1,100 people, or roughly 20% of the total plaintiff population. Having the largest client group of any firm, but being the youngest, least-established and least-experienced among the scores of firms now involved, you'd think I'd have felt proud. But I didn't have time to feel proud. I was too busy trying to stay afloat.

When talking to that reporter at the courthouse way back when, I couldn't have fathomed managing this volume of clients. I was working sunrise to bedtime most days, living and breathing the Unocal case through the Summer of 1995. Somehow, I found a few hours here and there to take on and settle a couple of very small employment discrimination cases anyway. But, as small matters, they provided me with meager financial reserves.

Luckily, those cases settled fast—just in time too, since work on the Unocal case was on another uptick. I took what money they generated and hired a couple of administrative support staffers to help with Unocal. From that point forward, we worked on virtually nothing else.

For my new assistants, I needed a place to put them and, so, for a couple hundred dollars a month more, I rented an additional 12-by-12 foot room, adjacent to the two little rooms I already leased. We immediately dubbed our new digs the "War Room" and dedicated it to all things Unocal. Maps, checklists and memoranda adorned every wall, partly for their utility and partly for inspiration. Since my new staffers almost never left this little box, I tried to make it a visually intriguing space but it was probably wasted effort. These staffers were way too busy to consider the wall art—or even sit down. California law requires employers provide seating for their employees, and so I brought in two swivel chairs. To my knowledge, no one ever used them. When I was in there, which was roughly half of my time, I never used them either.

Instead, we opted to sit on desk corners when we sat at all. I suspected it was because it saved seconds when moving from box to box or file cabinet to file cabinet. Ultimately, dozens of open banker boxes lined each wall, our makeshift filing system for handling open projects on a massive scale, which meant the workers were constantly mobile. Archived documents like client retention agreements and medical and work records went into the metal file cabinets; everything else stayed out, ready and accessible. I ran several phone lines in, and they were used constantly.

Ultimately, my ever-revolving workforce worked in that room, virtually all day, Monday through Friday, some weekends, many evenings, for the next couple of years. For each of our 1,100 clients, we tracked every detail, on some particular form or another, copied it, stuck it in some file or another, and moved on to the next detail. Check, check, check. The tedium of the work caused a lot of staff turnover, but a virtual flood of entry-level job candidates was always just a want-ad posting away. For the remainder of the case, those people rarely left that room. The energy in there was high. It was insane.

We spent our days tracking down medical records, talking to doctors, faxing authorizations to our clients for employee personnel files, medical/psychological records, interviewing witnesses, collecting evidence of our clients' exposure locations. Telephone receivers in the war room were always warm, with workers fielding client calls all day long. "For how many days during the release were you at home?" They'd ask. "Did you work during this period and, if so, where? How often were you outdoors? Did you have pets? Are they all right? Are your kids all right?"

We'd ask about their relationships and how their spouses felt, sometimes tiptoeing around their sexual relations, recent divorces, often caused by the stress, by the sickness, or from all the bickering over how to deal with it. We recorded everything, often in a narrative format which made comparing and grouping litigants impractical. We developed forms, but the forms evolved constantly as our understanding of the claims and damages evolved. We'd then go back and create new and better forms.

This was an overly labor-intensive process, and it seemed tremendously wasteful. I thought it was absurd. This wasn't efficient. We were duplicating work constantly and had no way to spot trends or quantify the strength of our own case. Anecdotal information was interesting, but it would have limited value at trial if it couldn't be shown as part of a larger pattern. We needed a vehicle for more comparative analyses.

We needed to build a better mousetrap.

CHAPTER 18
MOTHER OF INVENTION

I'd been thinking a lot those days about an easier way to demonstrate for Kenecke's office the seriousness of my clients' symptoms. Unocal's lawyers had sent us written questions and document requests for the hundreds of victims I represented and the effort to respond was grueling. And it was just a matter of time before Kenecke's team repeated the exercise for my newer clients. If I was right, that new discovery would not only be a daunting amount of work, but collecting details of my clients' damages would be as piecemeal and inefficient as ever. Kenecke's questions called for answers nowhere near exhaustive of everyone's experience. In fact, they barely scratched the surface. That meant a second round of discovery for everyone was just around the corner.

Kenecke's prior requests sought information about only the most common symptoms, the most common claims, and the typical exposure scenarios. But there was so much more to these victims' stories, and Kenecke was missing most of it. What's more, many of Kenecke's broader questions called for a long, narrative response. That wasn't an effective format to compare and value different claims. You simply can't rank or easily group the victims say, by location or by injury, if that information is buried in long rambling paragraphs about their families, property and exposure circumstances. How can you find out how many people suffered from one symptom if you're forced to sift through page after page of unstructured rants about how their employer wouldn't give them time off work to recuperate or what a bad neighbor Unocal had been? Weeding through that much paper to locate each data point was absurd.

So, we needed more uniformity, better organization. And we needed comprehensive answers, but how does one categorize a massive number of people by things like exposure location, symptoms, wage loss and a hundred other factors when each answer is long prose? What you need is a surveying tool, something with true-false answers, check-boxes and multiple-choice questions, not narratives. We needed a master document, a form, something to which both sides could agree and which asked about every condition, damage and background detail we might need at trial. That's a tall order when you're trying to capture the experiences of thousands of people.

But we got lucky: Unbeknownst to me, our Committee already had a good template. Apparently, a couple of months earlier, some of the attorneys in our case had negotiated a huge settlement against the General Chemical Corporation, a sulphur-manufacturing company located in Richmond, California. When I heard the news of that settlement, I figured this must have been what that unscrupulous Steering Committee lawyer was talking about in the hallway after our first meeting—the thing that, as he promised, was motivating those out-of-towners to sign up for virtually anything.

The General Chemical incident was devastating in its own right. Starting with the rupture of a railroad car in 1993, its six-mile-long sulfuric acid cloud blanketed an enormously dense residential area. Almost immediately, residents streamed to hospitals complaining of respiratory problems, headaches and nausea and, ultimately, more than 60,000 of them filed lawsuits. A Questionnaire was used there to determine the extent of injuries and damages, but also as a prerequisite to each person getting paid. Without some kind of survey, the

General Chemical case would have been utterly unmanageable. If a Questionnaire worked there, it could certainly work here.

But, the Unocal release was quite unlike the General Chemical event. The General Chemical event was limited to a four-hour incident, whereas Unocal released Catacarb for 16 days. That fact alone guaranteed that designing such a discovery tool would be challenging. Complicating matters further was that Unocal's three subsequent chemical releases had been folded into the Model Complaint. But, while we knew the kinds of symptoms one could expect from the more recent events, Catacarb's potential short and long-term effects looked endless.

While the General Chemical survey was a good starting place, it needed to be expanded considerably to account for what was released here, its duration, changing wind patterns in the area over many days, and many other factors. To do that, we argued with Unocal's lawyers about its format and contents for months. We wanted check boxes. They wanted space for narratives and essays for our clients to describe their symptoms. They wanted to prove to the judge that no two plaintiffs were the same. They wanted to say the case was totally unmanageable, that trial would be unmanageable. Maintaining a class action requires you show the claims are very similar. Without that commonality, a verdict for one person cannot extend to anyone else. That's what Unocal claimed. Long, flowing, highly-individualized narratives would support that argument.

I also knew Unocal wanted the Questionnaire long since every additional page reduced the likelihood that a plaintiff would read, understand and complete it. For our side, a long document would also be more cumbersome and expensive to process. Just processing the mailing, copying and service of 1,100 Questionnaires would be daunting for a little operation like mine. Add to that the hundreds of phone calls to help fill in the gaps left by what the clients sent me, the collection of their medical records, employment personnel files, and property appraisals and you can quickly see how it would become a project that might deny justice to all except the most determined victims.

And the Questionnaire was supposed to be user-friendly, or why use one at all? That meant no Legalese, since that would significantly threaten our chances of a big turnout. Based on the demographics I'd seen, our clients' experience with lawyers and litigation was probably limited, meaning excessive jargon would serve only to scare them. In 1994, Crockett residents had a per capita income of less than $27,000, with roughly 7% of the population being below the poverty line. These were not people with a lot of positive experiences with our judicial system.

In Rodeo, the numbers were even more dire, with a per capita income of less than $21,000 and 6.8% of residents being below the poverty line. And these statistics correlated with education levels. In Crockett, only 18% of the adult population held a four-year college degree. In Rodeo, only 13%. Lower education and income levels usually translate to a greater apprehension toward the legal system. They just do. They also suggest more instances of people with reading and writing challenges. In other words, these were the people who most needed a financial award and, yet, their unique circumstances would most handicap them from ever collecting it.

With all these considerations and agendas in mind, our Committee's negotiations with Kenecke's office continued in earnest. Unocal struck first, with a proposed Questionnaire that was nearly 100 pages. *No way*, I thought. *No one would ever fill that out*. If I had sent that out, I'd have lost all my clients. I expected something of more like 25 pages, with a lot of multiple-choice and true-false questions—something simple and streamlined (i.e., the opposite of what Unocal wanted). The battle continued with Kenecke's lawyers well into the fall before a compromise was reached. It was in true-false and short-answer format, but it was still 40 pages. Still better than 100 though. Plus, much of the

Questionnaire addressed real property damages and business expenses irrelevant to most clients.

Forty pages was a manageable monster although the list of agreed-upon symptoms alone was four, full dense pages, one for each of the four chemical releases at issue and consistent with what Ms. Eisenberg's work showed, with highlights including: "Asthma. Choking. Chest pains. Sore throat/Throat irritation. Nausea. Vomiting. Diarrhea. Vision problems. Dry eyes. Blisters. Headaches. Tremors. Dizziness. Numbness/Tingling. Memory loss. Depression. Mood swing. Insomnia. Autoimmune condition. Joint pains. Liver problems. Thyroid problems. High blood pressure." And these were just the most common symptoms. The list went on and on, and, next to each condition, was a matrix of check boxes allowing each client to select how frequently and for how long after that fateful Labor Day weekend each applicable symptom occurred. Be careful what you wish for.

As if trying to remember how long each victim suffered each symptom a year earlier wasn't challenging enough, the Questionnaire also probed medical and psychological treatment and medications taken, and pre-existing conditions such as asthma, emphysema, asbestosis, or other respiratory and skin conditions. It asked about home ownership, and about educational and employment information going back years, and about smoking, diet, and family health histories. It asked where each client was during each of the releases, even providing tables so they could, for each eight-hour time block over the 16-day release period and for those other releases, check a box indicating whether they were mostly indoors or outdoors. The moment the Questionnaire was ready, I wasted no time making 1,100 copies of it (44,000 pages in all)—and sending it out.

In the cases I'd litigated before, there had always been periods of intense effort, followed by days or even weeks of downtime while I awaited a reaction from the company's lawyers. During that downtime, if I needed a break, I usually got it. No such luck here. I had hoped that, after mailing out the mountain of blank Questionnaires, there would be a short respite before more major activity. Within 48 hours of dropping off boxes of Questionnaires at the post office, the flood of phone calls began.

What also began was receipt of piles of undeliverable mail. I was awestruck by how many of my clients had moved and left no registered forwarding address—scores of them. I was alarmed that I'd become so disconnected from so many people who'd once begged for my help. If we couldn't reconnect, it would mean no completed Questionnaire, which would mean their likely dismissal from the case. As the prevailing party, Unocal could recover its costs, maybe from me, putting me in the poorhouse for sure.

I got on the telephone immediately, trying to reach those whose Questionnaire packets came back undeliverable. I called their neighbors, family members, doctors and employers, using any telephone number I could dig out of their file or extract from their friends and neighbors. We did a good job, but we lost more than a few. There was nothing more I could do about it. It was a write-off, both of money and time, when I had little of each to spare.

This represented a major shift. In the first year of litigation, whenever we needed records, questions answered, telephone numbers weren't disconnected, letters didn't come back undeliverable. But now, to the extent they could, people were attempting an exodus out of Crockett and, to a lesser extent, Rodeo. With four major chemical releases over the course of a single year, who could blame them? That would make most people want to get as far away from a refinery as possible.

When I heard this, I went to check it out, and, once there, what I saw was an eerie sight. "For Sale" signs lined the sidewalks of Crockett, on some blocks almost every home. Homeowners wanted out fast. Many renters were already gone. Friends, families, doctors at the Good

Neighbor Clinic, real estate professionals, even the attorneys were advising it. In the rush to get away from this danger, it was no wonder calling me with their changes of address wasn't first on their minds.

This was going to make my job more difficult but it was also going to make the case tremendously more valuable because it offered a unique kind of damage no one had anticipated. It added a series of claims that could be made by nearly every Crockett and Rodeo family and could be proven without regard to exposure circumstances or physical symptoms. You didn't even need to be in town during the event to recover on this one. It was a claim based on home ownership, and all you had to do was produce a deed.

Even where environmental catastrophes lead to horrible personal injuries, the victims usually find a way of coping. They buckle down, see their doctors and care for their kids. They don't ordinarily put their homes on the market but they were doing that here in large numbers. For that, they could potentially recover broker commissions, closing costs, relocation expenses and the loss from selling their houses at dramatically reduced prices. Even renters who moved and incurred moving costs and longer commute distances to work could jump in on that theory.

But a more interesting theory concerned the homeowners who could *not* sell. The bad press now tainting Crockett and Rodeo, coupled with the new glut of houses on the sales market were red flags for potential purchasers, and so most properties weren't selling. Committee members were in agreement that there had to be a remedy for this.

For those who could and did sell, measuring the damage from buying high but selling low would be third-grade math. That's easy. Putting a price tag on the interference with the enjoyment of your home would be more subjective, but the law recognize that as a damage too. Compensation to homeowners who couldn't sell at all, who remained prisoners in a community repeatedly hit with toxins, remained a wildcard.

Anyone who understands microeconomics knows that the forces of supply and demand largely determine the price for anything, in any marketplace. Generally speaking, a thing is worth only what somebody else will pay for it. But after four dangerous and highly publicized events, almost no one was willing to buy homes in Crockett for, seemingly, any price. Did that mean they had zero value?

I reached out to real estate experts with this question and what I learned was a gold mine. Apparently, for investment property owners, where their renters left out of fear of future releases, we could use the amount of lost rents. That would be a simple formula. For owners occupying their own homes, I was more skeptical but was told that the experts could quantify that too, so long as they could calculate the reduction in the "fair market value" of the houses, before the Catacarb release, and then after. The tricky part to that was determining the fair market value of homes that, seemingly, had no market value at all.

Having never owned a home, the basics of valuation were new to me, but fairly intuitive: among other things, you look at the "comps" (the price of comparable homes recently sold in the area). That made sense. Recent sales history of homes in the area tends to drive what someone will pay for a new offering. But, with no indication of Unocal's recklessness slowing down, home prices were falling fast all across the area. How could we find these all-important "comps" in a zone where almost nothing was selling?

And, let's take it a step further. Even if you were lucky enough to find a comparable property that had sold recently, that comp was already likely severely devalued. Owners who were selling wanted out so quickly they'd accept almost anything. Those lowered comp prices meant your sales price would also have to be lowered dramatically. Then, if you could sell, your property became the new comp for someone else's sale, and so on, and so forth. Soon enough, the value of every home in town would be spiraling downward. The experts called this phenomenon the "neighborhood effect"—the reduction in one property's fair market price attributed to the falling prices in neighboring areas. It was a fascinating, albeit relatively untested theory, in the courts, but I loved it.

Apparently, the Steering Committee loved it too. The Committee decided to hire one of the top property appraisal experts in the field to testify about it, starting with an analysis of Crockett home values. Once hired, he got to work reviewing all residential home sales there, looking at historical data, Crockett market trends, the number of days properties were on the market and sales prices in nearby cities. In the end, he determined that the "adjusted sales price" per square foot averaged $111 for the 16 months prior to the Catacarb release, but only $101 for the 20 months following it. This represented a huge drop in value in the affected area during a time period when residential sale prices were rising in most nearby cities.

Of equal significance was that his findings represented an average for the *entire* town—not merely those homes closest to the refinery—and that meant fair market values for homes *closer* to the refinery probably dropped even more. It was a remarkable discovery. Every homeowner, personally injured or not, was now able to make a claim for tens of thousands of dollars, and on claims no one had before considered. With a few thousand homeowners, just within Crockett and Rodeo, we'd figured out how to add more than $50 million of value to the case, virtually overnight.

In my search to track down wayward clients, I visited Crockett and Rodeo a lot, oftentimes by going miles out of my way to take the "scenic route" past the refinery. I told myself I was keeping watch over it, but, more importantly, these excursions were inspiring me to keep up my typical 12- to 14-hour days. Each time I passed by that hissing, bubbling, energetic facility, I thought to myself, "I want in there."

Week after week I made that drive and, after more than a year, my wish was granted: our Committee agreed it was time for a tour (a.k.a., a "Site Inspection") of Unocal's facility.

Site inspections are an important part of this kind of litigation. They are also a lot of fun. This inspection would be the Committee's only opportunity to view and photograph the areas and equipment involved in each of the releases. Touring these important parts of the refinery, we'd also get to feel what it's like to work there. The pictures we'd take could be shown to a jury at trial, or to witnesses during depositions, or in meetings with consultants. They'd be immeasurably helpful, saving time and long descriptions, and avoiding ambiguities. If a picture really is worth a thousand words, a Site Inspection would be critically important.

For precisely these reasons, Unocal didn't want us anywhere near its property, nor did it care about making our jobs easier. It fought us on every aspect of the request, despite the fact that such tours are routine. In the end, we'd win. We knew that. Unocal just wanted us to work for it.

After much negotiation, we got our tour, but not without limitations. The visit could last no more than a few hours and the group would be required to stay together at all times. Everyone on our formidable Committee was allowed to attend, along with our refinery-operations consultant and photographer, but we couldn't touch anything, ask workers any questions or record areas or equipment unrelated to the case. We'd also have to sign a liability waiver, meet before the inspection for a safety and security presentation in Unocal's conference room, wear safety equipment provided by the refinery and bring our own steel-toed shoes.

Upon hearing we'd reached an agreement on these terms, I ran out and bought some boots that could do double duty if I decided to go backpacking anytime soon. Sitting at my kitchen table the evening before the inspection, my new boots waiting by the door, I studied every blueprint, map and photograph I had of the refinery. I felt like I was preparing for war.

Pulling into Unocal's Administration parking lot the morning of the tour, I looked around rapidly, wondering if anyone who'd seen my little red car during the prior year's reconnaissance mission with Doug was watching. I'd driven on the main road by this lot many times since, but stopping to get more photos this particular day felt like I was returning to the scene of a crime. Other Committee attorneys were showing up at the same time, most of whom were driving cars far more expensive and cleaner than mine. To avoid scrutiny, I parked at the far end of the lot.

I had long-since been sized up by everyone as the new kid on the block and, at my age, it would've been tough to convince anyone otherwise. Still, I was uncomfortable displaying anything that would suggest my lack of experience or success. I turned the car off, waited until no one was looking in my direction, and then hurriedly walked across the parking lot, past the Benz's and Porsches, toward our meeting area.

Once there, our team filed into Unocal's large conference room and excessively ceremonious introductions were made. The whole event was pretentious and inauthentic, as if the lawyers were over-compensating for the fact they were told they could wear blue jeans—as if anyone could really forget that these attorneys spent most working hours in custom-made suits. As I surveyed the room, I was struck by the formality of the display. At each position around the long table was an identical collection of safety equipment, including earplugs, hard hats and safety goggles, meticulously arranged by company officials with the care of one setting places for a formal holiday meal. I felt like we were back in school, preparing for some science-lab experiment, and I couldn't wait to get started.

After too much coffee, a lengthy safety presentation and the signing of liability waivers, we were fitted with flame-resistant Nomex coveralls and were good to go. All this deliberation made clear the refinery intended to run today's tour by the book, but it felt like a farce coming from a company with such a robust track record of neglect. *Well, good for them for at least trying now,* I thought, but I remained jaded. I suspected that Unocal merely wanted to avoid an accident involving the same lawyers already suing the company. Symbolically, a head count was repeated and a brief pause taken before the Safety Coordinator pushed open the door and stepped aside. It was time for the tour.

Walking single-file out of the conference room's side entrance and down the few short stairs that dropped us into the refinery was kind of like Alice stepping out into Wonderland. It was an enormous, fantastical place, bubbling with energy and smells, hissing steam, workers pointing in all directions and managers yelling commands over the din. I'd driven through refineries before but had never *walked* through one, but no matter; I had already made my mind up about them. I'd already decided to loathe this place, condemn it, right along with those people who managed it.

It wouldn't matter what amazing things I might see there that day. My mind's eye envisioned a wretched, grimy scene, driven by brawny, defeated men with sweaty, oil-blackened faces, unappreciated slaves forced to toil down dark corridors and under a canopy of rusty, decaying machinery with steam and liquids of dubious origin dripping everywhere.

Prior to our tour, it may even have been that way, but not today. My God, that place was clean, too clean. I knew a good whitewash when I saw it, and I knew Unocal had a talent for it. This was all window dressing for the unsuspecting, but I knew. The other Committee lawyers knew too. The company had mapped out with precision our walking route through the labyrinth of piping to the places specifically designated in our inspection request—the only places we were allowed to go—and then fastidiously scrubbed that path, and only that path. It was spotless, and we were shepherded through it with care such that we'd see only Spotless.

Lagging behind or drifting more than ten feet away from the pack was met with an admonishment by Kenecke's lawyers to get back in line, little dictators that they were. Unocal's attorneys, appointed as watchdogs for this outing, barked at us frequently in ineffectual displays of authority but, ultimately, knew our Committee would be back if we were denied the opportunity to see everything. And we knew that they knew this, and so we had no intention of backing down just because some corporate lawyers wanted to impress their client. This was our time to soak it all in, and so we went where we wanted.

Our cameraman pushed the envelope too, being hired to shadow us and take shots until forced to stop. Clearly, he'd done this sort of thing before, been hired to go places where he wasn't welcome and asked to keep shooting in the face of controversy. He wasn't fazed by any of it. We'd stop and point at alarming yellow and red labels on oil drums, and the cameraman would scurry over to snap a picture; then the Unocal lawyer would dart over to see what we were doing. If we caught an employee in the frame, the little dictators would scream about privacy and stand in the way.

Whenever we took pictures of anything Kenecke's team perceived unrelated to the case, an argument would erupt, followed by much arm waving and loud threats about taking the dispute to the judge, about postponing the tour until a later date. The company really hated us being there but hated even more that it lacked the power to do a damn thing about it. I didn't hire the cameraman so I stayed out of the fracas but would stand close by so as to be able to watch the sparks fly, snickering and feeling eminently satisfied that we'd so gotten under their skin. This was vindication. With the Catacarb release, the company thought it could get away with murder. Flashing our warrant to walk into Unocal's home was beautiful payback.

As far as I was concerned though, this was supposed to represent payback only to Unocal, not to its workers. I never blamed the rank-and-filers for the Catacarb release. They were just following orders, and they'd been tricked, like almost everyone else had been tricked. I knew these workers meant no harm. I also knew many of them repeatedly pled for management to shut down the tower. Indeed, hearing that one guy even seriously considered sabotaging the plant to end the release bolstered my faith in humanity.

Still, I wondered what these workers thought about us being there that day. As we walked through the maze of pipes, I noticed harsh looks and dark eyes peering out from under hard hats, following our movements, evaluating us. They'd undoubtedly been told an important tour was happening, but what information accompanied that message? What did we represent to them?

Some gestured in our direction and, while not exactly giving us the finger, no one was waving enthusiastically or offering us a thumbs-up. It was obvious we weren't welcome, if for no other reason than we were on their turf. That we weren't wearing three-piece suits wasn't fooling anyone into thinking we belonged. We didn't have that refinery-worker swagger or the ease of knowing our way around without a guide. But was that enough to justify the cold shoulder?

Refineries being 24/7 operations, I had anticipated seeing a lot of refinery operators, some who would have been on shift for hours already. I also anticipated they'd know who we were and that our point in being there was to ensure such a disaster never happened again. I didn't need their applause, or for them to consider us the cavalry but—maybe—the good guys? We represented a threat to their jobs. We were meddlers in their routine, their system, dirty and corrupted as it may have been. Apparently, I was naive to have thought otherwise.

I remember driving away from the refinery that day feeling, on one hand, the satisfaction of a job well done and the optimism that we were one step closer to our goals. I felt good, mostly. We got all the shots we needed. I learned about how work flows at a refinery. I saw the bustling of busy hands at work, turning valves, checking pressures, and climbing up scaffolding. On the other hand, I had to remind myself not to let the workers' disapproval ruin my good mood, the progress we'd made. I tried to chalk it up to old-fashioned employee loyalty, but thinking about industrial psychology wasn't soothing me. Nothing was. I knew we were doing the right thing but, on my drive home, I was feeling pretty bummed out.

CHAPTER 19
THE IN-BETWEEN

Completed Questionnaires were expected by mid-January 1996 and yet, by that point, we had received responses from less than half of our clients. Just as I felt during the prior year's barrage of discovery, I was worried we might lose hundreds of people and face an unmanageable fine. I'd felt cocky after having performed so well in the prior effort, but we had far more clients this time. Motivating them to complete a dense 40-page survey would be a far-larger undertaking. More than ever, I was busy, and I was worried.

Luckily, we caught another break. Kenecke's team backed down again, giving us continuances to keep submitting Questionnaires through later in the year. I kept waiting for the other shoe to drop but, frankly, I think they were just too busy processing the thousands of responses they'd received already to push us harder. Sure, they reminded us of our obligations frequently. They just didn't do anything definitive in response to our failures.

With this breathing room, I adopted a "Leave No Questionnaire Behind" policy at my office, although I acknowledged that such a level of success was probably a ridiculous goal. I pushed my tiny band of support staffers pretty hard, and I wasn't the kindest of bosses. I was stressed to the limit and often forgot it wasn't their fault we faced these pressures. I demanded they be creative, given how many of our clients had moved but not provided forwarding addresses or telephone numbers. It was tough to snap at a silent telephone receiver. We snapped at each other instead.

For the few dozen people who just never responded, we said "good riddance" and wrote them off, thinking we would never hear from them again. But we never formally dismissed them. Maybe they'd resurface someday, we thought. Had Kenecke's lawyers asked the judge at any point to cut them for failure to return the survey, he would have agreed, but the company never asked, and I never asked why. At the time, I almost wished it had though, since a court order would have saved us a lot of calls, not to mention the reassurance these people wouldn't surface later to claim we should have tried harder.

This was a project where my idealism did not serve me well. I thought ours was supposed to be a partnership; the clients provided the facts, I provided the law, and we teamed up to make the defendant pay. But many clients didn't see it that way. For those people, it seemed like, the moment they became "clients" and their suffering became a "claim," we became polarized. The moment they began viewing me as a representative of the System, many lost all interest in helping me, even though these efforts would also help them. We tried anyway. We spent months making calls, literally thousands of them, but the objections were endless.

We encountered people who wouldn't put the phone down long enough to walk to their mailbox and see if the blank Questionnaire we'd sent had arrived. Others swore they'd filled it out truthfully but refused to sign their name to it. Others claimed they completed it but were just too busy to mail it back. I'd sometimes offer to send someone from my office to pick up the packet from their homes or to deliver new ones. They would reject those overtures too.

Breakdowns in communication I could understand. Moving away and forgetting to update contact information I could also understand. I could remain patient about those things. This was different. This was something deeper. This was litigation fear, or indifference, or a rejection of success as something they deserved. It was confounding and I would be on the hook for a lot of money if I didn't figure it out. I was already going into unmanageable debt with maxed-out credit cards and little revenue.

Worst of all, I lost my sense of humor, the thing that, theretofore in my life, was always there for me when I needed it, when things seemed dire. I could always laugh at life before. Nowadays, I was grumpy, tightly wound and my levity was waning. By February 1996, I knew it was gone. That month, I was wrapping up calls to clients we called "Incompletes," the people for whom we lacked some Questionnaire data points. Nancy, one of the younger moms in the case, was one of them:

"Hi. I'm calling for Nancy Watson. This is Scott Cole, one of your attorneys in the case against Unocal."

My script was well practiced, and I launched into it casually and folksy, as always. "Nancy? Good. Hey, so I'm calling about the Questionnaires we mailed you a couple of weeks ago. I got the one back for your daughter, Sandra—and that one's fine—but I had some questions about the one I have here for you, and the one for Bennie. Do you have a minute to go over these?"

Happy to talk, but mildly defensive, she argued, "Sure. You know, I tried to fill them out as best I could, but what they're asking is kind of confusing."

Feigning sympathy, I explained, "I hear you. Believe me that we tried to make these forms as short as possible, but there are a lot of people with different kinds of injuries, and it all needs to be represented. Plus, Unocal needs to understand how badly everyone was impacted by this." All of this, of course, she liked, and I was in.

After addressing the issues in Nancy's Questionnaire, we turned our focus to Bennie. "So, first off, is Bennie a nickname?" I asked. "No, that's his real name," she explained.

"OK, fair enough, so, can I go over Bennie's Questionnaire with you, or...," I trailed off.

"That's fine," she said.

Re-reading Bennie's answers, his medical situation was unclear. I wondered if Nancy could help with that. "So you have down here that Bennie had some nose and eye irritation. Are those conditions continuing today?" She indicated that they were not.

"OK, good. That's good," I responded, and then continued, "And in response to those symptoms, did he get any medical treatment?" Yes, Bennie had, indeed, gotten treatment.

"All right, well, unless you have them now, we'll need to get any doctors' names, and we'll need to get those records." Nancy said she had those and would send them soon. That wouldn't be a problem.

I figured Nancy might know if Bennie had any economic claims like wage loss or property damages. She paused briefly after my question about that, awkwardly, and then responded, "No, I don't think Bennie would have a claim for anything like that." Apparently, my question had confused her but I was way too tired of making calls like these to bite as to why.

"All right—well that's all I've got for you," I wrapped up. "So, if you can get to a fax machine, I can send you these pages. If you and Bennie can read and verify your respective answers and then sign and send back the last pages of each, I'll get them over to Unocal's lawyers."

She agreed, "Sure, I'll sign them."

I couldn't remember anything suggesting Bennie couldn't sign for himself. "I forget how old he is, I'm sorry, but, if he's an adult, he'll need to sign for himself," I explained.

"Is that going to be a problem?" I pushed, after an awkward pause.

"Yeah," Nancy responded. "Bennie is our dog."

And that's when I knew I'd lost it—my sense of humor. This was an absurd interaction and the punchline should have made me laugh, at myself. Clearly, I'd been careless and hadn't reviewed all Bennie's information before picking up the phone. Clearly, I overlooked that he neither went to school nor had a job. Clearly, being a dog was why he still lived at home. I just thought Bennie was a loser. Clearly, I was *projecting*.

But I had good reason to be disturbed. I just realized that I had signed a contract with a six-year-old collie, and that I had included his name in my very-public Complaint and that I'd now have to contact Kenecke's office and explain all this. I told Nancy I'd have to call her back. I needed time to cool down and think. *What is wrong with these people?* I thought. I was starting to wonder if I had the patience for this kind of work.

At the same time I was advancing my representation of household pets, Unocal's defensive effort was mounting in earnest. By early 1996, our Committee had taken the depositions of seven Unocal representatives and scheduled 26 more. We'd reviewed more than 100,000 pages of company-produced documents and even more from third-parties from whom we'd subpoenaed records. We were aggressively increasing the tenor of the litigation. And why not? Our billion-dollar case deserved it.

Having thrown down the gauntlet in a big way like this, we weren't surprised when the company began scheduling its own depositions—for our clients. This was another tit-for-tat, but I knew it was probably one of the last before trial so my spirits lifted. Negotiations over my clients' deposition dates gave me a small window to take on some short-term hourly work and generate some income, but it was modest and fleeting. The last year's efforts on the Unocal case were intense and without much human assistance, volunteer or otherwise. By the spring of 1996, I knew I couldn't hang on physically or emotionally if I had to continue working until 10 p.m. each night. I was just treading water.

But the brief work on a few non-Unocal matters was a welcome distraction. In no small part due to the stress of this case, my marriage was over. Liz had returned to complete her Master's degree and was cultivating a new academic and social life, and I was doing nothing but working. The relationship we developed in a simpler time eight years earlier as carefree undergraduate students had since become heavy and unsalvageable, and she moved out.

The day she left, I came home from work to see our small apartment half cleaned out and several closet doors left wide open. There was an unusually loud echo to my footsteps. After taking a few minutes to contemplate what it all meant, I gathered the few dust bunnies created by all the commotion, topped off a glass of red wine and got back to work on some Unocal files. It hurt, but I was busy. I told myself I'd mourn it later.

CHAPTER 20
JUST THE FACTS

It was of some consolation that the legal team at Kenecke, Peters and Wade had been just as busy over the winter as I had been. For our side, "busy" meant tracking down clients and producing Questionnaires. For Kenecke's group, it meant reviewing them, examining exposure circumstances and reported symptoms, determining which plaintiffs' claims warranted closer examination. In litigation-speak, a closer examination means depositions.

Taking the deposition testimony of parties to the case is at the core of the discovery process. Like other forms of investigation, these Q&A sessions are intended to collect data that you may use, or at least that you can threaten to use, at trial. Unlike most other forms of investigation, however, depositions are highly interactive and, for that reason, extremely powerful, real-time fact-finding tools. In our case, many plaintiff depositions were expected. We'd already questioned Unocal's workers; it was just a matter of time before Kenecke's team would seek to grill as many of our clients as possible before the judge made them stop.

For those who have never sat for a deposition, let me tell you—it can be dreadful. However, if you sue a big company, the chances are that, sooner or later, you'll have to sit for one. Once there, you'll be asked sometimes extraordinarily personal questions that, except for a viable objection, you'd better answer; when you're in the hot seat at a deposition, the questioning attorney will make sure you do and can be relentless in the approach to getting those answers. How uncomfortable you are simply doesn't matter. Depositions aren't meant to be exercises in cruelty, but the hammering is commonplace and it can last for days. The lawyers would tell you it's an acceptable means to an end. The problem for the witness, however, is that this excuse has been known to justify a lot of nauseating tactics.

For those people who haven't experienced it, here's how it works: First, you receive a Notice of Deposition from the other side. It tells you where and when to show up for the beating, usually at the offices of your opponent's lawyer. Hurray. Now, you're a "deponent."

Next, following some negotiation between the lawyers over a date for the appearance, location and other logistical matters, you show up at the deposition site, hopefully well-prepared for a day of questioning, accusations, innuendo and legal bickering. Usually, you are represented by legal counsel—and Lord help you if you are not—who will sit beside you for the purpose of making objections from time to time and otherwise ensuring a smooth process. That's what they'll claim to be doing anyway, but the reality is that the deponent's attorney often seeks to interfere, obfuscate, block and/or otherwise muddy the process and the transcript of the proceedings, so that no one reading that record later can tell exactly what was admitted or denied.

Indeed, while claiming that they are simply "preserving objections" for a later time, good lawyers can make a mess of the transcript with long-winded challenges since, at deposition, there is no judge present to preserve order. And some lawyers love doing that—making a mess of their adversaries' testimonial record, aiming to make it hard to decipher later what the deponent said, trying to render the process useless.

And the stenographer is of no help here. The stenographer (also called the "court reporter") is retained to transcribe verbatim everything said in the room but has no other role and no authority to chime in on disputes between the lawyers. Despite who pays his or her fee, the reporter is expected to remain neutral. The same goes for the videographer, if one is hired, and that's optional at the election of the lawyer asking for the deposition. With all these observers, if you are uncomfortable being interrogated, or suffer from poor recall, or your case involves particularly embarrassing facts, sitting for a deposition can be a nauseating experience.

Consequently, being served a deposition notice is never a welcome event. It is, in fact, so unwelcome that many lawyers will do just about anything to avoid bringing their clients to them. Sure, the parties themselves may be eager to "tell their stories," but, I assure you, their attorneys are not. The attorneys are mindful of the benefit of surprise, and, if they could sequester their clients until trial, they would. You see, a deposition is the only time the other side can talk directly to your client before trial and, when they finally get your client in that room, it's for one purpose only: to punch holes in your side's version of the facts and browbeat your client as long as necessary to do that. Nobody truly understanding the process would welcome that.

But, despite your best efforts to block it, your client simply must, at some point, show up. Knowing this, when deposition notices for a few of my clients arrived, I exhaled slowly and deliberately. *Here we go*, I thought. *Now, Unocal will see what it did to these people.* At first, I was thrilled that a record would finally be made of these residents' stories because I was still thinking like an idealist, not a shrewd advocate.

When logic finally kicked in, my excitement disappeared. I realized there was zero benefit—either to me or to my clients—of those stories coming out now. I could call my clients on the telephone and hear those stories whenever I wanted to. I didn't need a formal deposition for that. But Kenecke's lawyers did. It would be unethical to talk to my clients without it. That meant the only benefit of deposing my clients would be to Unocal. Its lawyers wanted to get at my clients' testimony to mount the best possible defense and, at trial, to crush us.

Kenecke's lawyers had set deposition dates a few weeks out for several of our plaintiffs, and, while we didn't know why they chose these people in particular, there was little we could do to avoid producing them. The more I thought about it, the more I worried, not just for the harm it could do to our case, but for the time it would take to sit through weeks of these, and the expense of buying pricey written transcripts.

And I worried about my own performance. At the depositions, would I be experienced enough to recognize when real damage was being done? Kenecke's lawyers were slick. My clients might give up information relevant to some novel or esoteric defense I'd never considered, and the case might be over before I even realized it. Kenecke's lawyers wouldn't tell me when they were scoring points. Without a doubt, poor performance could end these plaintiffs' cases on the spot, not to mention damaging every one of the remaining claims, just by association.

With the first date of these depositions rapidly approaching, I quickly phoned each of the deponents and gave them the bad news. I half expected them to bolt and say they didn't want any part of this anymore, but they didn't. Nothing had changed for them. They were eager to help. Each of them had questions, but, preferring to answer all of them at once, I set a group meeting at my office. I told them they could come one particular evening the following week, and they jumped at the chance. None of these people knew much about legal procedures, and, so, when they showed up, I expected they'd be wide-eyed and tense. My goal would be to get them to relax, explain the process, and teach them to think like defense lawyers.

A week passed and, at around 6:30 on the appointed evening, they all showed up for their prep session at my Alameda office, ready to get to work. Feeling they needed little in the way of additional motivation, I dove right in, starting my lecture with an explanation about why these depositions were happening and the pitfalls to avoid. I explained that the questioning attorney's job was to pin them down about what facts they currently had and to observe how they'd present to a jury, should they ever take the stand in court. During my introductory remarks, I handed each of them an instructional packet of what I called "Depo No-Dos" and said we'd discuss its contents for as long as it required to ensure everyone was ready.

To achieve the best result, I told them I needed them reacquainted with every medical record, every pay stub, and every invoice for damaged property. I told them they needed perfect recall of which medications they took, and for how long, and in what dosages. I told them to memorize which days they'd missed work because the Catacarb made them too sick to come in. In short, they needed to rehearse everything about their lives ever since the first day of the release. That wouldn't be easy or comfortable, would make them defensive and want to speed up. I told them not to. I told them to slow it down once under oath, stay relaxed, or mistakes would be made. I told them what I wanted them to do, but, mostly, this meeting was centered on telling them what not to do.

Everyone says plaintiff depositions aren't supposed to be memory tests, but they really are. If you don't remember important facts, you're not going to make your adversary uncomfortable enough to pay you big money for your case. There's an assumption shared by most that, if something really important happened to you, you'd remember it. Also, having great recall gives the other side little opportunity to trip you up. In the make-or-break context of a deposition, lawyers can get fiercely competitive and determined to make you say what you don't want to say. If you remember events well and are consistent in your storytelling about them, that won't happen, and that really gets under their skin.

After a few introductions and pleasantries, I directed my clients to the circle of chairs I'd arranged. I wanted them facing each other, and me, to ensure their attentiveness but it was mostly logistics; the conference room table I shared with the other tenants on my floor wasn't big enough for more than about six people, so we met in another space that was much larger. Once they were seated, I walked them through the checklist of everything that could get them into trouble when testifying.

"So, let's get started. No-Do number one: Don't answer the question *not* being asked. Focus. Just answer "yes" or "no" or "I don't know" whenever possible. This is at the top of the list," I explained. Lots of heads nodded to communicate their assent.

I went on to explain why. "In my opinion, it is human nature to want to help others, particularly when they appear to be struggling or confused. The questioning attorney knows this and will feign confusion to bait you into offering more information than the question requires." I explained that the Kenecke lawyers were our legal enemies. "We don't want to help our enemies hurt us, right? If someone has a gun to your head, would you start handing them bullets?" I hoped they were paying close attention to this point. If not, they'd be easily suckered by a smiling face when they sat down in that deposition chair, and they'd fail.

I continued the conditioning. "When someone asks you a question that starts with words like *Did you* or *Do you*, they're not asking for an explanation. So, don't give one. If they want an explanation, let them follow up with another question. These lawyers are very good. They know how to ask for what they want." I wanted this group to answer the questions being asked, not the questions they thought ought to be asked. It's a robotic but necessary approach. Since it's the questioning attorney's job to lull the deponent into a false sense of security so he gives away the store, being surgical in answering is critical.

I continued down my list. "All right. Let's move on. "No-Do number two. Don't speculate. A witness is someone who can attest to a fact based on *personal knowledge*. That's what you are, witnesses, but only to what you actually know. Speculating is to make guesses at something. I promise you that Unocal isn't spending thousands of dollars a day on lawyers and transcripts just to have you guessing at things. What's more, when you guess, they're going to ask you to back it up. It's like a lie; it just keeps compounding, and it makes the whole process take longer." I didn't want them getting called back for more days of testimony than needed because they lacked the self-confidence to admit they weren't omniscient.

But most people have a hard time with this one. They prefer to avoid conflict. They see not giving a substantive answer as interrupting the smooth flow of the deposition exchange, and so they'll randomly guess at answers just to avoid appearing difficult or evasive. In everyday life, little harm usually comes from speculating or assisting your audience, but, under oath, it's a problem. A deposition is not a conversation, and, ironically, the smoother the process goes, the more likely the deponent ultimately suffers. "Don't do it, "I told them. "The discovery process is about collecting facts, not creating fictions."

Heading down the list to point number three, I cautioned them. "Don't rush to answer a question. Take your time. You're the star of the day. It's your deposition, and no one's going anywhere while you think about how to best answer each question." What people don't usually know is that deposition transcripts almost never show how long the answer took and, even when they do, so what? You're *supposed* to be thoughtful and accurate; even the questioning lawyer says that when the deposition starts. You can't be thoughtful if you're rushing or wilting in the heat of the other side's pressure tactics.

"Take each question in isolation; think about it, and then give a calm, brief answer when *you* are ready," I told them, but the warning alone wouldn't be enough. Every seasoned lawyer knows that a deposition is a game of catch and release. A lot of psychological manipulation goes on there. If the witness' testimony is not what the questioning lawyer wants to hear, the lawyer may berate, guilt or insult the witness. If the witness is an open book, however, he will get rewarded with head nods, patience and a smile. Lawyers know that displays of anger can produce hurried answers, so ploys to excite and fluster the deponent are common. I told my clients we could take breaks as needed, but they had to self-soothe and slow it down while in session or they'd get hammered. Almost no one is immune to the tricks of a master interrogator.

I carried on with this approach for a while, offering anecdotes and best practices from my limited deposition experience. "Never offer opinions. That's for the experts. Don't promise to get information later. If I object—and hopefully you'll pause after each question so I can—don't talk. Let me make my statement. My objections are for your protection." They got it.

The role-playing was the fun part, where they could practice what they learned and build some camaraderie. It was also timed to end the night on a lighter note; interactive games are always more interesting than lectures. And it allowed the clients to laugh at each other. I liked that. No one chooses to be injured, but this lawsuit was uniting otherwise disenfranchised, disconnected people against a common adversary, and that was empowering. We all felt it and so the levity was an ideal way to close out the evening.

As they got up to leave, I reminded them of the deal I'd made with Kenecke's office that our firms would exchange particular documents three days before each deposition. I reminded each client I needed evidence of any pre-existing and ongoing medical conditions, their exposure circumstances and their property damages. We'd get whatever Kenecke had on each person too, before each appearance, so we could be ready.

This mutual exchange of information in advance was critical. I wasn't about to get sandbagged by documents from my clients' distant pasts. I also didn't want to happen what almost always happens: the plaintiffs show up for questioning, reveal their document search was inadequate, and we all come back for more days of deposition. Each of my clients assured me that wouldn't happen, not to worry. Clients always assure you it won't happen, and then it does. Still, for some reason, I trusted them. In those days, gullibility, like hope, sprang eternal.

Plaintiff June Potter was first up. I'd been to Kenecke's offices before, to review all those boxes of documents, but that was a long time ago. Still, I was more confident today. I walked in with June like I'd worked there for years. I chuckled and smiled knowingly when the receptionist escorted us to the same conference room I'd previously shared with Doug, Brian and a mountain of paper.

Terri Armstrong, the Kenecke partner I'd dealt with since the beginning, was leading the deposition process, and would be taking this one too. I'd really hoped otherwise. There was something about it being a woman deposing my female client that unnerved me, as if Terri might use that nurturing gene to disarm June, making June let her guard down. Unguarded clients worried me. I wanted clients who were wound as tight as a drum, such that they'd never forget Terri was the devil to them. I wanted clients who would look to me throughout this process for guidance, as if they needed my permission before speaking.

My interactions with Terri had always been cordial, but I certainly couldn't tell my clients this. They might think we were in cahoots or, at least, that Terri could be trusted. I had to act like she couldn't be, even when I thought she was being authentic. That's a lot of acting, but, sometimes, behaving like a bitter obstructionist lightens the job for your client just enough to get through it. If that's what it took, I was willing to play that role as long as necessary.

Day One of June's deposition started promptly at 9 a.m. Without much small talk, we dove right in. First, the Admonition, which is the interviewing lawyer's speech about deposition ground rules and such—the same stuff I'd covered with my clients already. Please don't speculate, she'd warn. Here is what you do when objections are made. Take your time answering. *Take your time? What a load of garbage*, I thought. Terri was telling June she had the right to be thoughtful and take her time, but I knew it wouldn't be long before Terri was complaining about the pace and pushing June to hurry up.

The first couple of hours were very dry, as is the opening act of most depositions. These were the background questions about June's home life, her educational background, kids, spouse, cats, dogs, fish, career and eating habits. Her medical history and then a segue into more relevant issues wouldn't come until much later. I acted impatient and urged Terri to recognize the wastefulness of each line of questioning, no matter what I really thought of it. I was hostile and eristic. We'd take breaks at least every hour, during which I counseled June and reminded her of our strategy. Terri didn't like that frequency. I didn't care what she liked. We took a long lunch break. I knew this would not be a one-day event, so why rush it? When we sauntered back into the room after our meal, Terri was tapping her pen in an anxious staccato rhythm. Good. I wanted her to know who was in charge.

When we were in session, I sat on the edge of my seat, and not just figuratively. I was itching for opportunities to object, to make a fuss and put up roadblocks, to stay relevant in a process where I was expected to be a glorified baby-sitter. If the goal of these depositions was to punch holes in June's claims, maybe enough to get her case dismissed, it was my job to derail Terri's train. Even at the risk of being a complete jerk, I wasn't going to let lawyer tricks and pressure tactics stop my client from doing great. This company had hurt June, and now it wanted to silence her and rob her of her day in court. Not on my watch. I questioned everything,

Terri: "Do you regularly drink coffee?"

Me: "Objection. Vague. What do you mean by 'regularly'?"

Terri: "Well, on how many days during a typical week do you drink coffee?"

"Objection. What do you mean by 'typical week'? Vague as to time." I allowed her to answer anyway. Then, more questions about coffee, then vitamins, prescription medications, etc.

Then, Terri would tack and hit her sideways: "Have you ever used cocaine?"

"What? Objection! Are you serious? Don't answer that," I'd intervene loudly. This wasn't a serious effort on Terri's part though. Terri knew I'd fight her on this, and that was the point—to make my client anxious, to show June that this was a no-holds-barred exercise and that Terri had no boundaries. And that's precisely why I had to shut it down, no matter whether my objections were valid.

"Scott, I'm entitled…," Terri would start. *Don't let her finish that sentence*, I'd think to myself, as I rudely interrupted. "No, Terri. You are not. That's absurd. Cut it out, and move on," I retorted dismissively.

Terri: "Are you really saying…"

Interrupting more vigorously this time, louder, bullying her, I couldn't back down. "I said what I said. Move on."

After a short debate about California's privacy laws, Terri dramatically announced that she was having the transcript "marked" for later review, and then she moved on. "Has anyone in your house ever smoked cigarettes?"

"Objection. 'Ever'? That calls for speculation. Why don't you just depose *them*?" I'd suggest.

"Well, Scott, right now I'm deposing her," Terri sassed back.

"Fine," I snorted, dismissively. "But depose her about what she knows. I don't want her speculating as to whether somebody in her house might go hide in the woodshed from time to time to smoke cigarettes."

Now that's called a "speaking objection," and, not only is it frowned upon, it suggests that you're worried about your client's ability to stay on course—not that I cared or anything. I let June say she didn't think so but couldn't know for sure.

Moving on. "Are there any particular foods that you try to stay away from?"

This was kind of a big question, but I let it go. It was unlikely to get June into much trouble, no matter how she responded—and I needed a sip of coffee.

June responded, "Fat."

Terri: "And why is it that you try to stay away from fat?"

June: "Um, because it makes you fat."

Good one, I thought as I snickered softly. *No need to object here, though*, I figured. June had this one, and it was nice to get a short break from battle.

And that's the kind of dialogue that went on all day, that day and every day I was there, and there were an awful lot of days. The process was tedious and the level of minutia unexpected, but I was hardly in a position to complain. These were seriously impacted people, some of the same folks we'd proposed or even selected as representatives of the community in our Model Complaint. Being our choice to put them center stage, I knew the judge would allow Kenecke's attorneys a wide berth to ask almost anything they thought necessary—but it didn't mean I wouldn't make them work for it. I just had to ensure I could justify my objections. Interfering *too much* would just lead to more delay, maybe even a fine and a dressing-down by the judge.

June's narrative, in that first of many depositions taken, still stands out. Maybe it's just a Primacy effect thing (being the first deposition) or that she looked so sad as she told her story. Maybe it's just because it was the first time Unocal's lawyers were hearing it. June had worked at the local school district's administrative offices, located almost directly across from the refinery. While there during the Catacarb release, she observed a brown, oily substance on her vehicle. Unocal promised to wash all the workers' cars for free, but it was too late. The Catacarb had already eroded the paint on her dark vehicle, turning much of it white.

Around the end of August, June started experiencing cramping and diarrhea three to four days a week. Later, when she discovered a chemical release had occurred, she called Unocal. The refinery representative who answered promised her symptoms would quickly dissipate, but they didn't. Two years later, here she was, still suffering, and not just from Catacarb poisoning. As a Rodeo resident, she was there for all four of the releases. Being a homeowner there meant she couldn't avoid getting pounded by Unocal's recklessness again and again.

As I did when I heard most stories like this, I just sat there fuming. Her biography was not terribly unique; with minor variations, everyone's experience shared common themes; they all lived or worked within the Catacarb plume area, all experienced an onset of symptoms at the same time, yet most had been in good health, and they were still suffering and still living in fear. I almost wanted these plaintiffs to scream at Terri, to make sure they sent a strong message back to her client. In retrospect, however, I think their quiet factual recitations, letting the agonizing experiences speak for themselves, amplified the message.

After closing out her last day of deposition, June and I headed downstairs to the street to recap the day's events and part ways, at least for a while. I had more depositions to defend but her work was over. We stood on The Embarcadero, San Francisco's famous bayside promenade, with its endless wind blowing in our faces and we talked. The gusts were making my eyes sting and, for a moment, I considered how little regard we normally have for wind, including what's being transported by it. I was certain the symbolism wasn't lost on June either.

I told her she'd done a good job, and she thanked me for my dedication to the cause. I said she'd get the chance to review the transcript of her testimony soon but that she had nothing to worry about. I explained that our case was very strong, and I had high hopes.

Suspecting she'd driven to the deposition, I wondered if I should ask for a ride back across the bay. I'd taken the subway to get there, not able to afford high San Francisco parking prices. But then I thought better. It's not smart to let on to your clients that you're poor. They want heroes without blemishes, ones who can easily throw money around. They don't want ones who can't afford parking. We said our good-byes, with me wondering if I'd ever see her again, and just how muggy the subway car would be.

As I walked away from Kenecke's brick fortress, I geared up for the ride home. The few times I'd ridden the subway before June's deposition taught me that, well, I hated the subway. It seemed dirty, I didn't like that panhandlers always, somehow, made their way on, and you could rarely get a seat when you needed it. But this day I got a seat. This day was different for a lot of reasons.

This day, cloaked in warm self-righteousness and sacrifice, surrounded in that train car by all those bodies and all their smells and quirks, I smiled. Suddenly, I was happy, part of the human experience, doing what average folk do. I'd just finished a day on the side of justice, on the side of the *people*. Being among those people again, even if just for a 30-minute subway ride, felt fitting, and I glowed. I've loved the subway ever since.

It was probably inevitable that I'd come to enjoy these rides home—or at least that I'd become well-acquainted with those trains; four months of depositions, and none were without colossal frustration and needless delay. Despite the clients' best intentions to follow the rules I laid out, each one was required to come back several times, sometimes just to answer questions about documents they failed to produce. Had they more conscientiously heeded my warning, this would have been easy to avoid.

These weren't anomalous events though. They happen all the time in every kind of case. Usually, a deponent first testifies he or she had made a diligent search for whatever documents were requested. The interrogating lawyer then pushes further, asking all the places where the deponent looked for those documents—maybe there was a storage locker or a desk drawer at a workplace where more material was kept. Invariably, the deponent admits the search was incomplete, and the whole thing falls apart. Rinse. Repeat. Back for another day, this time after a more comprehensive search and even more questions about where else such records might be found.

By my estimation, this doubled our work, but only doubled it. Nothing runs in perpetuity, and, finally, after those four months, we were done. While I never welcomed Terri's attempts to box in my clients, or the lost time listening to the minutia of these people's lives, or the sitting at attention, ready to pounce after every question, walking out for good on the very last day of depositions left me feeling cleansed. It was as if we'd put it all out there, shown our cards, and now just had to wait to see whose hand won. We had arrogantly snapped "Take that!" and thrown down the gauntlet, a declaration of war, but also an invitation to negotiation.

On that last day, I expected some small talk, some telltale sign that Terri was worried about anything she'd heard. But none came. It just stopped, ending with a simple "Thank you. I have no further questions," and then Terri walked out. And then we walked out. It was the most unfulfilling 30 seconds of my career.

CHAPTER 21
VINCENT

The problem with many personal injury attorneys is that they often see their clients' suffering only in terms of evidentiary issues, and legal jockeying, and how to translate pain into the best financial recovery. It doesn't mean they're heartless or unsympathetic, but it does mean they're expected to turn off their emotions in favor of objectivity, particularly when they have to give bad news. Attorneys are supposed to offer a balanced view of the case and be candid about how a neutral audience might view the situation. That's hard to do if they're feeling what their clients feel. Knowing this, when my Crockett clients came to me, even when they told me the most heart-wrenching stories, a little voice in my head always warned me to stay neutral.

So, if staying dispassionate is part of what makes a good personal injury lawyer, did I do a good job? No. I guess I did not, and that's a big reason why Unocal was one of the last personal injury cases I ever handled. It taxed me far too much to hear about people's suffering, daily and for years, knowing the only remedy I had for them was money—when what I really wanted to do was go over to Unocal and punch someone in the face. I felt this on behalf of nearly everyone I represented, even my most difficult and unappreciative clients, but the urge was especially pronounced when it came to children. Time after time, I winced as I witnessed the cruel impact on them since, of course, the little ones were those most deserving of our protection.

As hard as it was for me to watch from the sidelines, it must have been nearly unbearable for their parents. I witnessed it, firsthand. I saw the pain in those parents' eyes, convinced they'd failed to protect their families, regretting not leaving town when they *just knew* something was wrong, letting their children go to the outdoor public pool, and then seeing them choking, developing rashes all over their bodies that burned so badly they cried, becoming so dizzy they couldn't walk straight, sneezing and seeing blood. It was nothing short of horrible. I saw it in how the parents screamed at the town-hall meetings, and I heard it when they wept over the telephone countless times. There was such guilt on their faces and in their voices.

I have to admit that, as a much younger man then, I wasn't well equipped to address others' feelings of this magnitude, and so my empathic learning curve was steep. Knowing how uncomfortable these interactions made me, when my assistant told me Mike Arnett had made an appointment to discuss his situation, I nearly cancelled the meeting.

I already knew a lot about the Arnett family. Being Ralph's neighbors, Mike had heard about the Catacarb release even before the news story broke, but his family didn't sign on as clients until early the next year. Mike disliked lawsuits. He was strong and independent and didn't need anyone's help for anything. If the family had a problem, Mike handled it. In fact, but for how Catacarb was ripping apart his family, he may never have called me at all.

Mike was an Assistant Fire Chief at the C&H Sugar plant in Crockett, where he lived with his wife, Nicole. Now in his late 30s, Mike had worked for the iconic sugar producer for the past 14 years with no plans to leave any time soon. He was a conservative, blue-collar, career guy who loved Crockett's safe, small-town feel. Like his wife, Nicole, he had been in excellent physical shape prior to the Catacarb event—a self-described "health nut" with respect to his diet and exercise—no smoking, drinking or any history of significant medical problems. In other words, he was the perfect plaintiff.

When I first met Mike, he immediately struck me as a no-nonsense, self-starter type, someone willing to do almost anything to help others, but extremely reluctant to accept theirs. I liked him right away, and sensed the feeling was mutual. I think he knew I wanted to help his town and, by hiring me, he figured he'd be helping Crockett too. But that was as far as he was willing to go. His family had suffered tremendously, and he'd provide me with whatever details the lawsuit required, but he wasn't about to tell me how any of it made him *feel* or show much worry for the future. For him, emotional revelation was simply not part of our bargain.

By contrast, his young wife, Nicole, was more of an open book. From what I gathered, before the Catacarb release, she was an optimistic, vibrant woman. All signs pointed to a wife dedicated to her husband and wanting little more than a happy, healthy family. These days, however, she was not so optimistic, or vibrant, and she'd long since discarded any realistic expectation of ever feeling those ways again.

Mike also had a 10-year-old daughter from a prior marriage. I never met the daughter, but I knew of her circumstances. She had been living with Mike and Nicole (her step-mother) during part of the Catacarb release. I heard stories about the playful, energetic girl she used to be and, by Nicole's account, the daughter seemed like a typical, silly, hopeful little kid. I learned that, during the release, she spent a lot of time outdoors roller blading and playing with friends. From what I had picked up, she'd enjoyed several good friendships with neighborhood kids who'd seemed just as happy and energetic. All in all, before the release, life was good for the Arnetts.

Like her parents, the daughter was mostly exposed at her home in Crockett. When the release first hit the little girl, it triggered heavy coughing, which became so fierce it made her vomit. That was Day One. But then the vomiting continued on other days. Then came the vision problems which made outside play difficult, if not outright dangerous and, ultimately, forced her inside altogether. And then came the headaches, and a malaise and then depression, and away went the happy, energetic little girl who loved to roller blade and socialize.

Now, a year later, episodes of the daughter's coughing and blurred vision continued, albeit with less frequency. She still carried around an inhaler due to the asthmatic condition that started after the Catacarb release—the condition that put a virtual end to strenuous activity. Hers was a sad story, but not terribly unique; all over the Arnetts' neighborhood, parents reported similar situations.

In July 1994, a month prior to the Catacarb release, Nicole became pregnant. This would be her first biological child, and she was determined to do everything just right. Like Mike, there was nothing of concern in her family's health history, and so she was off to a good start. Also like Mike, she had been conscientious about her nutrition and exercise for years, and would be just as diligent about getting excellent medical care throughout her pregnancy. Needless to say, when she and Mike discovered that the pregnancy had taken, they were ready and ecstatic.

But that was several weeks before the Catacarb incident, before the bottom fell out of their lives. To speak to her back then, I bet she'd have talked my ear off about how much she loved Crockett and her growing family. By the time I first talked with the couple in early 1995, however, Nicole was just about losing her mind. She was approaching the end of her pregnancy, and she knew something was terribly wrong.

In my initial conversation with the couple, I just got bits and pieces of their story, but the one thing that stood out was her panic about her unborn baby, Vincent. And she was right to be panicking. I'd long since talked with medical experts about the potential *in utero* effects of Catacarb exposure; Nicole was hardly the first expecting mother to retain me. Among other things, I'd learned that ingestion of Catacarb could seriously affect a fetus at this point in its development and that the effects could be endless. I don't think Nicole knew the science behind it, but she didn't have to. She knew her baby was in trouble. If you were to ask her, she would tell you "a mother just knows."

After our introduction and signing of contracts, I didn't have much contact with the Arnetts for a while. They were facing an excruciatingly emotional series of events, and I was just very busy. In fact, as best I recall, our next significant conversation wasn't until around mid-Summer of 1995 when Mike called to let me know things had not gone well with regard to his son's birth—and that's putting it mildly. Some of what he told me was vague, other parts far too technical for me to understand, but I figured I'd grasp it all once their medical documents showed up.

At that time, I asked Mike to provide me with authorizations so I could obtain these records. I'd already intuitively tied Mike's symptoms and those of his daughter and Nicole to Catacarb exposure but was more tentative about Vincent's link. His health problems were present at birth, and they were severe, and maybe that alone made me cautious. Until I ran his records past my experts, I would need to reserve judgment. If everything Vincent suffered could be tied to *in utero* exposure to Catacarb, however, his case would be huge.

As good a tool as the Questionnaire was, the complexity of the Arnett family's situation exemplified its limitations. The Arnetts had returned their responses quickly, but, rather than detail every claim there, they largely incorporated by reference various medical and psychological records. Some families with document-heavy claims did that. The option of simply attaching records, versus distilling them, was a nice feature of the Questionnaire process—again, so long as you already had those records.

For Vincent, I didn't. The Arnetts had seen many specialists for Vincent, and I was still underwater trying to obtain those files. That's how it often goes—some records arrive quickly, other sources take longer to respond.

Given all that, by the time Mike requested a sit-down meeting, I was still very much in the dark about Vincent's prognosis—huge information gaps. I concluded that getting those details directly from Mike would cut down on a lot of work. That would be a perk of the meeting he proposed. The downside was that the meeting would be very uncomfortable. Talking to parents about their kids' suffering was always uncomfortable but I had no choice. When a client demands a meeting, you simply have to oblige.

My assistant set time for us one afternoon, but I called Mike back to bump it to that evening. This was a particularly busy time for me; the holidays were upon us and my days were frenetic. Plus, this meeting was going to be emotionally taxing; I didn't want it interrupted by phone calls or my workers walking in on us. I asked Mike to meet me at the front door of my building around 6:30. He said he'd be prompt and that Nicole would be joining us.

It was already dark outside when I opened the building's main door and invited them in from the cold. Clearly, this wasn't a social visit, but I felt compelled to make small talk about things like the traffic and their holiday plans as we walked up the creaky staircase to my suite, and they did their best to play along. I apologized for not calling them sooner and for my messy office as I swept documents off the guest chairs so they could sit.

Walking back around my desk to my worn out chair, I clicked on a table lamp giving my poorly-lit space a warm glow and unintentional intimacy. Taking my seat, we jumped right into it. They were antsy, unsure how this was supposed to go, and they fidgeted in their seats. I tried to calm them with my status report on current projects in the case but, not wanting to entirely steal the show, I kept my comments surface and brief. I wanted them to know that I was working toward a resolution, that their goals were my goals. I didn't know why they were there, except that it was important enough for them to get a sitter, and drive 27 miles through rush hour traffic to Alameda, just to meet me in person. When I finished my update, I just settled back into my chair, interlacing my fingers and signaling that I was in no rush and had no expectations.

Mike took over, while Nicole watched me, evaluating, wondering if I was really up for this and whether she could trust me. Mike wasn't sure how much I knew about their situation, he said, and so he wanted to "start from the beginning." Not knowing where this was headed, I gave him a wide berth. He explained that the C&H plant where he worked was directly in the wind path of the Catacarb fallout, but, like everyone else outside Unocal's walls, he had no idea a release was occurring. He talked about what a cover-up this event was, how everyone in town was hurt, but he was preaching to the choir. I knew all this, and, yet, I urged him to keep going.

He explained that those were warm days in Crockett that last summer and, so, he worked outside at the plant as much as he could. Nicole was at home a lot in those days too, and who could blame her? Their street was atop one of Crockett's highest hills, with a gorgeous, panoramic view of the Bay. But it was also one of the breeziest hills in Crockett and that was a problem. Sure, keeping their windows open was a great way to stay cool in late August, but it let Catacarb enter their home at a high rate. Still, I imagined that must have been a nice time for Nicole. She'd recently learned she was pregnant, and so she was busily dreaming about motherhood, calling friends and family, preparing for a life she'd wanted since she was small—while Unocal was busily ruining her chances of it.

Mike went on to explain how the volume of Catacarb started out small but grew quickly as the hole enlarged and the workers increased its concentration. Again, this had become common knowledge to thousands of people, but Mike was clearly looking to impress, so I kept quiet. As Mike walked the C&H grounds in the latter days of the release, he mentioned to coworkers that the air tasted metallic. That was weird, he thought, and his colleagues agreed. They'd tasted it too, but chalked it up to something innocuous being released at their own plant, maybe pollution from the nearby freeway or just pollen. Still, they looked into it but, when they found nothing out of the ordinary and all the levels at the C&H plant checked out, they spoke of it no more. Mike, like the other plant workers, wasn't about to start whining about something as silly as bad air. He put it out of his mind as best he could. He never suspected danger.

Nicole's schedule was flexible in those days, and Mike loved it. It meant she could bring him lunch at work, and Mike loved that too since she fed him well. She'd often walk from their Crockett home to the sugar plant in the late mornings to stay connected with him and since she knew exercise was important to making a healthy baby. It was a sweet story, and, as I listened, I wondered what having that kind of loving support would feel like.

In fact, as Mike talked, the appreciation for all of his wife's gestures was obvious but, oddly, Nicole wasn't fully embracing it, not fully taking in the gratitude. *Have they been fighting?* I wondered. I could feel their love for each other—anyone could have felt it—but it seemed strained. The gulf between them was undeniable and I suspected Mike's story was building up toward why.

Although Mike mentioned her often, I sensed Nicole was starting to feel like a third wheel. Apparently, I was right. Not happy in that role, she jumped in to echo how she tasted metal and felt a wetness in the air, both during her walks downtown and while at home. One morning in late August, in fact, she said they'd noticed their car windows covered with an oily brown substance, so sticky and thick they could write their names in it. A different day, Nicole accompanied her husband to pick up his paycheck. As they walked from the plant back to their pickup truck, an oily mist rained down, covering them so heavily that they skipped their errands, went right home and took showers to scrub the residue off their skin. By this point, that something extremely unusual was happening was unmistakable.

Mike then picked up the narration. He explained that, while oblivious to the cause, the metallic taste got worse during the Labor Day weekend. That first Saturday in September, Nicole and Mike were standing outside their house and felt a moisture cake their skin, compelling them to retreat back inside. Neither of them understood why they felt wet. There wasn't cloud in the sky. In fact, Crockett had enjoyed perfect weather for days, yet this wasn't the first time the couple had felt this sticky while outdoors.

Venturing outdoors later that afternoon, Nicole felt the mist yet again. She complained to Mike about how this oily substance had, for days, been in her hair and on her skin, and was staining her clothes. For the first time, Mike mentioned how the lunches she'd brought to his work tasted weird, especially when he was eating outside. Sharing these experiences made it obvious something far worse than pollen was falling from the sky, but, by that point, it was too late.

That night, Nicole started feeling really sick with flu symptoms, a headache, respiratory difficulties, violent stomach cramps and vomiting. Mike wasn't feeling well either but, then again, he hadn't felt well all week. Like his wife, he'd noticed oiliness in his hair and on his skin, so much so that he had started showering every day upon arriving home. He just hadn't told Nicole about it. Alongside his wife, he began suffering severe nausea, a sore throat and headaches, but had never suspected a connection between these experiences and anything threatening to their health. And why would they? If they were in danger, surely somebody would have told them.

Clearly, they assumed wrong and, to pay for that misplaced trust, they felt horrible for weeks. Mike couldn't afford to miss work and so he powered through, while his pregnant wife stayed home with near-constant headaches, burning eyes, rashes on the parts of her body exposed to the air and severe breathing difficulties. Whereas several of his coworkers missed work for days, Mike assumed they'd all start feeling better soon and, so, he rejected medical treatment or any changes to Nicole's pre-natal regimen. In fact, no one in the Arnett household suspected anything life-threatening had occurred until the town-hall meetings.

But, by then, the damage had been done. And that was always the part in these stories that made me the angriest—that people weren't given the chance to save themselves. That felt so unfair and I told Mike I thought it was unfair, while signaling it was okay for him to pick back up the storytelling. He concurred over the injustice but shrugged it off with a "whatever" type response, as if being unable to change the past meant you should just ignore or accept it. He wasn't looking for my concurrence. He just wanted to get through the facts, and any effort to communicate sympathy was just slowing him down.

I watched him and Nicole closely as Mike talked. Something was definitely off. It was as if they'd rehearsed this script, but Mike wasn't following his lines. She dutifully let him control the dialogue, but she was becoming depressed and withdrawn. She wanted more but Mike wasn't going deeper—down to the place she needed him to go. She probably suspected he'd do this but kept the hope that this meeting would be different. I didn't know him like she did, but it was clear to me as well that he was skimming the surface, not telling me something. It was contrived and mechanical, like a busy nurse giving report to a busy doctor on a patient's condition.

He was sure full of details about the release itself though, Nicole's exposure to it, his exposure to it, when their symptoms began. Most of this I already knew from their files, the Questionnaire, and those records that had already arrived. Their entire family had been affected—no question about it—and yet, as bad as Mike and Nicole's own injuries were, they were the least of it. Really, it was the kids I was curious to hear about, especially baby Vincent, including the emotional toll his situation had taken on his family. But Mike wasn't touching that, not getting anywhere close to it. That would be unsafe and flannel-shirted Mike didn't do "unsafe."

Conversely, unsafe is exactly what Nicole wanted, at least to the extent it might get Mike to show some vulnerability, to express the pain that was so obvious to everyone else in the room. I could tell Mike was conflicted but he wasn't giving in. I can't say I ever expected he would—talk about his feelings, that is. I wasn't even sure what that would look like for a macho guy like him. And, even if he could, I wasn't sure if I would be ready for it. Had I met Mike in a different context, we might have smoked cigars, drank beer and talked about the kind of guy stuff that would make a wife like Nicole sigh and roll her eyes. I never thought, even for a moment, that Mike would be getting touchy-feely with me tonight. He just wanted to get through this, give me whatever I needed to do my work, and then go home.

And, yet, now after 30 minutes in my office, Mike hadn't told me anything new but was squirming in his seat, signaling he wanted to leave, telegraphing that it was my turn to do something. Whether that meant to take the conversation in an entirely different direction or to tie a bow on the evening, I couldn't be sure, but I was leaning strongly toward the latter. I'd skipped lunch and this conversation was going nowhere.

"What you've gone through is horrible but, believe me, you're not alone," I explained. "Everyone's story is so incredibly sad, and we're doing everything we can to make the company pay for this." I didn't mean to sound dismissive. I was trying to give the meeting some closure while appearing sympathetic. I accomplished neither.

I expected my summation would prompt them to say "goodbye" and leave, but it didn't. No one moved. I also thought it would prompt some kind of verbal response, but it didn't do that either. There was just silence—a very long and very awkward silence. Surely, I'd offended them somehow. I was convinced of it and, yet, they were still there. Suddenly, I realized I wasn't going to be eating anytime soon.

I didn't understand precisely what had happened, but it was now clear that Mike was back in, committed to seeing this through. Apparently, all it needed was for me to show him the door, so to speak. With nothing left to lose, I picked the ball up again. "So, tell me about Vincent," I probed, staring into Mike. "Some of his records came in, and perhaps you could help frame what I've already seen," I egged him. It was abrupt, but, like I said, waiting for him to stop dancing around the elephant in the room simply wasn't working.

I was prepared for a defiant reaction, but my approach took Mike completely off guard, and I'll never forget his face. It looked like he was going to throw up. Maybe he didn't see this part of the conversation coming, but how couldn't he? Vincent's situation was the one I was least clear on and the most complex. From what I could already tell, Vincent's situation was astonishing. Mike simply had to know we'd discuss it. The topic of his deformed son had to be addressed.

But Mike was a guy used to being in control, and, yet, this had leveled him—the Catacarb, his son's response to it, his failure as a father and a husband and, now, me saying it was time to talk about it. He was out of his depth, and so he just stared back. Time stopped for what seemed like an eternity, but I held strong, didn't rescue him and, for a moment, I really thought I had him.

I was feeling unusually brave, and I wanted him to join me there. I was challenging him, saying I wasn't afraid of him, and that we were probably wasting our time if we didn't get a whole lot more personal. I knew he had a hard exterior but I also knew that Nicole and I could crack it. Mike just needed to feel somebody would listen and not judge him. But, for now, he was calling my bluff. He wasn't ready. He just stared.

By this point, Nicole had reached her limit. At first, I thought she was rescuing him by ending the silence, but she wasn't. She was upping the ante. She saw what I saw—a guy right on the edge, and so she decided to push him. She did it by diving in deep about their most intimate details, about the crying, the medications, about the marriage counseling. This was Mike's Intervention.

Nodding as Nicole talked, I alternated glances toward her and then Mike, witnessing his discomfort, wondering how graphic this was going to get. I had asked about Vincent's condition and how the parents were reacting to it. Nicole was now answering me but in a way calculated to bring Mike to a boil. Nicole was pitching strikes at Mike, baiting him to swing, but it was the ball thrown at me that was so beautifully executed.

And it was thrown absolutely accidentally. "In the marriage counseling, actually ever since Vincent died," Nicole explained, "we've been talking seriously about a separation." She was just giving me facts, arming me with information, but its effect was so much more. Upon hearing this sentence, in that moment, I knew I'd failed them. I could already tell they were having marital problems, and knew about Vincent's birth defects. I just had no idea that he'd died.

A horribly uneasy feeling suddenly overtook me, but I couldn't show it. Clearly, Nicole assumed I knew of Vincent's fate and I needed her to maintain the fantasy. Her disclosure was intended to reveal the couple's separation plans, not Vincent's passing, and so she keep talking without missing a beat, while I sat there feeling nauseous.

Luckily, I wasn't stupid enough to correct her. I couldn't admit that level of ignorance. They'd have walked out immediately and never come back if I had. The trust would have been gone. Instead, I said nothing. I furrowed my brow as if this was horrible common knowledge, whereas, in my body, I felt a rage that, sadly, I couldn't share.

I think I hid it well, but I was growing progressively uncomfortable as Nicole went on. This was more than I'd bargained for, and I needed a release I knew I wouldn't get. She said they were fighting hard to keep it together, day by day, but the agony was almost too intense to bear. Some days she wouldn't get out of bed at all.

Their teenage daughter was also in counseling for her grief, having had suicidal thoughts frequently after her brother died. Her school grades had plummeted, and no one expected much improvement any time soon. The long-term impact of what this family had gone through seemed to be growing exponentially as I sat there listening. Meanwhile, Mike's posture in his chair had shifted, and he was now staring at the floor. I was, by this point, past the shame of my own ignorance and had re-focused on him.

I couldn't tell what he was thinking, but I knew what I thought. Despite his rugged exterior, I took him for a coward, a guy who was willing to let his wife bleed. Her heart was emptying all over my office carpet, and, yet, he seemed determined to ride this out just a little bit longer and then go home—yet another silent victory against having to vocalize his grief and admit defeat. I saw him as a guy willing to sit in shame and do nothing, and I pitied him for it.

Nicole, not dissuaded by any of it, stayed focused, confessing to the drugs she was now on, about all the counseling, and how angry she was, and about the injustice. She didn't equate full disclosure with weakness. She shared her fears for her family's future and how she hated that they'd been compelled to join this lawsuit. She shared about her worry for her step-daughter. But, it wasn't until she turned her disclosures back toward Mike that I knew for certain why they'd come, and that, about Mike's cowardice, I was dead wrong.

Apparently, Mike was now on anti-depressants as well and, according to Nicole, he was barely hanging on emotionally. Looking over at Mike, it was evident he didn't like me knowing any of this, but, when she finally declared how Mike's rage scared her, enough that she'd run out of the house sometimes, Mike reached his limit. Cutting her off mid-sentence, leaning forward, embarrassed over what I now must have thought of him, but mostly just angry about having hidden so long in the background, he was now in a fury.

"Look, let me tell you what I think," he stormed in, loud and aggressive, his adrenaline and impatience surging. "I *know* guys that worked at Unocal, and they were threatened to not say anything or they'd lose their *jobs, and who knows what else.* And they were told the Catacarb was totally safe, and so they dumped this shit over our town for more than two weeks. Two weeks! We could have left if they would have just told us. I mean, Nicole was fucking pregnant!"

I was taken aback by the outburst. *My God. This guy is on fire.* He was still in control, but teetering on the edge of a kind of emotional flood I'd never experienced. And I was scared, mostly because he was scared, and that's not always a safe place. I had no idea what he was going to do or say next, or of what he was capable. I wasn't a grief counselor. I had no wisdom to offer or tools to fix what he was going through. I just sat still, said nothing, and hoped to God none of this would be about me.

Pausing briefly, recomposing himself slightly, Mike went on, a little calmer and more reflective this time, but more hopeless. "I really wanted him to be okay, you know?" he said, his jaw clenched tightly and shaking as his tears welled up, but so fiercely determined to beat this, to keep suppressed what must have felt like a tornado inside. He was resolved to not break down, or full-out sob, or end up on his knees but he now wanted me to know everything. He needed me to know, as if I could then fix this somehow. "Nicole takes really good care of herself, you know, and we did everything right. We knew about some of the issues after the ultrasound, but we had no idea about how bad his heart was going to be. We just didn't know," he trailed off, almost whimpering, silently begging for some divine intervention to make it all stop.

Breathing shallow and rapidly, almost convulsing, he'd break periodically, and then start in again. Nicole, however, was like a stone, unmoving. She was the one who'd wound him up and, now unleashed, she had to let him go. Her face was wet and contorted with a look of pride and relief but of such incredible pain, more for Mike than for herself. She was glad he was now on target, but his suffering was killing her.

I found myself wondering if any of their therapy had led them to this place. I also wondered if Nicole had ever seen him in quite this light before and if this was what terms like "total empathy" and "unconditional love" were about. I had so many questions. I'd never seen someone disintegrate like Mike was now, and I realized I was far from home, way out of my league, beyond the point of directing anything anymore.

And Nicole. Oh, how she loved him. It was obvious. It was so very obvious, and that fact made me feel small—wonderful, that love like that was possible—but small. I couldn't touch what they had, not to mention what they'd lost and so, very meekly and still, I continued to sit, doing what I could to calm my nerves and my envy, and not break into tears myself. I needed to keep it together, but so badly did I want somebody to pay.

Mike didn't get into the details of Vincent's condition, which was good. It would have just turned the conversation technical, and we didn't need that. We were past all that now. Mike was evolving, right there in my tattered guest chair—and he really needed to. It was time. He'd been blocking out Vincent's death. He'd blocked, I suspected, a lot in his life. His path toward healing compelled an emotional cleansing, not the recitation of more medical data points. Plus, other than the death itself, I already knew Vincent's story, the one authored by that shameless refinery.

To start with, Vincent's deformities were horrible. I don't know how else to quite capture it. His little heart was malformed, with an extra hole in his right ventricle, causing it to beat out of control, among other concerns. His head was also terribly misshapen, ears set low, and he had a very narrow windpipe, all results of Catacarb exposure *in utero*, according to our experts. But pre-natal testing and sonograms in 1995 could show only so much, and so Mike and Nicole remained as optimistic as they could during the pregnancy that his condition would be manageable. Within seconds of his birth, of course, that all changed. In those seconds, which probably seemed like hours to them, they knew their baby's chance of a normal life was completely gone.

Immediately, Vincent was taken into intensive care, specialists were summoned, and the joy and hope new parents are supposed to feel left and went—elsewhere. Vincent needed around-the-clock care, and, as little as I knew about parenthood back then, I couldn't fathom making a sterile hospital room your new residence, or coming to terms with the fact that an intensive care unit might be the only home your baby would ever know. Vincent's condition was just too uncertain not to be monitored constantly.

And so, for five and a half months, every day, one or both of Vincent's parents would be there. And each of those days, nurses would come in and take readings, and Mike and Nicole would ask if the results showed signs of improvement. And doctors would stop by, sometimes to perform tests, and then they'd give bad news, and then sometimes some good news, followed by more bad news. Mike told me about the emotional roller-coaster it kept them on, and it left me feeling dizzy and lost.

Not completely forgetting that I was his liaison to the court system, Mike's questions would occasionally come back to how I might help, but they were all over the map. "We've incurred almost a hundred grand, just for our portion of the medical expenses. Is the refinery going to cover that? And, then, what about what we've been through emotionally? How do they figure out what that's worth?" Mike asked rhetorically.

I didn't even try to answer. "Nicole bought these books and...we did everything we were supposed to," he trailed off again, with more tears.

More indignant now, he asked about their parents. "How will they be compensated for losing their grandson?" he asked. He wanted to know about all of Nicole's girlfriends who'd attended the baby shower and brought gifts, and should they not get something. He was reaching now, and he knew it, and didn't expect a response. He was just identifying a question that defied an answer: How could this be allowed in a world where, to Mike, things made sense—where working hard and being vigilant usually led to fair results? He had a lot of questions, but all I heard was that the ripples from one reckless event were endless.

In Mike's mind, he'd lost Vincent, maybe even some part of his daughter, and his marriage was hanging in the balance. He was convinced he'd lost Nicole's trust that he was invincible, that he'd never fail his family, just as he'd lost his own conviction that things always added up, that he had a vote in how the world operated. His body was convulsing as he talked and, although he could have snapped at any moment and in a very bad direction, I knew by this point we were all going to be okay. He was at or near the point of acceptance, exposed and helpless, having given in that there was nothing else he could say or do to change any of it. And when he finally, fully ran out of steam, he just leaned forward, put his face in his hands and cried.

And when he broke, so did Nicole, but differently. Her tears were as real, but sweeter. Mike's torment was more—complicated. Sitting in a hospital room watching his son cling to life for months, and then watching him quietly pass was horrifying, obviously. Now, he had to come to terms with his failure as the protector of his family. His power was gone, and he was confessing it to me, a virtual stranger, and another guy at that. I knew that was hard because I knew his kind. He was my kind. I'd always acted like I had it all figured out too, that I could handle myself and whatever came my way. I sort of had to, growing up as I did. So did he. I felt sure of that. I couldn't fathom the depth of his loss, but I understood this piece of his sorrow.

About Nicole, well, what can I say? She'd lost her baby and, if they didn't get some serious help, she was surely going to lose Mike. The love was still there—that part was obvious—but she couldn't reach much of him anymore. Tonight was an exception. I could tell that. Being hollowed out by his loss and his defenses finally down, his presence was genuine that evening, but this was a rarity. I found myself really hoping they were going to make it.

Mike made some final comments, but Nicole was done for the night. As he spoke in low tones, Nicole silently pled with me to do something, anything, so her husband didn't have to feel this agony, and so her life could get back on the path she'd mapped when she first discovered she'd be a mother. A stack of money wouldn't do that and so I was of no more use to her. She didn't speak again beyond a perfunctory "thank you" as they each shook my hand and then walked out.

I felt like a failure.

Before that night, I had fooled myself into thinking that, as a lawyer, I had special powers to improve people's lives. I had never thought much about how far that power extended or what, beyond money, those improvements would look like. I just enjoyed the fantasy. It made me feel important, motivated me to take on risky causes. I lost that illusion that evening, thanks to the bad choices made at that damned refinery. I suppose I was past due for it, but I hadn't planned on growing up just yet.

That night, I was forced to swallow my fantastical beliefs and they went down like a jagged pill. I was forced to accept that there was absolutely nothing I could do but provide a safe place for the Arnetts to breathe, and try hard to not let the hate I felt consume me. I wish I could say I promised the Arnetts I'd do my best, and nothing more— no promises of vengeance, nothing overly empathic, no guarantees of success. I mean, under the rules of ethics, that's all I was allowed to do. I wish I could say I stayed neutral and dispassionate about what I'd heard that evening, but I can't and I won't, and I'm okay with that.

If comforting them that night, letting them believe their loss wasn't for nothing means I failed in my job, well, so be it. The way I see it, I may have failed as a lawyer, but I succeeded as a human being. Surely, even the Arnetts would've preferred it that way.

CHAPTER 22

LET'S MAKE A DEAL!

While I hadn't personally experienced it yet, I had heard that some class actions could go on for years, decades sometimes. I wasn't prepared for that and was starting to worry. The message to my clients—the Arnetts excepted—was merely that we'd do our best, but I knew they expected a victory and were starting to wonder why the payout was taking so long. With nothing else to report, and my clients' impatience mounting, I was thrilled to learn that Unocal's lawyers had agreed to attend a mediation session in an effort to settle the lawsuits.

The news could not have come at a better time for client control but, as importantly, I knew we were ready. By mid-1996, our Steering Committee had taken depositions of dozens of Unocal representatives, all the model plaintiffs had sat for multi-day depositions, and everyone had a well-informed perspective over the pros and cons of going to trial—the ultimate alternative to settlement. We could have chosen to proceed toward a jury trial, but its associated costs, delays and potential appeals would have been outrageous. What's more, a bad result, unlikely as that seemed, would have been devastating.

But just exploring settlement wouldn't delay our litigation effort, and the financial outlay was merely the cost of hiring a mediator to facilitate our settlement talks for a day. That downside was minimal. The Committee agreed the case was far too complicated to resolve through direct talks with Kenecke's lawyers, but we couldn't hire just any media-tor. We agreed, if we were going to hire a negotiations specialist, one who could handle strong personalities like ours, someone who could digest and make sense of all the data we'd collected but who also possessed the instincts of a first-rate salesman, we'd better pay well for one of the best.

In 1996, national figures comparing the number of new personal injury case filings to the number of state and federal court trials showed that well over 90% (and some statistics showed at least 95%) of cases were either dismissed or resolved through a settlement. Today, those numbers are even higher. Sometimes, those settlements were achieved through conferences with the judge, who, as you'd expect, put tre-mendous pressure on each side to make concessions. Other times, the parties did it themselves, through telephone calls, meetings on the golf course, handshakes following martini lunches. Sooner or later, we'd talk settlement too. While the specter of taking a case of this magnitude to trial was exciting, even I knew that cooler heads would likely prevail long before that ever happened.

Although lawyers have used settlement brokers throughout history, an uptick in litigation during the 1990s generated an even greater need to resolve cases short of trial, and, yet, there was a steadily-decreasing availability of busy judges to assist them. What's more, martini lunches were quite out of vogue by that decade, as were handshake deals. Each year, cases were becoming more complex, evidentiary issues more chal-lenging, parties finding increasingly clever ways to screw over each other, the practice of law becoming more specialized.

Facing these challenges, lawyers started turning, in record num-bers, to what's known as "Alternative Dispute Resolution" or "ADR," a catch-all term referring to techniques for resolving legal disputes outside the court system. ADR's two most common techniques—arbitration and mediation—were already proving a huge success, especially for higher-value lawsuits like class actions, and lawyers loved them for their expediency and relatively low cost.

Lawyers from our Committee and from Kenecke's camp also saw the benefit of ADR, but we'd need to agree on what form that would take, and those forms were quite different. Arbitration would provide us an opportunity to submit our dispute to a neutral third party, who would review the evidence and then impose a legally binding decision. The Committee didn't want that kind of finality, not yet anyway. By contrast, mediation served as a way for us to negotiate directly with Unocal's lawyers, still with the help of a neutral third party, but without losing control of the process. We liked that.

Unlike in arbitration, the third-party mediator we chose would leave the decision-making to us. We'd remain in the driver's seat regarding whether to settle and on what terms; the mediator would only steer the negotiating process, helping us push through snags and impasses common during big-ticket litigation negotiations. If that worked, we could walk away from mediation with an enormous result which, I was convinced, would catapult my career overnight to a place that might otherwise take a decade. To get this great result, however, we would have to hire someone extremely skilled, a "closer," if you will. Without a pro like that, we'd be wasting time and resources, perhaps even dooming the case from ever settling.

Mediation had come a long way since its Greek roots 2,000 years earlier. Even in the 1990s, there already existed numerous well-established and nationally known mediation services at our disposal. We picked one called the Judicial Arbitration and Mediation Services (JAMS), a national organization of retired judges and experienced attorneys that nearly every lawyer knows. It was one of the more expensive services, with even its most junior mediators charging several thousand dollars a day, but it could be well worth it to settle such a high-profile, high-value case. Luckily, a late cancellation allowed us to grab one of JAMS' best mediators for a session in September.

When clients hear their cases are headed to mediation, they generally forecast success. But they shouldn't. It doesn't matter how much investigation the lawyers performed, or how clear liability may appear. There are never guarantees. Sometimes, a defendant refuses to settle because the timing isn't right—maybe it had a bad year and cannot afford to pay you. Maybe, even in the best case, it still wants to lowball you, sending a message that your analysis could be wrong, shaking your confidence. The possibilities are endless. None of that mattered to me though. The moment I heard we'd locked down a mediation date, I was sure the case was over.

The realization that this was coming to a close gave me mixed emotions, but mostly one of relief. Settlement meant more than the prospect of wealth; it meant I could give good news to my clients, including some very persistent ones. I'd been fielding phone calls from people who'd received medical treatment at the Good Neighbor Clinic months before and were now asking where they should go for continued treatment. I was getting yelled at for not moving the case toward resolution faster. I was working daily to get back Questionnaires and to track down records, all while wondering how I'd further stretch my dwindling financial reserves. Everybody seemed to want to know when this case was going to end. Now, I could prove we were making headway.

With now 44 lawsuits consolidated under my case name, most of them brought by attorneys I'd never met, I appreciated our Steering Committee more than ever. The Committee needed to prepare for the mediation, and, had attorneys from the dozens of peripheral firms fought to participate in our work, the process would have been a logistical nightmare. We had to draft an extensive legal brief for the mediator, assemble a massive amount of data and choreograph an elaborate presentation. We couldn't block non-Committee lawyers from attending the mediation, but we weren't about to let them help prepare for it or take part in actual negotiations once there. Still, with so much interest in this case, we knew the crowd would be enormous. We reserved the biggest room the mediation service offered and hoped it would be large enough.

By the time the September date rolled around, we were ready for battle. We'd reviewed countless documents, edited dozens of videotaped depositions, briefed all the issues and explained how the amount of damages possible, should the case go to trial, would put the number in my original Complaint to shame. Unocal was staring at liability that could be in the billions, and I thought our arguments were very strong, not just for out-of-pocket losses and the community's suffering but also for an award of punitive damages—money to punish the refinery and make an example of it for others.

Riding the packed elevator up to the mediation center should have been a clear sign. I knew the event would draw a lot of interest, but, even in these final minutes before the start, I had never expected a circus. I never expected to walk into a 40-foot-long conference room and see it packed with scores of lawyers. It was surreal and, yet, at the same time, it brought so much into focus. The demand for a billion dollars in my original Complaint was meant to send Unocal a message; it was meant to be impudent, a challenge, a 28-year-old's display of bravado toward Corporate America.

I never actually foresaw a billion dollar result happening, but that was changing today. The spectacle I was now witnessing, this room of lawyers and all that firepower, convinced me that maybe I'd been right all along. I was sure our prospects for getting paid—handsomely and soon—were excellent, that my life would soon become something I'd never dreamed was possible, that my clients could move away and start feeling better.

After numerous introductions and signing of confidentiality agreements, everyone settled in for a long joint session. The mediator suggested our side go first. That's typical. Afterward, there would be a short recap by the mediator of what was said, or a short break, and then the defendant's side would present its evidence in rebuttal. That's the tradition, and that was the plan for this day.

Most mediation sessions conclude the same day they start, so we had to work fast. If we couldn't settle today, we'd probably not convince the company to come back for a second session unless we'd already made significant progress toward closing the gap. Our opening presentation took all morning and, as much as I wanted Unocal's team to hear about the tragedy they caused, I almost couldn't wait for our side to finish. We had a lot of work to do. Plus, I was dying to hear how Unocal would defend its actions. Not once since Catacarb was likened to soap had I heard about the release was defensible.

During our pitch, Walter did most of the talking, with a couple others from the Committee chiming in about particular issues. The rest of us watched. This part wasn't my project. I'd helped on the prep work for this, but the Committee had agreed someone well-seasoned at this sort of thing should run the show. That was Walter.

He took the lead walking the mediator and Unocal's team through our evidence of the company's profit motives for pushing back the plant shutdown and for continuing the release for 16 days. We presented expert opinions of how far the Catacarb traveled and the reports which detailed its health effects. I thought the evidence was remarkably convincing, and I was feeling pretty smug. *All those lawyers on Unocal's side of this conference table must be pretty scared right about now*, I thought. For over two hours, we referenced document after document, playing video-recorded presentations demonstrating that this had been one of the most outrageous acts of corporate greed in history.

Then, it was Kenecke's attorneys' turn. With such overwhelming evidence, I could barely wait to hear what they'd say. Finally, after two years of hearing story after story of suffering, I'd get to hear a different perspective. I was sure I would hear lies and more whitewashing, but it would be an answer, or at least a theory, to the question of why. With that much anticipation, I was thrilled when the mediator called on them to offer their rebuttal. Facing that mountain of evidence, however, they passed. They said nothing. They thanked us for our presentation and asked for a break. Kenecke's lawyers said they weren't leaving, but a public showdown wasn't of interest to them. They'd stay and proceed directly to a private meeting (aka "caucusing") with the mediator, but we wouldn't be getting the answer we came for.

They're not even going to try to justify this, I thought, but I cautioned myself not to overreact. Companies apologize with money. I knew that. *We can still resolve this, even without an admission. At least they're still here*, I told myself. But, while I knew the real work was done during caucusing, I was worried. Unocal and Kenecke would be talking directly to the mediator, without us in the room.

I trusted the skills of our neutral helper, but I wanted to hear Unocal's defense for myself. I also wanted our side to get the chance to respond to its defense, on the spot, before we went into hours of private sessions and lost the rhythm and spirit of the presentation we just gave. Instead, now, we'd be forced to rely exclusively on the mediator to sell each side's arguments to the other. You simply can't sit in the same room with your adversary all day and get anywhere, not with that many strong personalities being asked to be patient and listen to one another. We'd have to let go and trust the process, with the future of my clients, and me, on the line.

The caucusing process really is the heart of every successful mediation, and, after the parties engage in their joint session, it's always the next step. Per tradition, members of our Committee and Unocal's team were escorted to separate "breakout" rooms. Everyone else stayed behind in the big room. The idea is that, once there, we'd probably never see Unocal's reps again, but we'd be talking through the third-party mediator. The mediator would ping-pong, back-and-forth, meeting separately with each side in our separate breakout rooms, trying to understand how our positions were different, but where a deal might be struck.

While in those breakout rooms, the mediator's job would be to make us question our assumptions, see the strengths in the other side's arguments and evidence. The goal would be to soften us, to stretch the limits of our negotiation stance and, ultimately, urging us to enter the settlement range of our adversary. Picture a Venn diagram, with the respective circles representing the respective settlement positions of each party. The mediator is looking for where those circles overlap.

Although I'd been let down by Unocal's silence in the initial joint session, I was encouraged when the caucusing continued well into the evening. It wasn't tough to stay optimistic. My Complaint asked Unocal pay $1 billion to the community. That demand was followed by the filing of dozens of other cases by lawyers who, presumably, saw the same misconduct I did. Then, the evidence started rolling in—about Unocal's profit motives, about the science behind the injuries. Then, Unocal agreed to this mediation. There was no question that this case would settle big.

But, it didn't settle. At 9:30 that evening, the mediator came out to tell us to go home. Unocal's lawyers kept us there for 12 hours and weren't offering a dime. With a cash carrot, Unocal fooled us into making an elaborate presentation, into educating it about our legal theories and how we intended to use our evidence should the case go to trial—so it could better prepare for that eventuality. This wasn't negotiating in good faith. This was shameful. It was also a psychological game to demoralize us.

Adding a final insult to that injury, we left the mediation to Kenecke's threats that it would be scheduling depositions for an additional 100 plaintiffs. Unocal could easily afford to, so why not? It was the kind of one-two punch that demonstrated the uglier side of litigation. It convinced me we should never talk settlement with them again.

With no good news to give my clients and a seemingly long road ahead of us, the rest of 1996 and early 1997 was kind of a blur. The fall '96 deadline for submitting Questionnaires came and went, and, while our return rate was excellent, the frantic effort to achieve that result, once again ruined my holidays. Traditionally, Thanksgiving marks the beginning of a seasonal slowdown in the legal profession. Apparently, that tradition wasn't designed for me. I continued to negotiate with Unocal, making excuse after excuse for those people who'd failed to submit Questionnaires over the prior year while, at the same time, begging these clients to help me help them.

At the same time, our Steering Committee and Unocal's lawyers were busy talking about trial plans. How many plaintiffs would testify there? How would we select them? For how long would each of them be up on the witness stand? Should we phase the trial, such that the testimony applicable to everyone (e.g., from the real estate experts, toxicologists, refinery engineers, meteorologists) would go first, followed by the more individualized stories of the plaintiffs?

Then, after we finished presenting our case, Unocal would want to call its own long series of witnesses. How many of those would there be and for how long would each of them testify? The company would undoubtedly call its corporate people to deny knowledge of Catacarb's toxicity, to downplay the company's recklessness, to tell the jury what a great neighbor Unocal was to have washed down all those cars and houses for free.

Both sides could then cross-examine each other's witnesses, with us saying Unocal was a money-hungry ogre of a corporation, and the company painting our plaintiffs as gold-diggers who were exaggerating their symptoms and just looking for a handout. With the claims of now nearly 6,000 plaintiffs at stake, four separate events, and more than 50 distinct symptoms, this promised to be a long and laborious courtroom battle.

It would also be an expensive one. While everyone on the Committee was required to give money to our litigation war chest, each member's contributions, so far, had been relatively modest. The costs for the remaining pre-trial and trial work, however, could be jaw-dropping. I had no idea how I'd bankroll my portion of that, and, yet, I was more committed than ever. Being jerked around at that mediation, being treated like beggars, really pissed me off. Just paying us money no longer seemed like enough.

So, with trial in mind, I started making preparations. By March 1997, I had cut virtually every office service beyond my telephone and facsimile lines. It wasn't enough. I reached out to volunteers so I wouldn't have to pay for office staff anymore. That helped but, with almost nothing coming in, I still struggled with cash flow. I simplified my operation—indeed, my life—stripping it all down to where it had been when I started out several years earlier. I ignored most bills, ruining my credit in the process, let insurance policies lapse, and prayed that the next Steering Committee request for money wasn't going to do me in.

CHAPTER 23
COULD YOU REPEAT THAT?

The French term *fait accompli,* literally translated, means "fact accomplished." More loosely translated in the context of our case, it means we got screwed—at least that's what it felt like when I picked up my phone messages one morning in mid-April 1997.

"Scott. Hey, it's Jim Harrison. Good news. We settled the Unocal case for $80 million. This is a great result! Anyway, I just wanted to let you know. Give me a call back if you have any questions." Click.

Jim worked for the Walnut Creek firm where some of our Committee meetings had been held. In those meetings, I developed a sense of Jim as someone I could trust, someone deserving of my respect. He was an affable guy, and experienced. He'd gotten some decent results in personal injury cases and, when it came to his legal analysis and his strategies for how we could corner Unocal and its Kenecke lawyers, I generally supported him. That was, of course, before this call.

Hearing this message, I was stunned. *I'm sorry, but could you repeat that?* I silently asked. His words stopped me in my tracks, and, despite replaying them, they didn't get any more believable. *Is he kidding me?* I thought. *Where does he get off settling my case, for my clients, without even talking to me—without even telling me negotiations were continuing?*

I must have stood there for a solid minute, dumbfounded. Without as much as a heads-up that a deal was being discussed, the case had been settled for pennies on the dollar.

Needless to say, I was furious. This was supposed to be a billion-dollar case. This was supposed to improve the lives of our clients, or at least give them some vindication. As I stared at the answering machine, I did the math. Sure, $80 million may sound like a lot but, after reducing it to account for attorneys' fees and significant litigation costs, the average client would clear, at best, around $8,000. That number would not be a game changer, and, especially for people like Mike and Nicole Arnett, it wouldn't be vindication.

Jim's message sounded like he was bragging, but I couldn't imagine why. If I wanted to take pennies on the dollar for this case, I could have done that much earlier. Any of the lawyers could have, at least for their own clientele. Even Unocal's Catacarb Fact Sheet, the one passed out to residents early on, said that. The Fact Sheet spoke about how Unocal's insurance adjusters "quickly assembled" to resolve claims. That meant settlement. I even knew of some residents who had taken advantage of that and got paid. What the hell was Jim taking credit for?

And when exactly were these negotiations happening? Our Steering Committee was required to file statements with the judge in advance of each Case Management Conference. Those were supposed to let him know how the litigation was progressing, and that included updates about settlement negotiations. The last statement we filed told of the failure of the September mediation and that there were no further mediations scheduled. September was six months ago! I mean, why invite us all to the mediation if you're just going to settle in private?

The arrogance of it was appalling. I wasn't against settlement, *per se*, but I was sure against the secrecy and presumptiveness of what he'd done. If I had known Jim wanted to talk about a settlement with Kenecke's team, I would have been okay with it. I would have said, "Go for it. Talk all you like with them. Just let us weigh in on the demands you're making and, for God's sake, don't hint at an agreement without consulting us." Of course, negotiating in the shadows made that kind of transparency impossible.

Jim had invited me to call him back "if" I had any questions. Of course I had questions. I just couldn't bear to hear the answers, or Jim's voice, so I asked Doug to call. I felt stabbed in the back, even more so than when the SoCals poached my clients because I really trusted Jim. For a moment, I struggled to remain in denial and struggled to find an excuse for how this could be considered acceptable. Maybe Jim just drew the short straw in the contest for who'd have to call me. Maybe we were still able to back out of this deal. I was bargaining, pushing off what was already obvious. Jim was complicit in this act, and the deal was done.

While I was fairly certain that no contracts had yet been signed to finalize this agreement, it didn't matter. Once Jim signaled his willingness to accept $80 million, there was no going back. Even mediocre negotiators know this. It's intuitive. Once your adversary sees you soften, hears the pause, senses that you're on the fence about its offer, it's a fait accompli. You'll almost never see a nickel more.

Didn't Jim also know this? Didn't he know he'd painted all of us into a corner? If he didn't have that savvy, then he had no business negotiating on our behalf in the first place. If he did have it, then he blatantly betrayed our trust. His reasons—fear of trial, thinking this was a great deal, wanting the whole thing over—didn't matter. He pulled the trigger because he could. What we wanted simply didn't matter.

The only question was what to do about it.

I wish I could report, at least for dramatic effect, that I fought "the good fight" and rejected the deal. Ultimately, each Committee member needed to sign the settlement agreement if they wanted its benefits. Theoretically, I could have held out. I wish I could say I did that and then took my clients to our own successful trial years later. Some of my clients might have appreciated that bravery, or stupidity. Others, however, would have fired me immediately and changed over to a firm that was willing to take the deal, a firm that would have gotten them paid out sooner. I wish I could say I wasn't effectively forced to play along and accept what felt like a sell-out.

But I can't say any of that. I had to be fair to everyone, and that's tough to do when you have clients with such divergent interests. I had people who'd already waited for years to get paid, many of whom were still badly suffering and had no medical insurance to cover their treatments. Was I supposed to ask them to wait longer? And, if I was, how could a little firm like mine handle such a trial? I'd accepted more than a thousand clients. Sure, that was my choice, but it was predicated on a promise by all Committee members that we'd work together and that we'd try the case, if need be, *together*. If I was the only holdout, they'd surely break that promise, and I'd be stuck trying the case alone.

I had to think fast, and do some fast research. With another Committee meeting rapidly approaching, at which we'd be expected to support or reject the settlement, I had to consider if it outweighed the risks of trial and if the broader goals we'd set out to achieve had been met. Sure, I wanted more money, but I had to consider what was best for members of the community. In the end, this was, of course, their case.

But what was best for them wasn't obvious. When I filed the lawsuit, my focus was on getting my clients compensated for their injuries. Teaching Unocal a lesson also seemed like a nice fringe benefit. Now, however, for the residents who were forced to live in these towns, there was clearly more at stake. In evaluating the settlement being offered, I had to weigh all these considerations. I had to decide if we'd done enough since, in the three years since we'd filed, an awful lot had happened.

In the fall of 1994, there was no Good Neighbor Agreement, no solidarity between Crockett and Rodeo, and these towns had never done much to stand up for themselves. They had almost no voice at all. But this case changed all that meaning that a smaller financial payout, given these broader achievements, might still be considered a victory.

And I had to consider the impact of Unocal leaving town. In fact, just five months prior to our settlement, the Tosco Corporation, which sold gasoline under the "BP" brand across several states, had announced its intent to buy Unocal's West Coast operations for $1.8 billion, and that included assuming ownership of the Rodeo Refinery. As it turned out, the official transfer of ownership date had come and gone, and Tosco had already been operating the refinery for a few weeks when Jim's message arrived. That was a victory as well.

Tosco taking over the refinery meant that Unocal had been effectively driven out of the Rodeo/Crockett area. That was huge. At the time of the Catacarb release, Unocal was seeking that permit to expand its operations there. It had no intention of leaving back then. Now, in large part due to our case, Unocal was gone. Being gone meant it could never hurt these residents again.

Given Unocal's long history of reckless behavior, I knew this sale represented a tremendous benefit to these towns and had long-term value way beyond any realistic financial recovery from this litigation. The transfer was going to make Tosco the third-largest gasoline marketing company in the region and, with that status and wealth, it could easily honor the Good Neighbor Agreement obligations it adopted. As far as protecting these towns in the future, the sale meant we were on the right track.

And Unocal seemed to have learned its lesson in other ways. As it turned out, back in July 1995, Unocal agreed to pay $3 million in civil and criminal fines to the county. At the same time, company representatives pled guilty to 12 misdemeanor charges for public nuisances and failing to adequately notify state and county officials during the Catacarb release. I was thrilled to hear that, in no small part because it showed that the county reps who had been complicit in the release were finally stepping up and doing their jobs. I was also thrilled to hear that part of the financial penalty was earmarked to establish a community early-warning system for hazardous petrochemical releases. Nice.

Finally, and more recent to our settlement, the U.S. Environmental Protection Agency had proposed penalties of nearly a half-million dollars. Along with Unocal's new criminal track record, these civil penalties were far higher than most government fines for airborne releases and offered a deterrent that would undoubtedly make Unocal think twice about ever behaving this way again.

To properly evaluate this proposed settlement, I had to decide whether these intangibles were enough to bridge the gap between the settlement we deserved and the settlement we got, because there was no clear answer. Questions like these are rhetorical, and that's why settlements are common. With so many variables and vagaries at work, the outcome of most litigation is unpredictable, and that often unnerves people. Back then, I was unnerved too, and so I signed the agreement. We all did. Sure, I knew we'd been outfoxed by Jim and those who helped him settle without our input, but, without a better exit strategy, I'd have to make the best of it.

I attended the next Committee meeting annoyed but ready to move on. I grumbled and moaned during Jim's presentation of the benefits of the deal but signed the papers and pledged to present a unified front to the dozens of non-Committee lawyers not in the room. We all committed to that. And then each of us committed to not disclosing the settlement to the press, not yet anyway. I kept that promise. Jim did not. Just days later, there it was in the newspapers, an article on our tentative settlement, with quotes by Jim.

Clearly, he had no respect for us or for his own word. I got no advance warning and, therefore, no opportunity to brace myself for the onslaught of phone calls. Many of my clients saw the article before I did and started calling me the morning it ran, and the calls weren't nice. Being tricked again meant I couldn't get out in front of the information and tell people in the way I wanted. Instead, my clients were annoyed, convinced I'd cheated them, and asking questions for which I had not yet formulated answers.

Good job, Jim, I thought, sarcastically. Not only did he settle on the cheap, totally behind our backs and remove any chance of us negotiating for ourselves, but now he made our clients distrust us. We didn't deserve that. Like before, I didn't need to ask why he did it. I already knew. He did it because he could. It was his way of stealing the spotlight, upping his notoriety and boxing in any potential naysayers like me—just in case we had second thoughts about the deal. I vowed to never work with him again.

I remember the day the Woodworkers first appeared. With Unocal out of the picture and no right to participate any longer in the process, the Committee was charged with carving up $80 million of settlement funds and then presenting our proposed allocation plan to the judge. It was destined to be an arduous and protracted process, and we knew we'd be holding meetings frequently. The Committee had notified lawyers in the dozens of consolidated cases of the settlement but warned them a payout could be far off. That was eye-opening; I'd thought settling meant we'd get paid soon. Not so. We still had a lot of work to do.

At the first of these marathon meetings, one Committee member noted the presence of a lot of faces we'd never seen before. These were lawyers not appointed to our management team, people now coming out of the *woodwork*, as soon as it was known so much cash was up for grabs. Someone referred to them early on as "Woodworkers," and, between a few of us, the label stuck.

I thought it was a dubious moniker, perhaps even an offensive one, since it suggested their interest was exclusively monetary, but, for some of them, it undoubtedly was. While they hadn't been invited to Committee meetings before, they certainly could have attended depositions and court appearances along the way, or applied for Committee membership. But they didn't do any of those things and, yet, now they wanted to participate to ensure their interests weren't being bargained away.

If you asked, they'd say they had an obligation to protect their clients' financial stakes. They'd say that protecting those interests included monitoring Committee discussions and how the settlement fund was allocated, so to ensure *fairness*. I doubted that those were the reasons. Rather, I think their interests were more about ensuring the one-third fee they'd receive from their clients' awards. Their interests were secondary though. We needed transparency in what we now had to accomplish and, so, we begrudgingly invited them in.

I'd never met most of the Woodworkers before, but their names I recognized from lists regularly distributed during the litigation. Even before I met them, however, I knew their goals would be very different from mine, if for no other reason than they were late to the game. Most of them hadn't filed their cases until around the one-year anniversary of the Catacarb release, and that meant the low-hanging fruit—to put it crudely—had already been picked. The Woodworkers had little opportunity to represent anyone gravely affected and, so, many of their clients were people living far outside the demonstrable exposure zone.

It was crucial that our Committee keep the Woodworkers' unique interests in mind though. Our allocation plan—the proposal that would assign dollar values to each of the thousands of plaintiffs based upon factors like their exposure locations and symptoms, required consensus. The Committee could not design a plan that shut out the late-coming Woodworkers and their clientele from getting money altogether. Knowing that Woodworkers could cause big headaches and delays if our decisions threatened their pocketbooks, we concluded it was smarter to "keep our enemies closer" and opt for, at least, the *illusion* of their participation in a process where they, technically, had no vote.

Whereas some Committee members grumbled about what they saw as an intrusion by these new attorneys in our meetings, I thought that apprehension was short-sighted. Hearing their objections immediately would allow us to offer concessions, thereby reducing the chance of them from running to the judge and casting us as monopolists. We needed their buy-in on our plan. Our judge would be suspicious of a payment scheme designed *by* Committee members and which largely *benefitted* Committee members. He could scuttle the plan entirely and put his own in place. That meant our work was best done openly, with everyone present.

I welcomed Woodworkers' participation for that reason, but also because, now that the stakes had gone way up, I wasn't sure I'd have much of a voice in Committee decision-making. Having a voice now, as we divided up the kingdom, was more necessary than ever. If alliances with Woodworkers could be formed, they could do my dirty work for me, engage in back-channel politics, voice objections that couldn't come from me. As a Committee member, I was more visible than the Woodworkers. They could do my bidding. They couldn't vote on measures, but they could certainly complain loudly about them, and they could approach others without generating as much suspicion.

If I decided to befriend the Woodworkers, I had a lot of people to choose from. Before the settlement was announced, our typical Committee meetings totaled six to eight people. Now, dozens of lawyers appeared for meetings, a count routinely exceeding the number of seats at the large conference room table. To accommodate this, more chairs were brought in and lined up around the room's perimeter. That's where the Woodworkers would sit, staring sometimes for hours at the backs of Committee members, for whom seats at the big table were reserved.

While the meetings were in session, we'd hear nervous shuffling and grunts of discontent from the perimeter, oftentimes followed by a hand raise or outburst. The Committee members who cared would turn and crane their necks to see who wanted to be heard and listen with interest. Others sat motionless and poker-faced, careful not to signal to the Woodworkers that their veto power was any cause for concern.

Our sessions were debates over the scores of variables that would define our allocation plan, with any one of us members facilitating the conversation, jumping up to scribble ideas on the whiteboard, pushing each other toward consensus. Session breaks, however, were far more interesting to watch. Not a moment after a lunch or restroom break was called, attorneys from the table and perimeter would leap from their chairs and band together in little clusters, desperate to gauge support for whatever vote was imminent. Everyone knew this was a zero-sum game of trade-offs. We were frequently moving large sums of money from one pocket to another and back again. Each of us wanted every nickel we could get.

Since its inception, the Committee had a strict manner governing how it would make decisions—one taken directly from the same parliamentary procedure adopted by most modern legislatures. First, a Committee member made a "motion" for the group to take a particular action. If no one commented favorably on the motion, it was considered dropped. If the motion was "seconded," however, a debate on it would proceed, after which the proposal would be put to a vote. A majority vote won. Woodworkers were not allowed to make, or "second," motions or vote, but they took part in the debates and were loud enough for us to know exactly where they stood on the issues. I decided I could use that.

I'd never been a great chess player, but I was enough of a strategist to see the benefit of befriending these newcomers. Indeed, some Committee members saw Woodworkers' lack of voting power as a justification to remain unfriendly and aloof, but I saw that as a mistake. I saw their willingness to propose, support and/or reject ideas as an opportunity to test out arguments and positions I couldn't openly adopt. Had other Committee members tapped this resource, my strategy would have flopped.

Francois-Andre Philidor was an 18th-Century chess prodigy well-known for calling pawns the "soul" of the game. Analogizing that to people, I've always tried not to underestimate anyone's power just because that person lacked formal authority. By and large, the Woodworkers, even those with decades of litigation experience, were viewed by most Committee members as lacking power. In fact, young and inexperienced as I was, and despite my authority to vote, I think lacking real power was probably how most of the Committee members viewed me too. I worried about not being taken seriously at this critical time of dividing up the spoils, and while my vote counted as much as anyone else's, it was still just one vote. Plus, decisions are often made long before voting begins.

Whether my clients and I made out like bandits or flopped depended 100% on this allocation plan, but I was in no position to drive the conversations or lead members toward my best interests. What I needed was backup—vocal people who'd openly support my ideas—or I'd be effectively shut out of this process. Other Committee members could rest on their experience to get their terms met. I needed a Plan B.

Plan B would entail siding up with some of the Woodworkers. It would entail asking them to make certain proposals openly, touting them as their own, to see if they garnered any support. If they did garner support, little else needed to be done. The popularity of their idea would prompt a Committee member to adopt it and move for its passage.

But it could work for less popular ideas too. Woodworkers could suggest ideas even more radical than what I really wanted, fully expecting them to be rebuffed by other Committee members. After the inevitable push-back, that Woodworker could then offer a more moderate proposal—the proposal I wanted all along. Noticing the Woodworkers' flexibility, other Committee members might respond in kind, adopting the watered-down proposal without me having ever announced it was originally my idea. I think it would have made Philidor proud, but its ingenuity was secondary: it was my only alternative to going toe-to-toe with the SoCals, who would have acted as contrarians to nearly anything I proposed.

In return for these favors, I could offer the Woodworkers inside information I had, just by virtue of being on the Committee. The information wasn't confidential or off-limits—just data available to, but not yet distributed beyond, the Committee. Mostly, it was information from experts—outside reports discussing which symptoms were experienced most often, which geographic areas were affected, what concentrations were present in each and at what times. This kind of intel was extremely valuable. Everyone was entitled to see it, but few people outside the Committee knew it existed. And the people who knew of it weren't keen on advertising it. Even if they did, few could understand what they were seeing. But I could. If the Woodworkers were willing to help me, I'd share it with them.

What's more, I understood the personalities and agendas of Committee members largely shaped by the signature makeup of the group of people they represented. From this information—acquired through countless hours of Committee meetings and conference calls over the years—I knew who'd be receptive to particular arguments and who'd vote for what.

I knew one Committee member had a disproportionate number of Rodeo residents living at Unocal's southern fence-line but with shorter-term injuries. Maybe that was because he canvassed that area, maybe because he knew someone there and then word of his involvement spread to others nearby. Either way, that guy represented a disproportionately large number of clients, but he could handle it since each of those clients had relatively minor injuries. Minor injuries meant fewer medical visits, which meant fewer medical records to buy and review. That kept his cost outlay per plaintiff low. A guy with that sort of clientele would want an allocation plan that did not require plaintiffs to submit medical records to get paid. He'd also prefer a plan that stated the wind often blew south, into Rodeo, meaning more of his clients could prove exposure.

A different Committee member represented mostly Crockett clients, people unquestionably in the wind path and more seriously injured. In addition to the usual medical treatment, that lawyer asked many of his clients to visit psychologists, so as to document their fears of things like cancer. That lawyer would want a division of the settlement that rewarded psychological injuries equal to or even higher than physical ones. He'd also like most of the $80 million concentrated on paying the people of Crockett, where most of his clients lived, with very little left over for the lawyer with the fence-line Rodeo plaintiffs. With these opposing interests, these two guys would probably not agree on much. Without me, the Woodworkers couldn't predict how these two lawyers might vote on anything.

Luckily, my interests were somewhere in the middle. The signature of my clientele was Crockett and inner Rodeo residents (like the second guy) but with fewer medical records (more like the first guy) since many of my clients had been skeptical of the Good Neighbor Clinic and either didn't go at all or just didn't go early enough. Moreover, almost none of my clients had recorded psychological injuries, but they were as demonstrably physically impacted as any other group. Their obvious symptoms made them the quickest to retain counsel. Since I was the first counsel on the scene, that meant they called me.

The Woodworkers' clients were outliers, geographically at least, but their lack of medical records meant we shared an interest. Plus, the

Woodworkers' desire for a quick payout meant they were motivated to play along. It was those intersecting interests that made Plan B work so well. The Woodworkers couldn't vote; they needed me for that. If I tried to persuade Committee lawyers to downplay medical records, the SoCals would have pushed back, if for no other reason than out of spite. Woodworkers were the neutral messengers who could do my bidding on the most important proposals. They could come in under the radar and Committee members were compelled to listen to them, horse-trade and make deals. Nobody wanted them running to the judge to complain.

It was a good plan, so long as the Woodworkers didn't get ahead of themselves and become unreasonable. They knew they weren't going to get everything they wanted, but, with me on their side, they might get close (and vice versa). Still, sometimes, their ideas were absurd—like asking for money for people in small towns five times farther than Catacarb could ever have traveled. I rejected those on principle alone, but, even when I knew I wouldn't be going along, I listened and showed respect. That's not something most other Committee members seemed willing to offer.

Having locked my Plan B down early, I was quieter than most during formal meeting time but more vocal during breaks. Breaks were when I could reinforce my Woodworker alliances. Fortunately for me, many Committee members ignored the Woodworkers during breaks and exhibit outright hostility—seemingly toward everyone—during the open debates. I saw that as polarizing, unhelpful, and it sure wasn't impressing anyone. But I welcomed it. It allowed me to see early where each of them stood on the issues.

Even with the assistance of some Woodworkers, I couldn't completely avoid going up against Committee members, usually someone from the SoCal group. They were combative and abrasive toward anyone who disagreed with them so the battles were unpleasant. When I could avoid it, I gave the grandstanders plenty of rope to hang themselves, and I kept quiet. So long as things kept going my way, I didn't need the limelight.

Some of them just liked to hear themselves talk. Others were contrarians by nature. We'd bicker and, then, each time the Woodworkers observed our friction, they'd start advocating some crazy idea about people in faraway cities getting a big cut of the loot, or some such thing. The meeting would then turn chaotic, necessitating a break during which I'd remind Woodworkers friendly to my scheme of our plan and then we'd start the meeting up again, hopefully with better focus on the end game.

By this approach, we made a lot of progress. After numerous marathon meetings, over a period of several months, we reached consensus on how we'd value property, what symptoms couldn't be related to the releases, what days of the Catacarb release were most intense, what constituted proof that a victim was in town at the right time and so much more. At the same time, however, it became clear that the group was too divided on a few topics, like how far Catacarb traveled and how much money to set aside for the extraordinarily hurt victims. Clearly, back-channel politicking wasn't going to break this impasse. We needed some objective sources to call upon or this process could go on forever.

CHAPTER 24
SOLA DOSIS FACIT VENENUM

Paracelsus, the so-called "Father of Toxicology," was a 16th-Century Swiss-German philosopher and physician. Among his claims to fame is his axiom that "the dose makes the poison" (*"sola dosis facit venenum"* in Latin). This axiom holds that substances considered toxic may, nevertheless, be harmless in small doses while, conversely, ordinarily harmless substances can be deadly if over-consumed. We can all think of examples of this. All compounds—even water—can kill you if you take in too much, whereas small amounts of nicotine and the acetic acid found in vinegar are, generally, considered safe. Others, like alcohol or Botox, might even improve your popularity.

Half a millennium later, Paracelsus' maxim is still the starting place for understanding how humans react to particular substances although, as you'd expect, modern-day public health agencies take the evaluation much further. As Unocal's lawyers pointed out, the method of Catacarb exposure (e.g., ingestion, inhalation or skin absorption) and factors such as the victim's gender, age, health, and length of exposure were equally, if not more important, than the dose level when determining their acceptable/safe concentrations. This wasn't news to us; yet Kenecke's lawyers reminded us of it at every opportunity, in every

Case Management Conference Statement given to the judge, in how they questioned our clients at deposition, and at nearly every meeting they had with our Steering Committee.

Specifically, pre-settlement, one of the company's chief defenses was that, while Catacarb might be toxic in high-enough doses, its mixture with who knows what before it escaped the tower, the distance it traveled, and the unpredictable regional wind patterns made it impossible for any plaintiff to prove sufficient exposure to cause the reported symptoms. It didn't matter that Joan Eisenberg's study—even Becker Peabody's study—showed a strong Catacarb connection to our clients' symptoms. Unocal rejected those too.

But just rejecting the experts wasn't enough. The company even went so far as to argue that some of Catacarb's components, such as potassium, were already found in abundance in human systems and thus, were not harmful—an unabashed position, since what Catacarb contained wasn't ordinary potassium, and since Catacarb's own MSDS revealed it could kill. Indeed, all credible sources rejected the argument that Catacarb was safe. I mean, why would its Material Safety Data Sheet demand special handling procedures and adequate ventilation if it was totally benign?

Predicting Unocal's absurd defense, our Committee had retained a top toxicologist to vigorously refute it. Originally, we'd consulted with her in connection with the filing of our Model Complaint. Back then, we wanted to know if she saw a basis for Unocal establishing what's known as a medical monitoring fund and to help us develop the list of health effects we used in the Questionnaire.

As for the fund, she thought it was a great idea for persons exposed to carcinogens like Catacarb to be monitored regularly for the appearance of cancer. According to this toxicologist, this fund would be especially important for children who carried the highest risk due to the immaturity of their foreign chemical detoxification systems (not to mention the fact that they generally live longer after exposure, allowing more time for cancer to develop). Now, we needed her to quantify the level at which exposure to Catacarb and its breakdown products first became unsafe.

Our Committee's allocation meetings often devolved into yelling matches which threatened disintegration of the process altogether. There were a lot of strong personalities in that room, mine included. Needing a neutral and relatively incontrovertible authority, immune to politics and Committee members' self-interests, we agreed the toxicologist's findings should be used to start grouping plaintiffs. We could use her findings in tandem with the available wind reports from another expert, a more-recently hired meteorologist, to determine the distance and trajectory of the Catacarb stream (and the chemicals contained in the three additional releases). Sure, these experts' findings might threaten everyone's interests to some extent, but it was better than bickering.

Just like our toxicologist, the meteorologist was eminently talented. I have to admit, before this case, I thought meteorologists were all about preparing television newscasters to give weather reports. Given that misconception, I was blown away when I saw what ours could do. We needed a visual depiction of exactly where the toxins went—so-called "footprints" showing the outer edge for their different concentrations. This was critical since no one, not even our own toxicologist, could say definitively what concentration of Catacarb caused each symptom in each victim.

Apparently, within the field of meteorology, creating these footprints was common—the result of what's known as "wind dispersion modeling." Creating these models was our meteorologist's specialty, and he could give us the spread of Catacarb and other chemicals for any point in time, so long as there existed enough local wind data from which to work. But, while I thought this was a great basis for determining who should get paid, the Woodworkers did not. Their clients were largely outside every conceivable footprint and, as such, they were quite hostile to this approach, calling it "junk science" and/ or too speculative to be reliable. Still, this was the only way to fairly address each plaintiff, while warding off *legitimate* objections. I'd have to make it up to my new allies in other ways.

With the Committee's decision now made to commission wind models for each day of the Catacarb release, our meteorologist got right to work. He looked at the topography and terrain of Crockett, Rodeo and surrounding towns, horizontal and vertical variations in wind speed, and wind directions, hour by hour, based on data from government organizations. He even considered the likely size of the Catacarb droplets in the plume, determined by the volume of chemical released and the high pressure at which it exited D-409.

With this information, his computer model could tell us the concentration of the chemical, expressed in a parts-per-million (ppm) ratio to each liter of air which, conveniently, matched up with how the toxicologist measured the minimum safe exposure levels. What's more, our wind expert could provide that for virtually any place in the region and at any time. Finally, since different segments of the population— like the very young, the very old, and those with particular chemical sensitivities—suffered at different minimum exposure levels, we asked the expert to provide additional maps that considered these variables.

In the end, what he produced was impressive, at least for 1997 technology. It was dozens of concentric, amoebic-shaped patterns super-imposed over topographical maps of the area—one for each eight-hour segment of the 16-day release, and then another one for each of the three subsequent chemical releases alleged in our Model Complaint. Each eight-hour regional map was overlaid with what looked like the rings on a funky-shaped fallen tree, but more vibrant, with colors in each concentric ring softening from red to orange to yellow like the temperature zones of a candle flame, as their distance from the refinery increased.

With now roughly 50 separate maps, each showing unique air dispersion patterns over eight-hour periods, our first decision—whether a particular client could recover *anything*—was made a lot easier. We decided that, if you didn't live or work inside any of the footprints, you got nothing. If you were in one of the zones, however, you had choices, and those choices depended as much on the footprint within which you fell as they did on your symptoms, the evidence of your symptoms and how soon you wanted to get paid. We had clients who really needed immediate medical care but couldn't afford it. They didn't have years to wait for the highest possible payout. They needed an opportunity to collect something less, so long as it was something quick. They'd step aside for others willing to roll the dice for more.

Back at the office in those days, I remained inundated with phone calls from clients desperate to collect. I'm sure other offices were getting frantic calls as well. News of our method to quickly pay off low-value claims had spread through the community like wildfire, prompting even more calls.

We needed to hurry and close out this part of the process, at least for the clients who wanted their checks now. With the maps finished, but Woodworker challenges to our scientific approach continuing, the Committee made some small concessions to the newcomers by enlarging the recoverable footprints a bit, traded in the oddly shaped zones for round ones, and put the project to rest.

With our new Michelangelo-perfect circles drawn around the refinery to demark the progressive exposure areas, attributing settlement value to a client's location was as simple as scoring a carnival game. Depending on how far away from the refinery you were, you got more or less money, or nothing. This was our so-called "cash-out" plan, for which we'd allocate a few million dollars to pay off, by our estimation, more than half of the total claimant pool—thousands of them. It was a really efficient way of satisfying people who had little chance of winning anyway, and it didn't reduce by much the money we'd need to adequately compensate the more seriously impacted victims.

With this big decision made, we all got busy and, by late summer, each law firm was reviewing client files to determine who qualified for each of the four cash-out amounts we'd established. We picked the values of $3,250, $1,000, $500 or $250, depending on which exposure zone around the refinery the plaintiff was located. I was thrilled the values weren't higher, despite what many Woodworkers pushed me to support, since this meant that people who could demonstrate genuine injuries could collect a lot more than the ridiculously low $8,000 average I'd previously calculated.

The Committee desperately wanted these outliers to cash out and, so, we made collecting those awards quick and easy. Any eligible plaintiff could put in a claim, dismiss his case and get paid. Not a bad deal for just signing an attorney retention agreement and doing no real work. These cash-out plaintiffs merely had to show their whereabouts by producing some document such as a utility bill or driver's license. They didn't have to show injury, wage loss or any other damage to recover. For people living on the fringe of the affected areas, those with very short-term symptoms and/or with no treatment records, cashing out was the way to go.

But, there was one more prerequisite to getting paid, either as a cash-out plaintiff or otherwise. You had to complete the case Questionnaire, and a few dozen of our clients had not. Remember, Kenecke gave us multiple extensions to submit Questionnaires but then never asked the judge to enforce their return. That meant those clients were still in, and that spelled opportunity.

As it happens, allowing these recalcitrant plaintiffs a second chance to return Questionnaires turned out to be the best scenario for everyone; more clients could get paid and, by getting paid, they'd be forever dismissed and out of Unocal's hair—no chance to appeal. Unocal, of course, liked that. And, assuming our clients got paid, we liked that too since that meant Doug and I would start getting paid.

So, now, we had one last chance before the money was completely allocated. I hadn't given up on my lofty goal of a 100% Questionnaire return rate, and so I decided to make one more big push to get the last of these forms in. I knew, however, that getting responses from these remaining plaintiffs would require a different kind of work, perhaps something we had tried before. These were the fighters, the ones determined not to help us or to help themselves. Something about that felt like a challenge, and I love a challenge.

We had already called all of these people but hadn't gotten anywhere. In fact, by the time the Committee agreed on the cash-out plan, we still had dozens of clients who hadn't returned a Questionnaire at all. From that number, many were clearly outside the agreed-upon footprints. We didn't need a Questionnaire for them. They were out, done, dismissed. Others had telephone numbers and mailing addresses that were out of date. Despite all our investigative methods, they were also unreachable. We'd have to dismiss them too.

For the dozens left, the people injured and reachable, many of them were perfect candidates to cash out, given either modest injuries or the fact that it was just too difficult to get them to provide evidence of anything more. Since participating in the cash-out process required only a simple record of a plaintiff's whereabouts, bare-bones Questionnaire responses from these people would be enough to get them paid. We stepped up our efforts on the telephone and knocked out most of the simpler claims.

For the more recalcitrant people, however, we'd need a miracle or, at least, to do some serious handholding. Whether they intended to cash out now or hold out for later, they would need to complete the survey. It was 40 pages and Unocal could still challenge someone getting paid who didn't complete it carefully. A full return rate, therefore, meant working closely with some very reluctant victims, either by phone or in person. I knew I had to do that work myself. Clients really want to hear from their lawyer.

This project was destined to be labor-intensive. Most of the clients who hadn't returned this discovery, after two years of our begging, were quite poor—some of the worst in an already-poor community. There were telltale signs, but their home addresses alone revealed that. Many of them were disenchanted, sometimes outright frightened, by our legal system too. I could hear that in their voices, in their defeatist comments, even when we told them there were shortcuts, even when we told them a check was, virtually, waiting for them.

Worst of all, from what I gathered, some of them were also illiterate. These were the residents of places like the Bayo Vista government housing complex in Rodeo. Being situated right at the refinery's southern fence-line, these people were the most susceptible to the many chemical releases that plagued this area and, now, they were the most susceptible to getting no recovery for their troubles. Persuading them to complete and sign a legal document under penalty of perjury was simply an exercise in futility, unless we took drastic steps.

The final group of stragglers was those not living by the refinery but affected nevertheless because they worked in the exposure zone, yet lived elsewhere, sometimes in even more poverty-stricken locations like my hometown of Richmond. Oddly enough, it was these people who were the most non-responsive. It was these clients who fought the hardest against getting paid and, yet, they needed the money the most. It was a phenomenon that left me scratching my head.

And the frequency of the phenomenon didn't correlate with how immediate or large the financial payout might be. We could tell them they had $2,000 or $20,000 waiting for them and, yet, they'd make no more or less effort. Sometimes, we'd walk through each page of the Questionnaire with them by telephone, and we'd send them postage-prepaid envelopes so they could mail it back. We told them they could just scribble their name on their Questionnaire, sign it, send it back and that we'd find a way of getting the rest of the information ourselves. For them, nothing was working.

They hadn't always been this way. Over the years, many of them had talked to us, exhibiting great interest in how the case was progressing. Now that we had their money, however, many of them seemed paralyzed to do anything to collect it. I didn't like it but wouldn't let it change the outcome; if they wouldn't come to me, I'd go to them.

Remembering my uncomfortable experiences growing up in a rough neighborhood, I knew that going back into areas like it to collect the final outstanding Questionnaires wasn't going to be particularly enjoyable. With a couple dozen clients refusing to produce Questionnaires, I had little choice but to drive to them. I knew that visiting them in the areas where they lived would be dangerous, but, at least, it would be familiar.

I didn't have much time during the day to be out chasing clients. I would have to go at night, with Doug, since I certainly wasn't going alone. It would be an enormously labor-heavy project, but we'd focus on one client at a time until no one was left.

I directed my staff to call the stragglers daily to set house calls and be very aggressive about it. A "no" answer was simply unacceptable. Each time they reached someone who refused to invite me over, I'd take over the call. I smooth-talked, explaining that I had grown up in their area and had gone to school nearby. I'd always assumed they were embarrassed about their ratty homes and assumed that I, the big-shot lawyer, must live better. Without actually describing my sparsely furnished office and one-bedroom apartment, I dispelled that belief pretty fast.

I also told them a lot of my clients were their neighbors and friends and, together, this settlement was their reward for being brave and taking on Unocal. Most of these particular clients hadn't done anything particularly brave—these were the ones who were *avoiding* helping the case—but sometimes I had to talk about what I *wanted* them to do as if they'd *already* done it. Without that, they can't visualize success.

For the ones who saw through this, the extreme stonewallers, none of this worked. For them, I said I'd stop by their house anyway, if for no other ostensible reason than to drop off copies of the Questionnaire, to make sure they'd received it, and with duplicates in case they made mistakes. I feigned concern about the reliability of the U.S. Postal Service. I said I'd be in their area anyway, visiting other clients. I wanted them to know that I'd be seeing at least the front of their homes no matter what. If keeping me away was out of shame for what little they had, if it was to avoid shocking me, my approach was calculated to torpedo that strategy. I wanted them to surrender. If they assumed I'd come knocking anyway, they just might invite me in.

Once I had the green light for the house call (and I always did), someone at my office would take over again, grab my datebook and set a time for our evening meeting. Invariably, I'd look at the address, think *Oh, crap. I knew where that is,* and realize this wasn't just talk on the telephone anymore. I was committing to going to areas that were really sketchy, where I'd have to wade through territorial drug dealers and prostitutes and gang-bangers. That made me nervous enough when I was still a young punk who considered himself invincible, but I wasn't so scrappy or naïve anymore. Not only that, I felt responsible for Doug, who I'd convinced to come with me, without fully disclosing how unsafe these evening excursions would be.

Doug was always willing to help and, so, we went together, although his presence didn't make me feel much safer. This wasn't my element anymore and, no matter how good our directions were, we'd still get lost sometimes. That was scary. Areas like these often aren't lit well, their road signs are tagged with graffiti, and the streets are littered with broken glass, nails and other debris, just lying there, waiting to blow out the car tires of the unsuspecting and the unwelcome. Even at night, there are more people than you might expect loitering on corners, on porches and in driveways, looking curiously at you. You'd be well-advised to not ask for directions, or even look back. Knowing this from the outset, we were foolish to go.

Once on the cities' mean streets, I drove on high alert, furtively navigating danger. *Just roll through the stop signs*, I'd tell myself. *Don't make eye contact*, but I checked my mirrors religiously. If anyone walked near our car, I kept my hand on the stick shift and foot over the gas pedal. Doug kept the street map low to his lap as he unfolded and turned it in every direction to figure out how we'd wound up at the end of dead-end streets. There was no vehicle GPS in those days, and we dared not ask anyone for help. I knew we'd been pegged as outsiders; I wasn't about to draw more interest by confirming it.

It was dicey at times and, yet, when we got to the appointments, our greeters acted like we'd sacrificed nothing for it. But, at least, they answered the door and let us in—and they were hospitable. Some of them offered us coffee or water, and I would accept and then rarely drink it. I'd pretend not to notice the chipped, coffee-stained mugs, the clothes left on the floor, the dirty plates on the couch, but I'd already lost my appetite.

I can still picture some of the living rooms and kitchens where we sat across from those clients, sometimes late into the evening. Some were just modest post-WWII homes or apartments badly in need of repair, and some were downright disgusting—filthy, poorly lit rooms, paint-chipped walls. We'd show up, as dressed down as we dared while still looking lawyerly, but our attire was the least of their concern. Our WASP-ish appearance and mannerisms still screamed Establishment. With time, some warmed to the idea that we were trying to help. Others stayed cool and detached until we were gone.

I'd have preferred more of the "thanks" and less of the indignation. It wasn't like we were forcing ourselves on them; they could have asked at any time for their claims to be dismissed and avoided this. But they wanted the money, and letting us in guaranteed they'd get some; they just weren't going to show any appreciation for it. In their minds, opening their front doors for us *was* their sacrifice. Rarely did we hear anything that smacked of gratitude, but I told myself they must be thinking it. We were teaching them that not every outsider was a threat. I told myself that, maybe after we were long gone, and if they used the money for something meaningful, our help would register.

Still, I have to say, those were sad nights, seeing how these people lived—archetypical poverty conditions—and seeing how much they needed this money. The documents they showed us reeked of nicotine. Televisions were always on, sometimes with children sitting much too close, their eyes glued to their electronic baby-sitters. I tried to avoid sitting on the couches; that seemed a little too intimate. We sat in their dining areas instead, at greasy kitchen tables with cigarette burns in the laminate. We flipped Questionnaire pages for them and pointed as Doug and I explained what was being asked.

I worried constantly about my car outside, wondering if I'd discover it up on blocks or with a broken window or a flat tire when we left. I worried about who might walk in us as we spoke, how seeing strangers in their homes might trigger them, but couldn't let on that I was nervous. Revealing my anxiety would be as insulting as a verbal criticism. We just worked as fast as we could to finish and get out.

For the clients who didn't understand what they were reading, we read it to them, and we tapped our pens at where they should sign and, for no more than a couple of hours of work each, they got paid hundreds but, more often, thousands of dollars. Out of our 1,100 clients, everyone who hadn't moved and failed to provide a forwarding address, everyone within one of the footprints, and who didn't perpetually hang up on us when we explained why we were calling got paid. Some took their respective cash-out amounts, but others held out for a more-advanced process which held the potential of more money. Either way, in the end, they all got paid.

From start to finish, I looked at Questionnaires for one reason or another nearly every day for more than two years. In that time, I brought in staff members I could barely afford (if I paid them at all), turned my little apartment into a secondary repository for the hundreds of thousands of pages we were processing, and personally reviewed every one of them. Most of that was just a grind and unmemorable—the exception, of course, being the photocopying and delivery of the final Questionnaire. That felt epic, and, yet, it was driving into the ghetto for those kitchen-table meetings that was most satisfying, finally meeting the people who were so determined not to meet us, victoriously tearing down those walls.

I think it had something to do with their invisibility. The people we met those nights were the kind for whom most professionals had little time and little regard and, yet, I felt compelled to regard them. They frustrated me and sometimes appeared more interested in working the System and getting something for nothing than I would have liked, but I regarded them. And, once seeing how they lived, seeing their neighborhoods and their influences, understanding why people like this might not trust us, I didn't feel it was a viable option to leave them behind.

I think that's why I went to them. It certainly wasn't about our fees. These were mostly the cash-out people anyway, and we certainly had bigger fish waiting. It also couldn't have been about the full-participation goal I'd set for the office. That was just a worker motivational tool, and my staffers didn't need quotas to do their best. Going to these victims was more of a justice thing. I bitched and moaned for years about how these clients weren't keeping up their end of our bargain, but these meetings changed my tune and demonstrated how pointless my complaining had been. To meet with me like they did was, quite simply, the best they could do.

It might have been for just an hour or two, but we asked them to swallow their pride and to risk the disapproval of people in positions these victims would never hold. It was enough that I knew their seemingly small efforts marked the outer reaches of their comfort zone. That alone deserved a reward.

CHAPTER 25

THE HOME STRETCH

The moment our Committee reached agreement over details of the cash-out process, we started negotiations over how the remaining funds would be divided. I was glad we kept up the momentum, but my clients couldn't understand the delay. It had been months since people across the county had read about the settlement and that Unocal had left town. Now, they wondered why we were still sitting on *their* $80 million. I was being accused, almost daily, of unjustly holding their funds.

"It's been three years. Where's my money?" they would say. Other times, they'd point out how little I understood of their situation. "I've got bills to pay," they'd announce, or some other such thing. I wondered how they'd react if I told them how in default on bills I was. Either they didn't understand that mapping out victims' whereabouts, vis-à-vis our newly drawn circles, was so labor-intensive, or they just didn't care. Either way, this work would take weeks, as would my analysis of who I should advise to cash out. That each client was one of more than a thousand people waiting to get paid didn't seem to matter. The had my number and they were bent on using it.

They were tired of waiting and I understood. I was just as tired. I had put my career on hold, and definitely at risk, by spending the last few years working on almost nothing but this case and living hand-to-mouth as a result. That's the risk you take when you work on a commission basis for others. I assured them we were working as fast as possible, but being accused of not trying my best still stung.

On the upside, life on the Steering Committee had just gotten easier. As suddenly as the Woodworkers showed up, most of them split as soon as the cash-out process was announced—probably out getting more Questionnaires completed, just like I'd been doing. With our Committee meetings now back to a manageable number of participants, the members still bickered, but concessions and results were coming faster. Once we'd determined the mechanism for such a large number of plaintiffs to cash out—the people who should never have filed cases in the first place, who were only marginally injured, or just didn't want to wait any longer to get their money—the method to compensate everyone else became easy.

After reimbursing attorneys for their out-of-pocket expenses and paying the several thousand cash-out plaintiffs, the remaining settlement proceeds—still roughly three-quarters of the money with which we started—would be divided between two groups, both composed of people who could demonstrate severe personal injuries or large property damages. The upper-level group members could get virtually unlimited amounts, but with a much higher showing of damage; the lower-level group would have a damages cap but would be expected to offer less proof. For the time being, we left the qualifications for each group vague. First, we had to figure out where to draw the monetary line, and, to avoid unnecessary conflict, it was deemed best to look to an objective benchmark.

In 1998, California voters passed a constitutional amendment to unify our state's trial court system. That was a big deal, and the ripples were extensive. Before that point, all misdemeanors and most civil lawsuits involving disputes of $25,000 or less were handled in what Californians used to called Municipal courts. Cases involving felonies, family and juvenile law matters and civil lawsuits valued at above

$25,000 were, however, handled in one of the 58 counties' Superior courts. Using that model, which divided most civil cases by monetary value, our Committee voted to separate the remaining clients—those who, on their own initiative and/or at their lawyers' prompting, rejected the cash-out opportunity—into two camps. We called these two groups the "Serious Injury" and "Mid-level Injury" plaintiffs, a functional albeit admittedly non-innovational naming convention.

While the choice of clients assigned to each group remained highly subjective, the Committee established a few membership prerequisites—things like a minimum number of medical visits, real property owner-ship in the affected areas, significant personal property damage. And we set proof thresholds for each. Beyond this, however, participation was really up to the clients and their attorneys. Some attorneys, like me, decided to err on the side of being overly inclusive, cashing out fewer people and placing an inordinate number in the over-$25,000 class. Some of them did it because they were seasoned trial lawyers and knew a solid claim when they saw it. I did it because I didn't know any better.

Remember, to cash out, clients had only to submit a Questionnaire and sign a liability release form to get a settlement check. Submitting a Serious Injury or Mid-level Injury claim, however, was far more com-plicated. To begin with, those clients had to submit written statements detailing their exposure situations, their witnesses, their claims, and their current condition. Usually these were prepared by their counsel, but the clients took a big role in providing the data points. Mid-level Injury claims would be evaluated on the papers alone, but Serious Injury claimants would be allowed in-person presentations to a panel of one to three retired judges at JAMS' San Francisco offices, the same location as the mediation.

To what category we'd assign claimants also turned on how long they were willing to wait to get paid. Since Mid-level Injury claims didn't require a hearing, they would likely get paid out first. That, of course, was attractive to many people, particularly those lacking good presentation skills and those who couldn't easily travel to the hearings. Submitting a typical Mid-level claim required nothing more than a two-page summary written by the lawyer and some evidence to back it up—a doctor's note, an auto paint job receipt, some lost wages.

However, Serious Injury plaintiff claims demanded a lot more: a detailed 10-page brief (aka, a "write-up"), multiple doctor visits, property damages, oftentimes detailed legal or medical analysis of the more exotic claims. But, while there was a limit on the write-ups' length, the supporting evidence could be endless, and that meant a lot of records collection. Then, once the dossiers were finished, there would be some coaching of the clients to prep them for their meetings with the judges, then the presentations themselves, and then a lot of waiting. The panel would make settlement allocations for everyone, in closed-door meetings, outside our presence. While there wouldn't likely be a right to appeal those judgments, that process could still take upwards of a year.

Clearly the stakes were higher for the most injured claimants, but, from our perspective, the major distinguishing factor between the groups was the presentations themselves. And we wanted the dossiers as comprehensive as possible since, frankly, there was no way we could know which claims the judges would deem most valuable. I might assume one client had the better case, work that one up and be dead wrong in the eyes of the panelists, while virtually ignoring another claim that could have been a winner. So, I had to work everyone's case up vigorously while being careful about time management. You could research and assemble paperwork for any Serious Injury client for days but, with hundreds of people choosing this process, I didn't have days for each. I barely had a few hours.

Despite my eagerness to get started, finalizing the ground rules took our Committee another few meetings. But, once it was done, the Committee was done, forever. We'd spent an inordinate amount of energy bickering and backstabbing and back-channel politicking to get to what seemed like an easy procedure, and I wondered at what cost. When the Committee effectively disbanded, it was already October. The case settled in April. That's half a year of arguing, surreptitious alliances with Woodworkers, countless angry-client calls, and an enormous delay for residents who needed the money far more than most of our Committee members.

So, with that, each firm got right to work. By the time Halloween rolled around, Doug and I had established more than 300 clients as Mid-level Injury claimants and 230 as Serious Injury claimants. The rest were cash-outs, people who couldn't easily prove they lived or worked within the exposure zones and those who'd dropped by the wayside a long time ago. Most other attorneys placed almost all their clients in the cash-out category and had moved on to other cases. We, however, had a long way to go.

In the process of picking which people should cash out and which should stay in for the more elaborate process, I knew we'd have to break a few eggs, so to speak. We made the recommendations, but the clients had to agree, and I was relieved only a handful challenged our suggestion. It would have otherwise created an ethical dilemma. I actually assumed more people would request classification as Serious Injury plaintiffs, if for no other reason that they wanted the opportunity for a higher payout, but the victims were, generally, realistic.

As I explained to the few who were on the fence about what category they'd join, passing off ordinary claims as a Serious or Mid-Level Injury scenarios was like putting lipstick on a pig—everyone would still see it was a pig. By over-decorating bland claims, we'd lose credibility, perhaps for *all* our clients. Ultimately, only five people asked for the lipstick, and we gave it to them, putting them up as significantly injured. In the end, I felt relieved that they got roughly the same award as they would have had they cashed out.

With the enormous project of collecting records and writing elaborate profiles for half of our 1,100 plaintiffs, I was again feeling a sense of foreboding. By early November, I knew I was destined to spend yet another holiday season—my fourth one now since filing the lawsuit—miserable. While other people would be taking vacations and spending leisure time with their families, I'd be interviewing clients, doctors, employers, landlords, veterinarians, real estate brokers and family members, and tracking down receipts, reports, medical files, job resumes, and wage statements to justify reimbursement for all of it. I apologized to the few staffers who promised to see this through that there would be no time off, no vacations. I needed every hour they could give.

Since there would be no hearings for Mid-level Injury claims, we could submit that information as soon or late as we wanted, but our first few days of Serious Injury hearings—for roughly 60 of the 230 plaintiffs in that group—were set for early December, just a month away, with many more calendared throughout the following spring. Whether a client recovered $1,000, $10,000 or more than $100,000 (and us recovering 1/3 of each award) depended on us maximizing the limited resources at our disposal, and a month wasn't much time to assemble impressive dossiers that would outshine those of our wealthier and more experienced competitors.

With this light at the end of the tunnel—some guaranteed return on our investment—it was a no-brainer that I would put every last dime into the case. I continued to live cheaply, eat poorly, run up credit card bills, and defer paying everything so we could afford to purchase records and pay a few office assistants to help track down the data. Luckily, low-wage candidates were abundant for this kind of work, and I'm not too proud to admit that's all I could afford or that, once hired, I worked them to the bone.

I calculated we would need to maintain a quota of finishing roughly 25 Mid-level packets and roughly 20 Serious Injury packets *every week*, to which we'd append all available records, a colorful map pinpointing the client's location during each release, and the two- or ten-page write-up detailing their health histories, exposure circumstances, present and future health concerns and a request for a specific monetary award. That's like writing enough pages to fill a novel, every week, and that didn't consider the labor to track down, obtain, review and copy the supporting records, without the benefit of e-mails or online access.

Since *my* head would be on the block if we fouled this up, I would also need to check every word my staffers wrote, all while watching the clock every hour to ensure our team didn't fall behind.

As a kid, although a rebellious student, I was an avid reader. I loved the classics, good science fiction, anything that stirred up emotions, was high-concept or transported me to faraway places. I was sad that my opportunity for much fun reading disappeared in law school when my attention was redirected toward examining cases and statutes but, now, with this project, my chance was back. I would have an opportunity to read and write stories, hundreds of unique and compelling mini-dramas illustrating how this event touched people's lives in such different ways. It was a change of pace from anything I'd ever done before, and the days, late nights and weekends I worked on it for months thereafter unquestionably made it the biggest undertaking of my career.

Fortunately, for my clients, outside of this litigation, I had no life. I was now embroiled in divorce proceedings, with nothing promising on the romantic front, no children, no significant assets, much-neglected friendships and hobbies, and almost no other legal work. Other than for the cat my ex-wife left behind, my Unocal clients had my near-undivided attention.

But I told myself it was fine, that I was fine. I'd always been sort of an obsessive, ultra-focused guy anyway. Plus, putting my life on hold for just a bit longer for a good cause seemed like a sensible idea, as did transcribing my clients' tales of woe into word-processing templates as a surrogate for some of my own honest introspection. At the time, this all seemed perfectly sane, maybe even noble and compassionate on my part. Looking back now, however, working at this feverish book-a-week pace was terribly unhealthy, and I was utterly miserable. Even sadder, my only solace was the fact that many of my clients were miserable too.

And, yet, isolating myself, physically and emotionally, for months was probably the best way to tackle such a project. I didn't want distractions, and I'd been plugging along like this for a few years already. And who could speak with these people quite like I could? They lived like I lived. I never had money; these clients never had money. They never had a voice before—nor did I. I could identify with them and communicate with them in a way I was sure that my rivals—the other attorneys vying for as much of the settlement as they could get—simply could not. I mean, what did some rich lawyer with a nice home and a Rolex know about struggling each month to make rent? That lawyer probably didn't have my problems or my clients' problems. I remembered the refinery tour. I remembered their fancy cars. The probably weren't defaulting on *their* student loans.

Undoubtedly, we were in different leagues in that regard, and I thought that made me the better advocate for this crowd. These lawyers went to good schools and probably never had to wash their clothes in bathtubs because they couldn't afford the laundromat. They probably never had to take back used clothing for refunds just to afford food. Those were my stories, not theirs. I could really *talk* to the victims, and yet, was also trained to converse eloquently with judges. If I put enough money in my clients' pockets to get them proper medical treatment, maybe even get them out of Crockett, it wouldn't be the result of Ivy League word-smithing. It would come from knowing how to build their trust and draw them out, and then translate their little voices into a vocabulary the judges could understand.

Working around the clock as I did, it helped that there wasn't much outside to do, with winter starting and all. I worked best at home anyway, sitting alone in sweatpants and a T-shirt at a wobbly table in my shabby one-bedroom apartment, my lonely cat pining for more attention, distracting me often with his incessant meowing. Most cold mornings around Christmas that year, there I'd be, my coffee, bagel and a thesaurus within reach, my eyes locked onto my computer screen for hours, wrestling with every paragraph to make each new story vibrant and special.

Early mornings were when my creative juices flowed best, so it's then when I'd begin my days, routinely beating the sun by at least an hour. Winter daylight was short anyway, and so I was determined to waste no time starting the day's frantic journaling. I'd push my breakfast down into the toaster and have gamed out my morning before it jumped.

While eating, I'd work. While sipping my coffee, I'd work. I'd break every couple of hours to stare out the window for a minute or two, just to re-adjust my eyes, and then back to the screen. Sometime, usually just before noon, I'd throw on something casual and drive the dozen blocks to my equally shabby office where, until the close of business, I'd meet with staff, edit their write-ups and return client calls.

Evenings were spent back at home, distilling medical records, grabbing anecdotes from client conversations along the way, determined to paint their pre-Catacarb lives as exciting and hopeful but their futures desperate and bleak—and then sticking a suggested price tag on each head. I wasn't oblivious to the fact that just giving money to sick people was an unavoidable shortfall in the system, but that's all the judges could do, and they wanted individual demands.

But we had to be careful; if we asked for too much, we might get our hands slapped and a client's award sizably cut as a penalty. If we asked for too little, we just might get only that amount. But, if we did this right, many seriously injured victims could walk away with six-figure, tax-free recoveries. That would be a game changer for people barely making minimum wage.

Luckily, I've never needed much sleep, and, once I'm on a roll, I rarely take breaks. The flat where I lived had horribly poor soundproofing, so I'm sure I became a greatly appreciated, model tenant—never a peep. For that reason, the people in the other three units never knew exactly what I was up to, although they could see I was home a lot. I'm certain that I was "that weird guy in unit B who never goes anywhere" that everyone talked about in hushed tones. But they never directly pried into what I was doing. I think they were afraid the answer might be too bizarre to handle. Nevertheless, probably noticing I seemed depressed, the other tenants showed concern each time we did cross paths. That was particularly so for the Haitian couple just below me.

The couple hadn't been in the U.S. for long, and, so, isolating myself as I did must have seemed peculiar to them, being from a more interactive culture. They must have worried a lot about me since they would routinely bring me paper plates adorned with the most delicious home-cooked meals. I figured they equated reclusion with fasting or other poor eating habits, and they were probably onto something there. I could always smell when it was dinner time for them, and then, 30 minutes later, a knock on my door told me it was feeding time. Usually, it was Ronel, the husband.

Each night he'd stop by, I'd answer and act surprised that he and his wife had thought of me, and he'd smile back with his huge white teeth. We'd exchange pleasantries just long enough for me to graciously accept my supper, let him know everything was okay, and then slowly close the door. In the several years that I lived in that building, only twice did I head downstairs to eat *with* them, but they never took it as rudeness on my part. I think they knew I was biding my time, waiting for something big. Maybe they just knew I needed help.

I know that I should attribute some of my success in that case to them bringing me those dinners, allowing me to forego breaking from my work to grocery shop or get takeout. I also thank them for introducing me to some of the best spicy fish, plantains and rice I've had in my life, not to mention convincing me that someday I ought to see the part of the world they were from. Most importantly, however, their visits reminded me that there were things—people, food, places—out there, eagerly waiting for me when this torturous work was done.

Opening a card table and putting out a pot of coffee for my clients felt like I was setting up for an A.A. meeting. The JAMS panel of judges had given us a schedule for when we'd present each of our Serious Injury clients, and it included assorted dates from December through April. *So much for wrapping this up any time soon*, I thought, but at least the time line provided a slight breather just after the holidays so as to get most of our people ready.

Clients had been grouped, roughly 20 each day, for presentations in San Francisco. I arranged a separate meeting for each cluster, to be held at my office, a couple of weeks before each group's special day. The clients were required to show for these prep meetings or offer a really good reason why not. I wasn't willing to go in cold to hearings this critical, and I wasn't about to let them practice their speeches by telephone. Working out the non-verbal component to their performance was key.

Also key was getting them to let go of whatever fear they might be harboring about disclosing sensitive details to strangers. As a lawyer, a speech major in college, and a competitive debater in high school, I knew what could happen during a presentation. I had seen people fold under pressure when it counted, and I simply couldn't have that here.

I needed to push these folks beyond their comfort zone in practice runs, and that meant doing this publicly. As such, these meetings were to impart information as much as they were to elicit an emotionally charged rehearsal of each show. For these reasons, everyone simply had to be there.

I always set meetings on weeknights and asked parents to leave their kids at home. Whereas we'd identified several children as Serious Injury plaintiffs, I suggested their parents appear on their behalf. Children shouldn't have to retell stories of their pets dying, or watching mom and dad struggling with illnesses, especially to strangers. These were the same kids who'd sat on their parents' laps in those town-hall meetings and heard the crying and cursing at Unocal's spokespeople. It'd be cruel to take them back there. Plus, these pre-hearing meetings were the only practice we would have for the real deal, just weeks away. I wanted parents to express themselves freely and show their vulner-abilities. That would be hard to do if they had to worry about looking strong for their families.

From Crockett, my little island town of Alameda was a substantial drive—nearly 30 miles south on one of the most gridlocked freeways in California, and then over a little metal drawbridge that seemed perpetually raised. I worried the distance might be demotivating, but they came. Even the ones who'd moved away after the releases, who were being asked to drive hours to get here—they showed up too. Everybody knew what was at stake, and they must have foreseen how uncomfortable the meetings might be. That they came anyway spoke volumes about their commitment. At a point when I'd gotten fed up with complaints from so many of the cash-out recipients, it was refreshing to see really injured people arrive at our prep meetings still ready to power through.

Being a plaintiff's lawyer means being an educator and public speaker by trade, at least if you intend to have any success in the court-room. Knowing most of my clients had little practice with these skills but demanding they sit in the hot seat and talk openly about intimate, embarrassing life details felt insensitive, sometimes even a tad voyeuristic. On the flip side, this was the optimal way of desensitizing them to what was coming. If they were brave enough to open up to friends and neighbors, they could easily reveal themselves to some retired jurists they'd never meet again. I told myself the ends justified the means. Showing up proved to me that they agreed.

I'd also asked each Serious Injury plaintiff to prepare a personal written testimonial, a couple of pages at best, with no other guidelines except to dig deep and be authentic. Each client's dossier for the judges' panel would include this statement. I thought it would add an important personal touch that would distinguish them from the hundreds of claimants from other firms, and we needed every advantage we could get. I asked everyone to bring their testimonials to these prep meetings to serve as talking points, maybe even a crutch. In reality, it was a ploy to make sure they got them done and to reduce the number of last-minute no-shows.

Between November and March, I hosted a lot of these meetings, with little differentiating them except, of course, the stories. Upon arrival, I'd ask each attendee to quickly take one of the chairs I had arranged in a big circle, support-group style, around the room. While they dutifully, nervously complied, opening these gatherings with a few minutes of dedicated social time might have been smarter. Diving right in as we did left everyone too restless and inquisitive about the other participants' identities to fully concentrate on my directions or to be as brave at the outset as I'd hoped.

As the last client at each meeting took a seat, I'd launch into a description of the hearing process and my expectations, and then take a show of hands for who wanted to volunteer first. Never more than one or two hands went up, and it wasn't long before I was prevailing upon people to speak up to keep the ball rolling. These first few presentations were never fluid, but I didn't step in to relieve their jitters. They had to find their own way. They needed to know they could do it.

I'd heard each of their experiences reported before, often several times. First, I heard them when each client retained my office. Later, we discussed them over the phone, usually when we'd call for an update on their condition. That might happen several times per client. Then, when we vetted them to participate in the Serious Injury hearing process, we'd discuss their claims again. Now, I wanted to hear it in person. I had to make sure, when they sat down in front of those judges, they wouldn't freeze up, and practice makes perfect.

In fact, practicing now was more important than ever. It'd been more than three years now since the Catacarb release, and people with ongoing symptoms—chronic headaches, dry-eye syndrome, PTSD, frequent nosebleeds, were inclined to downplay them. Living this way was just part of their new lifestyle, and they were a little tired of talking about it. These practice sessions were calculated to fire them up again, to remind them that this *was* a big deal. They were also good opportunities to impart a few theatrical tips to make their performances more rousing and to square their recollections with the facts and time lines as I knew them.

While I insisted they come to the meetings, I wasn't going to guilt or threaten anyone into speaking. I'm not even sure it would have been legal to force public disclosure of their private medical information but, luckily, I didn't have to. A little nudge now and then did the trick. It had to be tough sharing such intimate descriptions with people they might see around town, but they knew why they were there.

Some tragedies, like the Arnetts' loss, were more poignant and took longer to draw out, but everyone was a little apprehensive. There wasn't an evening I didn't hear about a failed marriage, some physical or emotional wound that left the person unable to work, a chemical sensitivity so pronounced that he couldn't walk into public places like supermarkets or drug stores without having an intense reaction to the smells.

One man, a former amateur triathlete, reported that he gained dozens of pounds because he was now virtually unable to exercise. As someone who'd made fitness a huge part of his life, I felt particularly bad for him. Another lady developed an OCD causing her to scratch herself frequently. Apparently, she worried constantly about what airborne things might be landing on her skin. Lotions didn't help much; they just made her feel sticky and heightened her concern about what was on her. She jumped right in with her narrative; others were closed off and required more coaxing but were, ultimately, relieved to have shared. That was the benefit of bringing them together. In one way or another, the fellowship softened everyone.

Predictably, those with the most heinous and humiliating injuries were most at risk of shrinking once in front of the judges, and I worried this reflex would unfairly translate to smaller recoveries. The presentations were going to be capped at roughly 20 minutes. Whatever didn't come out in that short time would never come out. These judges weren't going to make the plaintiffs' cases for them or dig for data not put right under their noses. The panel was there to listen, evaluate and make rulings but not investigate or advocate for anyone. It'd be me who'd play gatekeeper for what they heard, and, whatever I failed to elicit would be my clients' loss.

At our evening meetings, particularly for these at-risk victims, the ones most embarrassed and reluctant to share, I suggested the group give them a little more breathing room, more time to find their rhythm. I worried the most for Mike Arnett—that he might freeze up. He didn't though. He was great. The couples joining us for that particular session interlocked fingers tightly and held their breath as Mike honored the short life of his son. He could more easily talk about it now and I was proud that I'd had something to do with that.

Unlike at his previous visit to my office, Mike held it together this time. I thought hearing details about Vincent again would be less sickening since I knew how the story ended. It still made even Mike nauseous but he got through it, and Nicole was right there by his side. That seemed promising. I wasn't worried any more about their marriage.

Ms. Boucher, who'd lost her husband due to Catacarb exposure, was there too, at another meeting. She came alone. The veil of confidentiality is pierced when people beyond the attorney and client are in the room, but I found myself wishing she'd brought a friend, at least to wait outside. Her soft, lamenting presentation about missing her partner and best friend moved almost every couple to tears.

When I first met Ms. Boucher, she was just starting her emotional journey through the stages of grief. She'd lost her husband of 26 years and was still very angry. Now, three years later, she'd apparently reached Acceptance. Oddly, I found it was easier to hear her description when she was still mad. It's always easier to hear victims' stories when they're mad since the anger takes center stage, distracts you. The venom directed toward their accused allows you to keep up your own walls so the anguish doesn't penetrate. That evening, however, she was just hopeless and empty, and the rest of us were inescapably pulled into the horrible void.

I wasn't skilled at leading this kind of support group, but, fortunately, I didn't need to be. Except for a few early, gentle invitations to open up, the group members' longing to commiserate was beautifully self-sustaining. Prior to our first meeting, I envisaged these assemblies devolving into bitch-sessions, but I worried for nothing. Group members nurtured and brought out the best in each other, evoking a startling degree of resilience and emotional bravery.

Susan's group embodied this.

It must have been meeting number three or four at my office. It was mid-January, and cold and dark outside as we sat for another evening in my poorly ventilated office. Introductions had been made, my prefatory speech given, and a few clients, including a 40-something-year-old, soft-spoken, divorced woman named Susan, had already taken their turns. One of the men was sharing an experience from his work when Susan leapt from her chair, her nose dripping blood and a look of horror on her face.

With her hand over her nose, she bolted out the door, muttering something incomprehensible, frantic to find a restroom. Everyone present, startled and wide-eyed, quickly panned the room for answers that never came. We knew this was Catacarb's fault; we just didn't know what to do.

As the energy subsided and a bleak, albeit awkward calm fell over the room, some people looked to me for direction, while others just stared at the floor, absorbed in memories of their own experiences and in a funereal capitulation to the fact that they were all in this together. I had no script for this, but, as the ostensible man-in-charge, I thought I should offer some pedestrian sympathies about the inequity of it all, hoping to get us back on track. My toolbox was limited and was forced to grab the first blunt instrument I could find.

After what seemed like a sufficient breather, I asked if the gentleman speaker wished to finish. Clearly, he'd been upstaged, but he tried to go on, more disjointed now, fumbling for the right words, no flow. I figured Susan would be back when she was ready.

Sure enough, Susan tiptoed back in around five minutes later, apologizing profusely for the interruption and for, I guess, being a human being in trouble. By that time, yet another guy, Jeff, was hunched over, elbows on his knees, humbly telling the circle about his ailments as Susan quietly passed through, a clean, neatly folded paper towel in her hand—just in case—and retook her seat.

As she settled in, a woman next to her touched Susan's shoulder, leaned in and whispered something about it being all right. Susan returned a demure "Thank you" but then quickly straightened up. She didn't want to steal the show any more. She didn't think she was special or deserving of the limelight when so many of her friends and neighbors had suffered too.

Jeff watched this exchange as he wrapped up his own state of affairs, trailing off with some concerns about his family's future and how his heart went out to people like Susan. Appreciating the recognition, Susan smiled meekly, but Jeff wasn't done. Recognizing her embarrassment over the scene she'd made, Jeff reached into his pocket, pulled out a handkerchief, flaunting it, his eyes locking on Susan, narrowing. Not sure yet of its significance, Susan cautiously regarded the white cloth in Jeff's hand as he made his point clearer. "Believe me. We understand," he said, as tears welled up in Susan's eyes, her lips quivering. It was a gesture too touching for words, and so no one dared offer any.

My ancillary role as the nights' cheerleader compelled me to end each session on an uptick. We'd sat there for a few hours each time, and it was always draining. I thought bestowing some profound but uplifting observations might be a nice, light finale after each evening's difficult journey. Perhaps tying it up that way might help my clients briefly forget about the nosebleeds and their shaky hands and their vision problems—all the stuff we'd just discussed, *ad nauseam*. Perhaps an upbeat summary would permit them to drive home in peace, but, in actuality, the bow I tied on each night's sharing was for me. I didn't want to feel guilty for pressuring them to unpack all that baggage.

So, I summarized what we'd heard, noting the commonalities, covered a few logistical matters, and expressed appreciation for them placing their trust in me. And I explained what they were doing was rare—enjoying the benefits of settlement and avoiding the potential of defeat at trial, but still getting their "day in court." They'd be given a safe forum in which to vent their frustration and point fingers all they wanted, and to an audience of judges who'd be captivated by their stories. I explained it really was the best of both worlds.

Finally, I reminded them that the first time any of them got an audience to their grievances was at those town-hall meetings, and that could not have been satisfying. There, getting attention required shouting, crying and threatening. There, nobody rewarded them for taking a stand. Through this litigation, by stepping up and hitting Unocal in the pocketbook, where it counted, they had changed all that. Now, they'd be getting their reward. After their short upcoming presentations, I knew I'd probably never see any of them again. In the evenings, at my office, while I still had their attention, I wanted them to fully grasp what they'd achieved.

CHAPTER 26
NO CLARENCE DARROW

To my mind, there are litigators, and then there are trial lawyers, and they are very different breeds. Once in a while, you'll run across the attorney who is both, but it's rare.

The skill set of a great litigator includes first-rate research and writing abilities, a nuanced understanding of discovery procedures, and the creativity to game out multiple scenarios, seeing several moves ahead. Litigators file the lawsuits, gather the evidence and build the cases, arguing motions and taking depositions along the way. They approach their work in a cerebral manner, but they usually see the end-game as settlement. In fact, it is not uncommon for a litigator to partner with a trial attorney once it's clear the case requires the verdict of a judge or jury. It is also not uncommon for an overly confident litigator to assume he can do it all, try his case, and lose miserably.

Great trial lawyers, by contrast, are like stage actors. Is that too noble? Well, maybe more like film or even soap stars, but rarely as strikingly good-looking or suave. They don't need to be powerful writers, but they have to understand human psychology, how to connect with lay people and how to weave dull facts into riveting, conspiratorial tales of deception, neglect and greed. They also need to artfully draw out witnesses, eliciting painful storytelling or, conversely, disclosures against interest during brutal cross-examination. If you live too much

347

"in your head," you won't be a great trial lawyer. You need to get outside yourself, be flamboyant, a facilitator, a translator of sophisticated legal concepts into stuff even a schoolkid would understand.

If you tell people outside of the legal profession you are a litigator, they seldom know exactly what you mean. Telling them you are a trial attorney, however, immediately evokes all kinds of images and scenes from television shows. Yet—and I probably don't need to point this out—trying a case has almost nothing in common with what's depicted on TV. Yes, of course you're expected to question witnesses, make objections and, if you're a real hotshot, present a blistering closing argument. You don't, however, get to threaten your opposing counsel in open court, date the judge, prance around and talk directly to jurors, or berate witnesses relentlessly in hopes they'll break down and confess their sins. Even try to do those things, and you'll get lambasted, fined or thrown in jail.

If I was anything at this early point in my career, I was a budding litigator—but one who longed to be a trial lawyer. In school, I read about Clarence Darrow, the iconic trial advocate, and I dreamed of being what he'd been—a controversial defender known for taking on the tough, unpopular cases, and winning through brilliant oratory. I wanted to be exalted for my masterful courtroom interrogations and exposé of all things unjust, and I thought I had the fundamentals for it. I aced my Evidence class in law school, so I knew my way around an objection, and my undergraduate communications degree and years of debate competition provided the groundwork for reading audiences well and thinking on my feet. What's more, I loved a good fight.

Still, by the time of the first Serious Injury hearings in December, I was far from finding my legs as a courtroom star. I'd conducted just one trial by that point, and it hadn't gone smoothly. I won, but probably out of sheer luck. I fumbled with documents, made grandiose speeches aimed at massaging my ego, and posed lavish, interminable questions that left my client's performance on the stand choppy. I was afraid to trust the system, or my client preparation, and I tripped over my own feet. With such a dismal performance under my belt, I wondered what skills I'd possibly bring to bear in the hundreds of hearings now being set, and if my youth and inexperience were finally going to be the death knell for my clients' chances at any sort of real vindication.

Thanksgiving came and went way too fast, and the first day of our Serious Injury hearings was rapidly approaching. Judge Monroe was completely out of the picture. So was Unocal. Settlement papers were fully signed and filed, and cash-out payments were underway. We were definitely in the 11th hour now, and the pressure to handle this one last ordeal correctly was causing me a lot of anxiety.

Sandy, my devoted office assistant, accompanied Doug and me on the inaugural day of hearings. She'd been working for my office for about a year at this point, and for not a lot of money. Her down-home Southern charm and easy rapport with the clients was invaluable though and, as much to streamline the hearing process as it was a bonus for her hard work, I invited her along for the kickoff. With so much to do each day of hearings, we needed someone there to help with the transitions and who knew the files and personalities like we did.

For each of the days we'd scheduled over the next several months, the judges' panel offered to start as early as 8:00 a.m. For me, that meant waking at 5:30 a.m. to suit up, eat and organize a couple-dozen files for each day. The panel also said we could push the presentations well into each evening if we wanted. We took advantage of both offers, opting to power on through at an aggressive pace versus reserving more days.

All three judges showed up for our December 3 debut, a number which dropped to one or two for most subsequent sessions. Prior to calling our first witness, Doug and I sat across the conference table from our arbiters and talked casually about the ground rules and a few logistical matters. They also wanted to know, before we called any witnesses, what we thought about Unocal's conduct, how we got involved in the case, and which injuries we thought were most prevalent. I didn't hold back.

I explained that it was Ralph's call to me years before that started everything, that blew the lid off Unocal's attempt to cover up, and then downplay, its crimes. We talked about the angry town-hall meetings and how most of those residents then cursing the refinery were now my clients—me being first on the scene and having virtually unlimited choices of who I wanted to help. This was my effort to *prime* the panel—offering evidence veiled as interesting anecdotes and letting them steep, conditioning the judges to think it was my clients who were most vocal, *because they were the most hurt* and, thus, should get the most compensation.

For the same reason, I mentioned the Good Neighbor Clinic, how my clients were averse to trusting the doctors Unocal selected, and that maybe I had something to do with that. Important groundwork, I thought, for hearings where clients would say they didn't see GNC doctors. And I explained that I was mad at how the company handled, well, virtually everything. Sharing your personal attitudes with a judge would never happen in the courtroom, but this wasn't a courtroom. They asked for my thoughts about the company, and I had nothing to hide. Nor did the plaintiffs. They'd be eager to talk about their outrage. Being able to put it out there first would make my clients' intense reactions later seem more reasonable.

The informality of this introductory conversation was unexpected. During their decades on the bench, these judges probably never sat this close to any advocate, but I welcomed the ice-breaker. It was disarming and helped frame what we'd be doing ten hours each day, for many days over the next several months. Spending that much time together meant there would be little need to keep the process uptight and ceremonial.

In keeping with the informality, we agreed food was allowed in, something also foreign to courtroom proceedings, and that we'd work through lunches, taking bites as the witnesses talked. Our 20-minute delivery for each new case would be broken only by hasty introductions and farewells, sticking my head into the hallway to summon Sandy and the next claimant, and pouring more coffee. To keep the lineup in sequence, participants needed to arrive early and be ready to hit the ground running when we called their names.

Sandy greeted the clients as they arrived at the JAMS offices. She'd then usher them to a staging room and keep them calm until their appointments. As they waited, she'd refresh their recollection with records and dates, and ask them to rehearse their most compelling details. She was also charged with moving the order of presentations if a client was late or failed to show altogether.

Executed this way, these hearings marched at a cadence as reliable as a Swiss watch. As each presentation concluded, I'd walk the client the few steps to the door, and we'd shake hands goodbye as I hollered over my shoulder for Sandy. She'd escort another candidate to our room, make a fast introduction, and then duck back out as the judges and I dove in, not missing a beat. With this revolving door, there was little time for pleasantries. From banker boxes behind me, I'd grab the relevant dossier and then launch into unabashedly dramatic detail about how each new candidate was more wounded than the last.

For every one of these 230 Seriously Injured plaintiffs, I had their data points down cold, discerned each one's emotional triggers, and targeted those triggers liberally. I had no shame and few boundaries, drawing out credible emotional responses but trying to show empathy and respect. I changed up the order of facts frequently, keeping my delivery fresh and punchy, usually leading off with some whimsy about their pre-Catacarb lifestyle—as much for character development as a baseline to contrast how lousy their lives had become. I'd segue between topics, from their exposure circumstances, to property damage calculations, to their bitterness over the cover-up and destruction of their once-safe, once-peaceful community. I'd ask about their continuing health problems and the welfare of their kids, deliberately rousing their anxiety, hitting nerves and then, as if I didn't already know the response, posing sappy questions about how this awful injustice made them feel.

It was theatrical, fast-paced work, and far more sensational than the normal brief writing with which most new lawyers are saddled. Don't get me wrong—I don't hate writing legal briefs, but I always found that work dry, predictable and never particularly challenging. At these hearings, however, I got to question witnesses, often receiving remarkably unpracticed answers, compelling me to pivot and take the conversation in a whole different direction. And, no matter how many times we'd rehearsed this, they would offer anecdotes I'd never heard, sometimes in reaction to my questions, sometimes to the unrehearsed ones put to them by the panel.

Indeed, the process was surprisingly *unpredictable* and kept me on my toes. That's why I loved it. I was doing the trial lawyer-type work about which I'd always fantasized, the only differences being that I was presenting a couple hundred witnesses (in courtroom trials, you rarely call more than a handful) and that I was allowed to do it with a sandwich in hand.

Looking back now, I can't say five months and 230 hearings made me a crackerjack trial lawyer, but it sure taught me how to digest, organize and condense mountains of information, and to inspire people, letting them blossom while I shut up. But it was an evolution to get there. I came into the first Serious Injury hearing like a bull seeing red. Even after living with the case for years, there were clearly vestiges of the outrage I felt the day Ralph called me, and those inadvertently flavored my interrogation. I micro-managed everyone that first day, and I made mistakes. As a result, there were no client tears, no pauses for reflection. I didn't give any margin for them. I was wound too tightly, and I boxed the victims in so they could barely breathe.

By the following day, however, I was more adroit. I had counseled myself to calm down, remembered that this was *their* time. I sprinkled dashes of theater as needed, set the pace, and then hovered in the background. That day, I let *them* shine. The judges listened and empathized as three years of torment poured out, and it was gorgeous. It was then I knew that I was learning.

While it might not seem that tough, I also learned how to ask a question, just by watching. In courtroom trials, the judge stays relatively quiet during witness examinations, but, like I said, this was not a courtroom. Collectively, these judges had overseen more trials than any lawyer could present in a lifetime and, just by paying attention, I learned more about how to cull sensitive material than I would acquire in my next ten years of practice. For every five of my tedious inquiries, the judges would ask one and get about as much information.

They were real pros. They could disarm these witnesses, emboldening them to speak openly about their fears of living near a refinery, what the pollution did to them. They weren't verbose, ambiguous or pretentious. They'd ask, "What happened next?" or "How does that feel?" or they'd direct the subjects to "Tell us more about that" so that the witnesses never forgot they were the stars or got bewildered by a meandering interview. When you're a young lawyer, you think you have to look good, which you also think means being clever. These judges were past all that, and the casual rapport it engendered was awe-inspiring. Theirs was a warming approach, which elicited stories I'd never heard before—clients' accounts of forgetting the routes to work, panic attacks, sexual impotence and divorces.

As energizing as was riding this steep learning curve, my clients' bravery in speaking so openly about feelings many of them normally kept bottled up was even more thrilling. It was almost enough to make me forget that we'd probably failed them on the monetary end—almost.

I hadn't actually forgotten and, apparently, Judge Emerson, one of our panel judges, wanted to make sure I never did.

It was an early morning in January on roughly our fourth day of presentations. The client blocked for that 20-minute segment was M.I.A., and nobody else had arrived to step into the time slot. Judge Emerson had been present for every session thus far and was clearly comfortable enough to offer her interim evaluation of what she'd seen.

"Scott, these people are *really* hurt. I've seen so many of these cases now. I just can't believe this case was settled for such a low amount," she said, shaking her head in disgust and sighing heavily as she looked down at the profile of the next scheduled candidate. I was immediately horrified and froze in my chair.

Then, as if the gravity of her observation could possibly have been overlooked, she started up again, saying how there wouldn't be enough money to adequately compensate all the victims. She explained that her panel had some hard decisions to make, whereby some significantly damaged plaintiffs might receive big awards, but others might get little more than the typical Mid-level Injury claimant or even the cash-out amount. Having done the math, I already knew this was a distinct possibility. Still, hearing her announce that these residents might get punished for our Committee's mistakes felt like I'd been punched in the stomach.

Judges don't usually engage in Monday-morning quarterbacking over the parties' settlement decisions, so I wondered why she felt compelled to tell me this. Was she just appalled by what our Committee had done and couldn't help herself? Was she bracing me for the bad news I'd get in a few months once all the awards were calculated? Was she telling me this whole endeavor, at least from a financial standpoint, was a phenomenal waste of my time? A mix of humiliation and desperation came over me.

"I know. I agree with you, but mine was just one vote," I begged her to understand. Eager to have my association with the likes of Jim Harrison excused, I explained that I didn't appreciate being forced into this situation but that, by the time I was told about the deal, there was simply no going back. Still, I'd been found guilty, merely by association, and by virtue of this jurist, for whom I had immense respect, intimating I should have done more.

I also urged her to consider how appeals might delay resolution for years, how many of our theories were untested, and so on and so forth, but, still, her comments made me second-guess my choices. In that instant, just as Unocal couldn't whitewash its greedy actions, I felt polluted, ashamed of what our Committee had done. As much as I tried to dust myself off after her assessment and not let it faze me, the conviction stuck.

And yet, all things considered, and despite my unavoidable feelings of guilt, it's tough to say if she was objectively right—the part about us settling so cheaply, or her casting me as a conspirator in it. Obviously, Judge Emerson didn't have our vantage point, nor did she know how I'd been boxed in to supporting the deal. And what did she know about my own sacrifices—like my failed marriage, financial troubles, stunted career and risk of bankruptcy and malpractice lawsuits? While I couldn't reveal these things to her, I sure wished I could. I certainly didn't want her thinking I was a sell-out.

We chatted more in those minutes before our next appointment, and I tried everything to make her understand. I explained that, when I drafted the Complaint years earlier, the only remedy for these victims I foresaw was money but that my perspective had broadened. I said I saw a much bigger picture now and viewed the accomplishments in broader terms than just cash payments. I said that I hoped others, herself included, would view what we'd accomplished through the same lens.

I explained that, when we started out, my clients were merely *victims*, panicked participants at town-hall meetings, screaming at Unocal, begging for information and for help, but getting nothing in return but derision, evasion and more lies. It wasn't much different from the disregard little unincorporated Crockett and Rodeo had gotten from Unocal, the county and others for decades. But, then, we filed the case, and people everywhere heard about the company's greed and how it hurt, sometimes killed, its neighbors—and things began to change. Unocal buckled under the weight of public scrutiny, started to negotiate, and the residents took back their power. With a microscope now focused on its every move, Unocal got too uncomfortable to stick around, and it left.

I told her that, when the case started, and my clients spoke to me about their physical and emotional problems, I could hear their shame. Many of their injuries were a source of considerable embarrassment, and they were averse to giving much detail about them. For them to openly discuss those experiences oftentimes demanded they venture into uncharted levels of vulnerability. They weren't usually prepared for that, and I didn't blame them. The clients thought these delicate issues were best kept under wraps.

But now, at these hearings, they spoke with determination and conviction, like we'd practiced, and their voices didn't seem so faint anymore. Those with ongoing conditions were coming to terms with them. Those who'd lost loved ones to Catacarb—and there were more than a few—were coping better. Everyone still hated what the company had done, but they didn't feel as helpless today.

Finally, I reminded her that these communities had been garbage dumps for Unocal and other heavy industry for so long—the four chemical releases addressed in our litigation being only the most recent spikes in bad behavior. I pointed out that, until now, the residents had never taken action, never organized, and rarely spoke of the oil giant.

But they were speaking now, taking action and had organized in a way nearly unprecedented for such small towns.

My role was to provide the microphone—perhaps, more aptly, the bullhorn—so their voices could carry. With that instrument and, now, these hearings, their confidence was soaring, and they were accepting their new reality with dignity, and it was transformative. I told Judge Emerson that having effected all this change, vis-a-vis our lawsuit, was an enormous win, independent of any monetary award. My words weren't a bluff, and I wasn't playing hard-to-get; of course, we still wanted the money, but I wanted her to climb up and sit with me at the top of my new hill, where I could see more, where I could see further than just the settlement funds in front of us.

From my hilltop, I saw members of this community who had banded together and self-directed. I'd seen them force sweeping changes in how the oil business operates. These procedures were now being applied across the nation, and that would save lives. I'd seen the community improve its own schools, launch health studies, become the test market for a revolutionary air monitoring system, and send packing one of the planet's largest oil refiners. Viewed from my new vantage point, I explained, a haircut on the settlement money hardly suggested a *defeat*.

Whether I changed Judge Emerson's mind, I don't know. Most judges are excellent poker players, and I couldn't get a read on whether she saw any relevance of my big message to her task of carving up an $80 million pie. Theoretically, what I thought about either Unocal or these victims shouldn't affect her decisions, but I figured it couldn't hurt to try. My willingness to say the money was secondary might even have bolstered my clients' credibility, but my comments weren't that calculated. I just wanted the world to see what I saw.

In late April, we closed out the hearings, but decisions over who'd get what wouldn't come for several additional months. At least the clients' work was over though, as was most of mine, and it was fitting we'd end this way—right back where we started. My first experience with each person was, of course, hearing his or her story. All lawsuits start with a story—hopefully, a deliciously juicy one—but then the lawyers and the games and the court conferences and the legal-brief writing ramp up, and the personal tragedies are often forgotten. It quickly becomes all about which party can out-spend the other, which lawyer is most clever, and which side is first in shattering the other's will to fight.

Sometimes, following all that, you never hear the tragedies again. Some cases get quietly dismissed because the Complaint is poorly written and unsalvageable. Other times, cases settle with provisions to guarantee confidentiality such that the horror of what happened never comes to light. And, while I support settlement in many cases, it's maddening that the people most damaged are usually the ones *least* likely to get what we might call their "day in court." Companies simply don't want those stories publicized.

But this case was different. Here, people could talk freely—to me, to their neighbors, to the press and, now, to the judges, who really knew how to listen. The people got their day in court and, by releasing the emotion, by revealing themselves, their fears, their rage, they could start to be free of it, and they could be clean. Never since those injury hearings has it become as obvious to me: in the end, everyone just wants to be heard.

CHAPTER 27
MONTEREY

The day the injury presentations were over marked the end of the Unocal case, at least the heavy lifting—but not the waiting. By April, I had cycled through in-person hearings for 230 victims and documented, in painstaking detail, the claims of another 300-plus Mid-level claimants. I'd visited dilapidated homes in very bad parts of town after dark and suffered a lot of misdirected verbal abuse from people who were too proud to accept my help, yet too angry to see I'd forfeited everything. I was exhausted and, for the first time in years, I was ready to concede I was spent.

We knew other firms were still presenting their clients at Serious Injury hearings and, even after those were done, it could be months more before the judges would announce how much everyone would receive. If it ended there, it would be a very welcome event, but there was no guarantee of such finality. If anyone dared challenge the panel's allocations, it could take months, even years longer to resolve those issues before any money was paid out.

Badly in need of a break, the Friday after my last hearing, I got in my car and drove down to Carmel-by-the-Sea with no particular plan. Not that I stayed anywhere posh or did much more than sit on the craggy rocks at Pacific Grove and enjoy the salt mist off the crashing waves, but I saw this as my Entitlement trip. I deserved to not work, even if just for a couple of days and, going down there, I knew exactly what to expect. On a foggy day at that particular end of the earth, I had little choice but to be contemplative, and that was the point.

I had committed to this career nine years earlier when I stepped into my first lecture hall in law school, but here I was, my cold chin tucked into my parka, staring humbly at the rough sea, for the first time feeling that I had absolutely no direction. I had since launched another, simpler environmental case, also involving an airborne release, but it wasn't shaping up as planned, and the facts weren't sexy, not like Unocal's. I had also taken on a mélange of small legal matters, sporadically, over the past few years—ones that generally required little work and, consequently, paid out just enough to keep me afloat. Sitting there on that cold, mossy rock, however, I felt like an empty-nester, and I was feeling sorry for myself.

I thought a lot that day about what it meant to be professionally successful, how I would define that, how I would recognize it should it ever happen to me—introspective stuff, to be sure. I wrestled with a range of possible answers, none of which seemed particularly satisfying. Ever since childhood, I compulsively *moved* because, frankly, I was never taught how or when to stop. No one ever chalked a finish line for me. My parents always said I could do, literally, *anything*, and so I was eluded by measures of achievement. As a result, I've always run like a racehorse, and yet, what I was running toward was never quite clear.

Others, however, would say the destination should have been obvious. Those people—usually, the ones with high-paying jobs and nice cars—would say the goal is money. They'd say that being rich, or at least being "comfortable," means you've *arrived*. But, if that was true, if accumulation of wealth really was the end-all, then I hadn't achieved anything. I had booked a cheap motel for that night. I was poorer than ever.

I had credit cards on which I'd racked up significant debt for office supplies, and I was barely making rent. I had student loans, the collection agents for which were relentless. And I had almost no hard assets to offset any of it, or any money coming into my practice. My cases paid out only when I won or settled, and I'd won or settled little recently. I'd been way too busy with Unocal for those luxuries. By any *financial* measure, at least up to that point, I was an utter failure.

But that might be changing soon. My tax bracket might jump considerably in the next few months when the judges announced the awards to my clients and, by extension, the fee award to me. If there was a dramatic spike in my bank balance, what would that mean? Should that alter how I measured the value of the risks I'd taken? And, if my financial situation didn't change, if the awards were paltry, how would I deal with that? In that scenario, could I stay proud of the *struggle* and not be tempted to feel like a martyr?

Sitting there, I was equally depressed that these answers were clearer. They should have been obvious to me. Idealism has always been thick in my DNA. Shouldn't that make it easy to dismiss money as the yardstick for success? I mean, I could remember what I might call my *achievements* just as well when I was low on cash. And what if I made some real money but then lost it? I did have overdue bills to pay, you know. Would all that work for the communities of Crockett and Rodeo—the work upon which I might handsomely profit—become less important just because I turned around and spent the loot? No, this question wasn't so elusive. Cash and other physical keepsakes were great rewards for hard work, but they didn't *define* success.

Fame didn't either, or at least I thought. In fact, the prospect of becoming a celebrity never enticed me. What difference would it make if I was widely known, and was that even realistic here? The television and print news media had reported on my case many times, not that seeing my name in the papers was likely to make me notorious or leave anyone outside my industry remembering me for it. And, yet, what did I know about success at the age of 32? If my eminence quantified my achievement, then I'd failed there too.

From these musings, I realized I was probably over-thinking things, that I had probably always over-thought things, and that maybe I should work on that. This wasn't an elusive riddle; I already knew that success wasn't about possessions or whether others dropped your name at cocktail parties to sound important. Success was about discovering what *moves* you, what comes *naturally* to you—and then giving it your all. If your work is an extension of what makes you unique, the embodiment of what you love, then your reward is knowing you're in balance and without limits.

My dad had told something like that when I was a kid and, yet, over the past four years, I'd apparently forgotten his words. My victories felt almost like failures since I'd traveled through those years on auto-pilot, not stopping to smell the roses and not giving myself a pat on the back once in a while. I'd forgotten that success, at least as I was taught, was in the *doing* and was neither a point in time nor a finish line. And so, I never thought of myself as a success; I just finished one project and then segued immediately to the next. It left me lonely, uninspired and miserable.

But this day, on that rock, I was starting to feel different. I still felt melancholy, sure, but a haze was lifting. Maybe it was just getting away like this, short as the trip was. Maybe a forced stop was needed to wake me up, to take stock in what we had done. Doug and I had leapt without looking into something that was, at least ostensibly, way over our heads, but we came out the other side intact—more than just intact, perhaps. With the community's help, we ran an irresponsible company out of town, forever, motivated the development of industrial safety rules considered some of the most protective in the nation, coalesced chronically competitive towns, and warned other local players that they'd better not mess with Crockett. I'd spoke of these benefits before—to Judge Emerson, to others—but, for the first time, I felt *proud*.

On the drive back from Monterey Bay late Sunday night, I formulated some plans about how I might start living better. I had been existing hand to mouth for a very long time and, frankly, I was sick of it. The Steering Committee had agreed there should be no further delay in reimbursing each firm for its cost contribution, and that was exciting. Throughout the litigation, each member had given money to the group's war chest. My particular contribution was only $15,000, but getting that back all at once, and with interest, couldn't have come at a better time. With that money, I could pay off my overdue credit card bills, throw a few dollars at my lingering academic debt, and maybe even get a new office chair. My existing chair was broken, and I knew I'd be sitting a lot over the next several months, fielding telephone complaints about payout delays. The last thing I'd need was a bad back.

As I cruised back up the coast toward San Francisco, I also considered how I'd get my business back on track and, indeed, if I even liked environmental law, the field that had clearly dominated the last four years of my life. Championing an environmental cause wasn't by design. In fact, before the day Ralph called me, this area of practice had never entered my mind. When Ralph called me, I was a budding workers' rights attorney. That's how I first met him. An employee advocate was what I'd wanted to be ever since my second year of law school. That's what Anita Hill had been.

Remember Anita? Do you? And do you remember Justice Clarence Thomas—and the Senate confirmation hearings surrounding his Supreme Court nomination? Well, I was in law school when those hearings dominated television newscasts. And, like many of my law school classmates, I was fascinated by it, and with Anita's experience. Who wouldn't have been? Whether you believed her or not, her drama had all the prerequisites for a great Hollywood film, not to mention an excellent sexual harassment lawsuit.

In the early 1980s, Anita Hill worked for Clarence Thomas at the Department of Education and the Equal Employment Opportunity Commission. Anita was a workers' rights attorney back then, and Clarence Thomas was her supervisor.

In October 1991, during Senate confirmation hearings over Thomas' Supreme Court nomination, Anita was called to testify. The press had just leaked her interview by the FBI, which called into serious question Thomas' character. Given what she'd already revealed there, we knew this was about to get interesting.

Overcoming great pressure to keep her mouth shut, attacks to her credibility, and extremely aggressive interrogation, Anita testified Thomas sexually harassed her, talked often about pornographic depictions of sex with animals, films showing group sex and rape scenes and that he, generally, created a hostile work environment. Anita didn't ask for this attention, either in the workplace or at those hearings but, in giving such lurid details so publicly, she became a role model for millions of women and men alike.

I liked Anita's courage, that she didn't back down. I've always rooted for the underdogs, those who stood their ground. Against Unocal, that's what I tried to do. Anita's bravery seemed to motivate a lot of people. Mine seemed to have the same effect. If that was true, maybe it was worth the long hours. But perhaps I could motivate people who were a bit more appreciative, and without running the risk of signing up household pets and clients who were so quick to defect. That would be nice.

By the time I hit San Francisco, I realized that being the underdog, a role that fit me well, didn't require that I take on any particular cause or practice within any particular field of law. It just required that I do something calculated to level the playing field for otherwise power-less people. To achieve that, I realized that I had options. I didn't have to work in a context where I was fielding nasty phone calls, shuffling papers for a thousand clients a pop and compelled to call the State Bar on other lawyers. Theorizing that personal injury law might not be for me, I decided I'd call those Oakland attorneys who used to refer me workers rights' cases and see what they had to offer.

Monday, the next day after my coastal excursion, I got right to work making big plans. No more Unocal hearings meant I could move some other simmering, slower-moving cases to the front burner. Getting them to trial or settlement wouldn't be an overnight project, however, and my cash flow was still horrible. Reimbursement of my cost contribution was already heavily earmarked toward bills, and I didn't know how I'd market my practice without more income.

Four years earlier, I was a nascent practitioner, but I was building momentum; one case would conclude as others were heating up. I was just starting out but was already enjoying a well-choreographed waltz of legal proceedings that kept me busy and supplied enough receivables to keep me above water financially. What's more, I was starting to make a name for myself as a young, uber-aggressive advocate.

But Unocal took me out of circulation just when I was finding my rhythm. I spent the summer after the Serious Injury hearings trying to get back on beat, but the leads were gone. I had lost favor with the Oakland attorneys who had referred me those cases; apparently, I'd turned away too many of their clients these past years because I was too occupied feeding the environmental beast. I tried to rekindle that relationship, but it was too late.

Desperately, I called old clients. I called everyone. I put up ads. The cases I had pending were few, and the wellspring for new matters looked dry. I would have to scramble to make this work. Now, in my sixth year of practice, I felt my career was worse off than when I started out. I'd really doubled-down on Unocal and, now, I prayed every day that, when the judges' award letter showed up, I could pull myself out of the hole I'd dug.

To add insult to injury, as I searched for new business, the calls from my Unocal clients continued, and some were exhausting. The Serious Injury clients weren't complaining, but others harassed me and my workers incessantly. The people with skin in the game—the truly hurt, the ones with real damages, big medical bills—were thankful and patient. The others, the folks on the outer edges of exposure and the ones who were now feeling better, weren't so kind. "You'd better call those god-damned judges and do something," they'd insist or, worse yet, more accusations: "Why are you keeping my money?" as if I had expropriated their checks.

Usually, it was a cash-out client whose check hadn't arrived yet, or who now had buyer's remorse. Cash-out distributions were taking a lot longer than expected. Maybe she'd talked to her cousin, the impudent law student, who had no clue what he was talking about but still claimed I'd advised her wrong—and that he would have done better, if he just had his law license already. Sometimes, when I reminded those clients that shooting for more money would have meant a full-blown hearing, I'd be accused of *rigging the system* to keep them down. Clearly, those were no-win conversations, and the fact that our contract promised me one-third of everyone's financial recovery didn't help to boost their trust in me.

But the worst of it was when it was about their *kids'* money. My Lord! Judges routinely require minors' settlements be kept in trust accounts until they are adults. That's what our judge did, and it drove some parents mad. They wanted to spend that money *right now* and weren't concerned about what some judge said or whether their kids might need the funds later, for college, for a car, to get an apartment.

These parents would say this was *their* money and I needed to go and fix things so they could get at it, even if that meant confronting the judge or doing something shady.

So, that was my summer—listening to a lot of complaints, accusations and threats. Callers didn't seem concerned about The Cause, or clean air, or the new environmental regulations prompted by our lawsuit, and they certainly didn't consider me a champion of anything worthwhile. For them, I was the guy at whom they could yell strings of obscenities and launch non-sequiturial personal attacks, and then slam down the phone. At me, they could take out a lifetime of frustration because I was an easy target and a captive audience. I was the guy in power, an officer of the same system that had, in their minds, perpetually mistreated them and was now separating them from their objective. The things they would say were just horrible, to me as well as to my hard-working employees. Those rants were unfocused, unjust and vile.

And there was nothing I could do to stop the barrage of calls. I couldn't change their attitudes, and, so, if I was going to get through this period with my chin up, unjaded, I'd have to change mine. I'd have to grow a thicker skin; I adopted a duality, of sorts—a thicker skin when on the phone, while remaining hopeful about whatever I'd be doing next with my life. It wasn't magic. It just required tuning people out, not paying attention to the rants, remembering that their discontent wasn't about *me*.

That got easier when I heard the Serious Injury hearings had ended. As much as it threatened my focus for anything else, completing the hearing process was the best news imaginable. It meant the award letter was in the works. It meant, finally, everyone was going to get paid.

By late summer, my practice was starting to pick up again, which was great, but I wasn't ready to fully embrace it. I'd had no closure on the Unocal case. We'd finished a massive amount of work, then presented it all for the judge's consideration and then nothing—just crickets—for months now. Being in limbo after years of stress was making me feel very uneasy.

Money was starting to come in by this point from newer cases, and that was exciting, but my daydreams were far more enticing—visions of beaches on tropical islands with palm trees flaunting real coconuts, and people who didn't swear at me. I told myself that I was virtually there, among friendly islanders bringing me frosty drinks with miniature umbrellas in them, and who wore bright colors and smiled a lot. Everyone has this type of fantasy, but, whether I could actually play it out, at least briefly, would depend on the settlement letter. Until that showed up, these tranquil distractions would have to serve as my only reward.

As the weeks rolled by with no word from the judges' panel, I was starting to go stir crazy and badly needed a change. My weekend jaunt to Monterey was moderately relaxing, but I knew I needed a lot more than two days, and sometime soon, to reflect on this journey and to rejuvenate. I had law school buddies who had been working long hours for big firms and were burning out after just a few years of it. I didn't want that for myself.

Going into business alone, without a safety net or a boss, was my choice to walk a different path than my defense-side colleagues and, yet, if I was going to accept earning a small fraction of what they'd made these past years, I needed to believe a better quality of life was waiting for me. That better quality might have little to do with financial rewards, but it did involve *slowing down* to appreciate what I had now and what I had done. The first step in slowing down was getting out of Dodge, and for more than a two-day road trip. No matter what the judges thought of my work, whether it persuaded them to pay us well for our troubles, I was ready to check out.

CHAPTER 28
PAYOUT

An award of money is a poor elixir for pain and loss and, to this day, I feel compelled to apologize for this inadequacy in our legal system. In American jurisprudence, there is a legal maxim that, for every wrong, there is a remedy. The problem, however, is that the remedy, even when in the form of a dollar-for-dollar reimbursement or some kind of punishment, rarely makes the victim entirely whole, or happy. You see, most people don't want harm and then litigation; they really just want to be left alone.

When the award letter arrived one fall morning at my office, I remember wishing it was a Friday. This needed to be a celebration, on a day fit for celebrations, no matter what the letter said. Reading the judges' translation of my work and sacrifices into financial terms was a long-awaited event, and yet, it also felt a little anti-climactic. I had already, months before, tried to push away the significance of whatever sums might be in there, partly for fear of jinxing the outcome but mostly since our victory now seemed broader than just the financial payout. In essence, fighting the good fight, especially in the face of overwhelming odds, frequently abusive attorneys and some unabashedly offensive clientele, had sort of *become* the victory. But that's not to say I wouldn't be cashing my check.

I opened the envelope in private, unfolded the long letter cautiously and immediately started grinning, really grinning. I'd always joked that I went to law school to avoid doing math, but the hundreds of client awards were written in a language even I understood—lots of zeros. Money like this was going to be a game changer, to me, and to most of my blue-collar clients. I always told them to expect nothing but hope for the best. I hoped they'd taken that advice to heart since I wanted them now to be thrilled.

Within seconds of putting down my calculator, I directed my assistant to go out and buy several bottles of the most expensive champagne she could find. We had a lot more glasses to fill in those days, given the recent infusion of many new cases and several new staff members to work them. Most of my new hires had only lightly touched the Unocal case, but that didn't matter. I wanted them basking in the light right alongside the veterans. I also didn't care that it was a Tuesday or that we were barely pushing lunchtime. I needed to get this party started. We closed the office early and sat around our conference room table while I read some of the award highlights and thanked everyone who had been involved for their loyalty and perseverance.

The awards to each firm's clients were to be kept confidential from the remaining offices and the public, but I could tell already that our group had received some of the highest individual amounts available. What's more, by my math, it looked like our average payout per client might be the highest of any of the firms, the SoCals included. That fact alone felt great, but it paled in comparison to the stuff that wasn't mathematical. We had surpassed our own expectations and accomplished something huge here, with a modicum of money and experience.

I sighed in relief as I remembered how bleak it had looked just a year earlier, back when the settlement was announced, and it appeared that roughly $8,000 per client was what I'd be delivering to people whose families had been ripped apart. I had never let on about those fears to anyone and, now, I'd never have to. I'd worried for nothing. The millions of dollars itemized in the judges' letter would compensate people handsomely and would validate their experiences. For four years, I'd waited for this reality-check that what Unocal had done was tragic, not to mention some objective statement that I hadn't totally botched the case. With this letter, I got both.

As we drank, I told stories from the Serious Injury hearings—some sad, some funny—and offered my perspective about all that we'd accomplished. I said it was *monumental*. Sandy echoed the characterization and proudly chimed in from time to time, excitedly adding dimension to the proud but often heart-wrenching events we witnessed. Among this team, only Sandy had been fortunate enough to see the hearing process unfold close-up, and from start to finish, but I needed the others to understand the gravity of what the refinery had done, how its effects had changed lives and the victories the community had achieved under our leadership. I'd seen, firsthand, what little voices can do when pushed too far. For my new workers, I wanted to make true believers of them as well.

Ours was a great party and, naturally, it was my job to keep this gathering upbeat. And, yet, I was worried. No amount of "Atta boys" and self-congratulation could alleviate my dread that relaying even such outstanding results to clients might leave some of them indignant. Some of the plaintiffs still couldn't work. Some of their physical and emotional conditions were permanent. Even these sizable awards might be considered an affront to some, despite their promises when joining the suit not to make it about the money. As we sat with our champagne, we debated how we'd address that.

Still sober enough to make good decisions, however, we closed out our celebratory afternoon with a solid game plan. First, we'd separate the clients who'd get phone calls from those who'd just get letters. Awards that were low but predictable got a letter; they could call us back with questions if that was warranted. Everyone else got a call. I would handle the people with whom I'd cultivated closer relationships, as well as those receiving extraordinarily high awards. I was the boss, and I needed to gloat. That was my prerogative. Plus, I was desperate for some appreciation after listening to so many people bemoaning for so long over the delays.

Not wanting to be a complete elitist, however, I would take some of the potentially difficult calls too. These were the people that no amount of money could fully compensate. These were the Arnetts, Ms. Boucher, the people with whom I sat in depositions, the chronically ill. This wasn't a small group, but I needed to make those calls myself. These required a nuanced approach that was simply beyond my entry-level workers' skill sets. And, when you get down to it, I was the one these people hired, not my college-aged file clerks. To my surprise, even the hardest hit of these victims seemed content with the awards, but should that have been such a revelation? It's not like many people would be terribly upset about six-figure awards, especially when considering the limited fund with which we had to work.

It took us a little more than two weeks to make the calls—scores of them—and the thrill factor increased after each "Thanks, and good luck." As my list got shorter and shorter, I started to wonder what I might do with myself after this was over. As for the calls that my employees made, those were moving fast too. To avoid any complications, I gave my staffers a script to follow. It did little more than communicate the award, explain that checks would go out shortly, and thank the clients for trusting and being patient with us. From what I heard, that's all the information those victims needed. The calls my workers made were just as low drama as mine. Frankly, I think everyone had just had enough.

As a guy normally fixated on efficiency, I would normally have delegated every one of these calls. Handling the day-to-day management of more than a thousand plaintiffs was precisely why I needed office support, but this was different. I needed the kudos, the personal validation—not so much for the work quality but for the not-giving-up part, the not-giving-in. I needed to hear that they noticed. They didn't know about my divorce, or me sitting at my computer on cold mornings and feeling painfully alone, but I quickly realized they didn't have to. Their "thank you's" made detailing my sacrifices unnecessary.

Before I started my calls, I gamed out a few scenarios, how I'd address inevitable questions, whether some moral to the story should be advanced. I even wondered if I should come clean about my steep learning curve over these years. You see, until these conversations, I thought I was fooling people. I was sure my clients had no idea how young and inexperienced I really was since no one had ever asked. In these calls, for whatever reason, I thought they deserved to know.

But, apparently, they already did, and I didn't have to make these calls confessional. It was obvious. They'd heard about my small office. Many had come to see it. Others had even heard the SoCals derogating me years earlier, for my under-whelming experience and resources. These people knew what they were getting when they hired me and, despite choices, they stuck with me. That was my final victory—that they took my advice regarding their medical and legal and financial affairs anyway, and that they shared with me their most intimate life details, even though they knew it was financially and emotionally risky. Somehow, they were convinced I was the one most likely to get results.

But their final victory, of course, was getting paid and, I hoped, using the money for something meaningful. The kind of money some of the residents got would have allowed for some big changes—leaving town, returning to school, leaving dead-end jobs, getting better medical care. I didn't ask much about their plans. I didn't think it was my place to do that, nor did I intend to circle back to find out whatever became of them. I felt the appreciation, to be sure, but there were no hugs, no promises to "stay in touch."

With my last client call, I was done with the lawsuit and never kidded myself that I'd hear from any of these people ever again. And, for the most part, I never did. I knew the attorney-client relationship wasn't supposed to be a friendship, and, yet, I felt a bond and a tremendous responsibility to make sure they got what they came for, be that cash or merely to regain their dignity. It was mission-critical to me that, when they said their "goodbyes" to me and to this litigation, they did it feeling hopeful and, if called upon, willing to do it all over again.

My employees handled the remaining accounting to get everyone promptly paid, and it went without a hitch. I had to oversee setting up trust accounts for the children with more sizable awards. That was labor intensive too, but a kind of routinized work that didn't tax my patience in the way other projects had done. We stripped the war room walls of its maps and checklists and silly motivational posters, packed away client records and shredded nearly everything else.

And then came the day—a moment, in fact—when it was unmistakable, and irreversible. I sat at my desk one afternoon and could think of absolutely nothing that needed to be done for any of the nearly 1,100 people for whom we'd fought so hard, many of whom we'd gotten to know well, engaged in hours upon hours of conversation, watched cry in front of us. It was unnerving. It wasn't like me to lack creativity. I looked around my office suspiciously, as if I'd forgotten something important.

For a moment, an anxiety enveloped me, crept into my bones and made me jittery. There had always been something to do, but not now. I pushed back my chair slightly and looked out at those train tracks than ran in front of my building for inspiration, hoping the nostalgia of seeing those rusty rails would calm me. They reminded me of Ralph.

I had recently put in motion the relocation of my growing firm to Oakland, to a more luxurious space, and I knew I'd miss those train tracks; they were my only view during those difficult years. And as the sentimental moment passed, so did the leaden feeling, and I knew it was time to move on.

My desk was normally covered with Unocal files. Now, it was virtually spotless, save for the predictable office gear and telephone directory. Instinctually, when bored, I'd grab a Unocal case file and make some sort of a plan, devise a project. Now, there were no more projects.

This four-year adventure started with me grabbing a telephone book. Today, I grabbed one again, but not to expose any corporate misdeeds. Today, I just needed a good travel agent. I needed a real break—and real time to reflect and figure out what my next chapter should be about. A weekend down the coast again wasn't going to cut it, and it'd been four years since I'd had anything more than Monterey. Until now, to wish for more would have seemed frivolous, an unnecessary expense, an exercise of poor time management. In hindsight, working without a respite seemed crazy.

Remembering what my neighbor, Ronel, had suggested—about me visiting the region he was from—I hastily booked an extended vacation between three islands in the lower Caribbean Sea, effortlessly persuaded a friend to join me, and we made plans to spend the next six weeks alternating between being beach-going sun-seekers and mountain rainforest explorers. Purposefully selecting islands where tourists were sparse, I already knew the trip would provide the detox I'd been craving.

My financial reward for the lawsuit had far surpassed my expectations, and, so, I felt entitled to live large, maybe just for this short time before I had to get back home and act like a grown-up again. Not wanting any distractions, I positioned my new cases and paid bills such that no one would likely need me while I was away. My employees would run things, holding down the fort while I was gone and contacting me only in a real emergency. Attending to these final details was liberating. For the first time in four years, I was finally starting to let go.

Feeling like a little kid counting down days to his birthday, the ones prior to my departure moved at a glacier's pace, making the morning of our outbound flight doubly exciting. I recall it was a Friday—a day fit for celebrations—when my friend and I boarded that plane out of San Francisco International for the islands. I booked it that way on purpose, despite the higher-priced weekend fares. Fridays mark the end of most people's work weeks, but I'd worked nearly every evening and weekend since I filed the lawsuit. I wanted to change that too. Leaving on a Friday to do something fun was my way of thumbing my nose at this tradition. Achieving the symbolism was worth the few extra bucks.

In almost every conceivable way, I designed this trip to demarcate the end of a chapter, and milestones like that tend to breed some nostalgia. As our plane ascended and banked out of San Francisco airspace, heading east, my eyes were glued to the scenery below. As I zoned out, I couldn't help thinking about what some of my clients were probably doing at that moment and how things might change for them. I flashed back to Ralph and, of all things, a fictional vignette of his dog furiously scratching its fur. And I thought about the ripples generated by one phone call and how I was, luckily, in the perfect position to have done something about it when Ralph's particular call came in. Until this moment, the weight of responsibility over so many people felt heavy, sometimes even suffocating.

That's why I needed this trip. I needed to feel light, and I was proud that I was now able to admit it. And I was starting to feel very light. I didn't care anymore about the SoCals or about the Kenecke lawyers' *quid pro quo* approach to litigation, nor was I thinking about the F-bombs so many of my clients dropped on me when I explained their settlement checks had yet to arrive. Instead, I was thinking about how, in this career, with the right attitude, a risk-taker's approach and a large enough war chest, I could do almost anything. And, of course, I was thinking about how checking out for more than a month on tropical islands—not to mention drinking champagne in the First Class cabin—was, for a guy raised as I had been, pretty cool.

As the clouds started blocking my view of what we were leaving behind, I began to grin. I realized then that I wasn't mad, or melancholy or feeling trapped anymore. Settling in at cruising altitude, I was prepared for an adventure that would forever put Crockett behind me. I'd wanted that for a while and yet, oddly, I felt a longing. I missed feeling needed. I knew, when the Unocal case was over, I'd be done with the fevered pace, the working without sufficient funding, the politicking. I wouldn't miss those. Helping elevate this community, returning to them some of their dignity—that I'd miss. I knew then that I'd forever be on the side of the people. Sitting back in my seat and closing my eyes, I felt full, proud of what we had done, but mostly, toward the people of Crockett, toward the people who took a chance on me, I felt grateful.

CHAPTER 29
GONE

Little-known Dominica is the youngest and most mountainous island in the Lesser Antilles archipelago, and you really must see it. Nicknamed the "Nature Isle of the Caribbean" for its unspoiled natural beauty, it is still being formed by volcanic activity and is home to lush mountainous rainforests, the world's second-largest hot spring, and a host of rare plants and animals otherwise extinct on surrounding islands. Dominica's few dark-sand beaches and frequent hurricanes render tourism there a relatively under-developed industry—bananas and other agriculture dominating her economy instead. For that reason, Dominica will never be a powerhouse among its neighbor islands; her fruit is just too vulnerable to weather conditions and to external events affecting commodity prices.

The fact that Dominica routinely hosts fewer visitors than any other Caribbean nation was precisely why I needed to go. I learned about its independence, just twenty years prior, and its fame as home to the only remaining Carib (now Kalinago) population in the Eastern Caribbean, and I felt confident I'd find a culture there devoid of the hostility and one-upmanship that had taken me so low at times over these past four years. We booked a hotel in Roseau, its capital, and used it as our launch pad for weeks of embedding ourselves in the culture, exploring waterfalls, and eating as much *roti* as our stomachs could hold.

Dominica was then still an unspoiled, untamed place—just as I hoped it'd be. We spent some days in town but, mostly, we avoided the commerce, opting to hike trails only locals new, see villages and meet people with no exposure to oil refineries or class action lawsuits.

One day, we reverted back to our Americanisms and hired a cabbie to tour us around the island, navigating us through some of the more obscure areas, and helping us haggle for goods with villagers. I had taken several years of French in school, but many of the locals in these remote areas still spoke only a derivation of it known as Antillean Creole, and that made connections challenging. Our guide had a rough command of their arcane dialect, however, making the insignificant sum he requested for the day's excursion well worth it.

We'd rented a car for this trip, but the four-wheel-drive of our guide's vehicle was essential for today's outing. I was impressed. Many of the roads seemed at first impassable, but our driver cut through overgrowth and around potholes with ease toward the most remarkably lush spots I'd ever seen. Clearly, he'd been born into this and had no fear.

After sampling some fresh fish at a roadside stand at the entrance to the Morne Trois Pitons Rainforest, we decided to trek in for what became a hilly, energetic hike. As our driver hopped out, grabbed his electrical-tape-handled machete from the vehicle and started walking, I tentatively followed, wondering if I could really trust this guy. The car, the road and the rest of the world quickly disappeared behind us as we entered the jungle on paths only he could see, with me especially watchful, wondering what creatures' eyes might be on us.

The rainforest is a damp, often brooding place and, without navigational guides, getting back out is not a certainty. As we pushed through mud and monstrous leaves, I had little choice but to abandon my ordinary skepticism and trust that this dark, little man knew his way around and had good intentions for us. We traversed the land like this for nearly an hour, kicking the ground to make hillside footholds and pulling on branches to negotiate obstructions. Cresting yet another peak—our driver still hacking at recalcitrant vines with his makeshift sword—I wiped the sweat from my eyes with my linen sleeve, curious how long this would last and wishing I'd brought water. Somehow, though, none of it mattered; I was done with things mattering anymore.

As we finished our ascent up hundreds of feet of slippery hill-sides—one of many slippery hillsides in this unpredictable, challenging terrain—our guide slowed a bit, seeming to know what was next, and summoned us to his side. We dutifully obliged and, with a final swipe of his knife at this living curtain, the veil was down. The jungle literally opened up before us, and we gazed down through the mist into a vast banana grove. I was awestruck and humbled and nearly forgot about my labored breathing, my tired calf muscles, about everything material. The splendor of all that color pulled me in.

Rejuvenated at the prospect of being among the majesty of this, I energetically pushed on, marching down from our hilltop into this valley of green and yellow. As the terrain flattened and a clearer walking path emerged, I fell back a bit from the driver and my companion to be alone and reflect on the events that had brought me there. Magnificently colorful Sisserou parrots flew in pairs and prattles overhead, loudly bragging about how good they had it. I wished I could talk back.

Despite walking some 50 feet behind the others through this magnificence, I felt beautifully connected—to everything. I needed this. I needed to feel covered in mud and not care. I needed to sweat in this insane humidity and not care. And, at that moment, nature tested me, just to see if I was ready. The cloudy sky finally gave in, opened up, unannounced, and dumped the warmest, most glorious rain on me. I stopped, but the parrots kept on. *Show offs*, I thought, as I smirked and watched them go.

As the sky nurtured me with a well-deserved shower, I smiled slightly and chuckled. It occurred to me that, back home in such a situation, I would have gone running for shelter, but I was far from home. There was nothing here to run from. Exposed and free, I stopped and removed my soaked shirt, arched back slightly with my smiling face turned upward in blissful gratitude to whomever or whatever allowed this moment, closed my eyes and just let it take me.

AFTERWORD

As of the first printing of this book, it is more than two decades since I received Ralph's call. Given the passage of that much time, you might wonder why I waited so long to tell this story, and why tell it now. To those questions, there are no *best* answers, but there were events that signaled it was time. My turning 50 was one of them. So was the encouragement of my wife—my most fervent champion—who said to me, "Go. Take a few days for yourself. Stay somewhere quiet along the ocean and just write." It was that simple, and it became the first small step of a very long journey.

I thank her and others for their support since this was a story that always needed to be told—and by the guy who most lived it. I realized that fact the moment the Unocal case settled behind our backs, the moment the rug was pulled out from under us, the point at which we realized we truly were on our own. And, yet, that was simply the last straw in a series of reportable events.

When I tell people what that refinery did and how it almost got away with it, they are disgusted. And when I reveal, albeit with some embarrassment about the association, how our colleagues—the lawyers entrusted to go to bat for the community—sold us out, people are outraged by that too. Even Judge Emerson observed that betrayal and, when a seasoned jurist points out that sort of thing, it stings even more.

As the years went on and it became apparent that fewer and fewer people had ever heard of what happened in those little California towns, I knew it was time to document it. "Maybe, when others read about the courage of those residents, they'll find their own voice, too," my colleagues would say. I wanted to believe that. That message kept me focused on what needed to be said.

As my work on the text progressed, a relative of mine—a writer herself—confronted me for an explanation. She asked to know, in as few words as possible, my point in writing it. "That's easy," I said. "To expose." That was always my goal. It's why I filed the case. Unocal's power, at least before I came along, was its ability to control the flow of information, to keep things quiet. By throwing a spotlight on its behavior and forcing it out of the shadows, I helped residents take back that power. That's one dividend of litigation, and I hope that writing about it here will show readers its potential for change.

My relative, appreciating both the substance and simplicity of my answer, got what she asked for. Her investigative tone fell away, and she sat back, her once-dubious expression replaced by a wide, knowing grin. She understood. To her, my reply was sufficiently lucid and calculated that she could trust the same of the manuscript. "Then your book will be a big success," she retorted assuredly.

"Thanks, but I'm not an author," I said, my natural modesty rebuffing her prediction. "I just want people to know what happened and to understand that they can make changes too." To this, she didn't respond, no elaboration on this prevision of hers, prompting my assumption that the conversation had run its course. And, yet, something didn't sit right about her statement. Maybe it was her overly wise expression, as if she had a secret, something I was destined to learn on my own. I didn't press her at the time, but the sense that I'd misunderstood something key bugged me for weeks. And then it hit me.

I'd taken her comment to mean the work would sell like hotcakes, that maybe I could quit my day job for this. I mean, she's family. She's there to support and motivate me, right? It's certainly not a mystery that few books achieve truly great sales levels, especially those produced by first-time writers. *She's just boosting my ego*, I thought. But, upon further consideration, I started to see broader meanings in her simple, prophetic statement. She wasn't making a forecast of book sales, at least not principally. She was communicating things we all know already—visceral things.

For starters, I think she was saying that people don't like being deceived, and they get super-excited when bad actors are called to answer for their crimes. People want, if nothing else, the *option* of self-empowerment, and being misled hinders that. And I think she was saying that people want a just world, where pretentious folks in high positions are exposed for their faults and frailties, shown to be as human as the rest of us. And then, lastly, I think she was reminding me that people want to believe anything is possible—"*Tutto è possibile*," as my Italian wife would say. We need that. We need to believe heroes exist, and that the balance of power can be restored with a display of the courage that, frankly, we all have within us. People just eat that stuff up.

If that's what she meant by "big success," then these are all good messages, ones with which I completely agree. In fact, it was with those same intended messages in mind that I wrote this book—to show heroism isn't relegated to fairy tales and Hollywood action films. And, in turn, this means that, directly or indirectly, I wrote this book for the people of Crockett and Rodeo. I'm proud of what they did, and I knew readers of this work would be proud too. When you accomplish with these townspeople did, it's hard not to be.

I imagine most residents of those towns think little these days about the 1994 Catacarb release. And, yet, you can see the effects of the release and the lawsuit that followed if you visit these places and look around; there are vestiges of it everywhere.

The Good Neighbor Agreement contained several provisions discussed in an earlier chapter, but, admittedly, those were just the high points of the contract. Altogether, it provided new roads, a health clinic, a safer elementary school in Rodeo and funds to other academic institutions, a state-of-the-art early warning system, an independent audit of the refinery, health studies, a vocational outreach program, community emergency response training programs, and new vegetation and local parks. Since the Joan Eisenberg and Becker Peabody studies, three additional health studies were performed, as was Unocal's establishment of a corporate risk communication policy that requires far more information than ever before be given to the public about health, environmental, safety and operational issues pertaining to the refinery. Wherever Unocal moved to, those policies would remain in effect.

That's what the company did, yet none of it would have occurred but for the chemical release itself and the activism of townspeople. But the citizens' movement and efforts to rebuild their towns and better lives didn't end there.

On their own initiative—and on their own dime—many residents, such as those living in or around Rodeo's Bayo Vista housing community (the one next door to the refinery) used some of their litigation settlement money to purchase air filtration systems for their homes, systems designed to reduce particulate matter suspected of contributing to the high rates of child asthma. Other residents, from across Rodeo and Crockett, donated portions of their settlement checks to improve local schools; others got involved in community service, particularly in advocacy and watchdog groups formed to keep an eye on local refineries and other heavy industry. Finally, and no less important, those who made it through the Catacarb incident and decided to stay feel a little warmer toward their neighbors. Everyone suffered, and facing a common adversary often builds lasting bonds.

With sizable tax-free settlement proceeds at their disposal, the continued health care promised under the Good Neighbor Agreement also became a little less important. Most residents, even those without insurance coverage before the release, finally got the attention they needed. That doesn't mean some of them didn't continue suffering well after—they did—but they now had options for medical intervention.

Others used their funds to put community interests almost entirely over their own, an altruism that, to me, was heartwarming. These residents commissioned an engineering firm to develop an inexpensive, easy-to-use air sampler so as to measure chemical levels when air quality seemed particularly bad. The device, known as the "bucket," was subsequently adapted for widespread dissemination, and it is currently used by fence-line communities around the world. Beyond helping neighborhoods closest to refineries know what they're breathing, the bucket has become a cornerstone of advocacy for more comprehensive air monitoring.

Both in the Crockett/Rodeo community and beyond, "bucketeers" use their trapped samples as evidence to point out the lack of information being provided to their communities during potentially dangerous releases, and to criticize industry and government agencies for their apparent lack of interest in finding out what fence-line communities are breathing. But, thanks to the community activism, our litigation and the Good Neighbor Agreement, people under siege from frequent chemical emissions now have the ability to respond to the releases themselves, taking five-minute samples that represent air quality during the worst periods of pollution.

Most of these changes occurred either during the life of our litigation or within a couple years of its settlement, yet it took almost two more decades of sustained community activism around air monitoring to push regulators to change their approach. In 2013, the (Northern California) Bay Area Air Quality Management District (BAAQMD) proposed a new refinery rule that would require monitoring at the fence-lines of the five northern California oil refineries it regulates (including the once-Unocal-owned Rodeo refinery) and in nearby residential areas. Fence-line air monitoring requirements are also a feature of the U.S. Environmental Protection Agency's (EPA) new refinery rules, adopted in September 2015. What's more, many refineries around the nation have tightened internal normal- and emergency-operation protocols in light of the devastation occasioned by Unocal's neglect in response to the Catacarb release of 1994.

So, what about all those attorneys?

As for the Steering Committee lawyers, some still handle cases like the one against Unocal. Some have passed away; others retired. Walter's firm was embroiled in protracted litigation over some of his settlement decisions, specifically, to dismiss claims for punitive damages. The litigants who filed suit against his firm disagreed with Walter's actions to do that, just like they disagreed that our settlement was a sufficient remedy for the devastation to their towns. Eighty million dollars may seem like a lot of money, but when you take out the fees and the out-of-pocket costs, and then divide what's left by thousands of people, some of whom lost loved ones, years of their own health, their livelihoods, it's actually not that much. Apparently, Walter's crew ruffled more feathers than just mine.

As for me, well, I don't practice environmental or personal injury law anymore and doubt I ever will again. Today, I handle class actions exclusively, but in different areas, for consumers and underpaid workers, people just as disenfranchised and in need of help. I did go on, for the next few years after Unocal, to represent victims in a handful of other environmental cases—sometimes as the lead lawyer with other firms in subordinate positions—but then I washed my hands forever of environmental and personal injury work. I'd had enough. It became too heartbreaking to witness the pain of so many people and, frankly, that particular brand of legal politics just got too dirty for my taste.

But, in those few post-Unocal years, I gave it my best effort. I had really hoped that, by using what I'd learned in the first lawsuit, by taking the hard-nosed reputation I apparently developed there and using it to lead those newer cases, it might rekindle something I'd lost. I thought the new battles would help me rediscover that starry-eyed, childlike quality I possessed when I first met Ralph, when justice was black or white, no shades of gray. They didn't. Those illusions were gone, and that was okay. It was time to grow up, anyway.

And yet, while I see things differently now, the passion for championing the underdogs I had when I was 28 is still there. At 28, I took on my first class action, and then got to be on my first Steering Committee and got to learn from some of the best. Since then, I've handled hundreds of class actions, with some record-setting results, made law that has changed the practices of entire industries and helped millions of people in the process. Those things may never have occurred if it wasn't for Ralph and our Crockett and Rodeo friends.

Having now considered all this, maybe I should have answered my relative differently. Maybe the goal wasn't merely "to expose." Maybe it had more to do with the next step after exposure: to motivate toward action. In fact, I pointed this out as, at least, one of my goals in my introduction to this story. In those prefatory notes, I confessed my efforts to retell these events will have been worth it if I could embolden others to stand up for themselves, and I still believe that. In decades now of law practice, I've seen a lot of abuse toward people who were initially afraid to fight back. Maybe reading stories like this can serve others as the nexus between their indignation and the actions needed to make things right again. I'd like to think so. Maybe that's what my relative meant by "a big success." If so, I'll take it.

If you closely follow American politics, you already know that ours remains a very divided nation, but I think many of us have forgotten or even been blinded to the real enemy. It's not the media, or a political party or even a cause. The real enemy, I think, is ignorance, and the true criminals are those who propagate it. By that, Unocal betrayed the trust of—and became an enemy to—the Crockett/Rodeo community because the company kept those townspeople in the dark. If you agree that friends don't obfuscate, tell lies and harm each other deeply and permanently, then you'll agree Unocal was far from being, as it so vigorously marketed itself, a "Good Neighbor."

The Unocal facility certainly wasn't the first refinery in history to pollute surrounding areas or harm the people living and working nearby. Nor is it likely to be one of the last, although it could be. How much more harm to our personal health and natural resources we tolerate, however, is completely up to us—the writers and readers of books like these, people interested in change, people unnerved by the awesome, seemingly limitless power of those with big voices. It's really not that complicated. Given that, to a profit-minded corporation, money speaks loudest, we already know how to make all the changes we want. We just need a push.

The Crockett/Rodeo community got that push in August 1994, and just in the nick of time. The battle between the Crockett/Rodeo community and the Unocal refinery was becoming one of life or death. It really was. If Unocal stayed, more people were almost assuredly going to suffer. I mean, four major chemical releases in one year may be unprecedented, and don't forget that the first one caused deaths and was predicated upon an extraordinary level of recklessness. But, to push back, these small-town residents needed sufficient organization and motivation. The company certainly wasn't willing to self-regulate. It had been polluting that area for generations with almost total impunity. No, the residents had to intervene. They just needed a catalyst. Catacarb gave them that.

By standing up against an industrial giant, I worked with those townspeople to make life in the San Francisco Bay Area financially burdensome for an irresponsible multi-billion dollar enterprise. Through our efforts, we drove it away and effectively silenced it, at least locally, forever. It wasn't easy and, yet, our techniques weren't magical. We did it with a one-two punch that combined traditional legal maneuvers with grassroots activism, and we succeeded, but that wasn't our unique genius. History is replete with examples of revolutions, unionization, and boycotts in the face of threats to health and safety. We followed those models because, frankly, they work.

Today, I tell my clients that Nature itself fights for equilibrium, so why shouldn't we? I tell them that the real invitation is to do something, to get involved. I tell them not to believe the hype about the "evils" of class actions or give credence to the violent pro-corporate movements toward "tort reform." And why not? Because we *need* the vigilant, watchful Little Voices—the people ready to step up and make course corrections when industrial facilities go rogue. We need people willing to push back.

To everyone who joined me in that push for change so many years ago—and I mean everyone—thank you.

If you enjoyed reading this book, please take a few moments to submit your review of it on Amazon. The success of this book depends on it, and your help in getting its important message to others would be greatly appreciated.

ABOUT THE AUTHOR

SCOTT EDWARD COLE still practices law and is the founder and principal attorney of California-based Scott Cole & Associates. He has represented countless victims in air pollution litigation, and today, leads class actions addressing workers' and consumers' rights on both a state and national level. He has authored numerous articles, is a frequent guest lecturer to legal professionals, and is well-recognized as an expert in plaintiff-side class action litigation. He is happily married to his wife, Diana, and lives with their three children in Northern California.

Made in the USA
Coppell, TX
21 August 2020

34178701R00225